Post-Socialist Political Economy

Post-Socialist Political Economy

Selected Essays

James M. Buchanan

Advisory General Director, Center for Study of Public Choice
George Mason University, US

and

Nobel Laureate in Economic Sciences, 1986

Edward Elgar

Cheltenham, UK • Lyme, US

Published by
Edward Elgar Publishing Limited
8 Lansdown Place
Cheltenham
Glos GL50 2HU
UK

Edward Elgar Publishing Company
1 Pinnacle Hill Road
Lyme
NH 03768
US

A catalogue record for this book is available from the British Library

Library of Congress Cataloguing in Publication Data
Buchanan, James M.
  Post-socialist political economy: selected essays/James M.
  Buchanan.
    Includes bibliographical references.
    1. Economic history—1990– 2. World politics—1989– 3. Post
-communism. 4. Communism. 5. Socialism. 6. Economics—Political
aspects. 7. Political science—Philosophy. I. Title.
  HC59. 15.B83   1997
  330.1—dc21   97–25019
                                                    CIP

ISBN 1 85898 534 X

Printed and bound in Great Britain by
Biddles Ltd, Guildford and King's Lynn

Contents

Foreword

As a participating member of several intersecting academic communities, and particularly because much of the material contained in this volume was initially presented in lectures and seminars throughout the world, I have benefited from discussions with many friends, critics and colleagues, whose number is too great to allow any attempt at personal identification. I shall, however, list those whose comments I recall as having been directly helpful on arguments advanced in one or more essays in the book. I shall not try to match names with titles. Instead I extend my thanks inclusively to: Peter Bernholz, Geoffrey Brennan, Roger Congleton, David Fand, Frank Forman, Hartmut Kliemt, Robert Tollison, Viktor Vanberg, Karen Vaughn and Yong Yoon.

I have been fortunate in being able to work within the congenial research environment available at George Mason University, and, specifically, at the Center for Study of Public Choice, under the leadership of Robert Tollison and as administered capably by my longtime assistant Betty Tillman.

It would be unusual to designate an editor for a volume of essays that I, as author, selected and organized. In another sense, however, Jo Ann Burgess should be listed as 'Editorial Director', because she has handled the processing of the materials through the several separate stages of production. For enterprises like this book we need a more extensive use of credits. We should imitate Hollywood, in which case I should, quite happily, list Jo Ann Burgess under either the title suggested or even as 'Producer', as, however designated, she deserves a billing that is more visible than mention in a foreword.

James M. Buchanan
Fairfax, Virginia

Acknowledgements

Several chapters in this volume have been published previously either as they appear here or in a modified version. I gratefully acknowledge permission to reprint them. Chapter 3, (1991), 'Economics in the Post-Socialist Century', *Economic Journal* **101**, 15–21. Chapter 4, (1993), 'Public Choice after Socialism', *Public Choice*, **77**, 67–74. Chapter 6, (1995), 'Economic Science and Cultural Diversity', *Kyklos*, **48** (2), 193–200. Chapter 7, (1996), 'Economics as a Public Science', in Steven G. Medema and Warren J. Samuels (eds), *Exploring the Foundations of Research in Economics: How Should Economists Do Economics?*, Aldershot: Edward Elgar, pp. 30–36. Chapter 8, (1994), 'Economic Theory in the Postrevolutionary Moment of the 1990s', in Philip A. Klein (ed.), *The Role of Economic Theory*, Norwell, Mass.: Kluwer Academic Publishers, pp. 47–60. Chapter 9, (1991), *Analysis, Ideology and the Events of 1989*, Zurich: Bank Hoffman, pp. 7–26. Chapter 10, (1990), *Socialism Is Dead But Leviathan Lives On*, The John Bonython Lecture, Sydney, Australia: Centre for Independent Studies, pp. 1–9. Chapter 12, (1993), 'Asymmetrical Reciprocity in Market Exchange', *Social Philosophy & Policy*, **10** (2), 51–64 as well as in (1993), Ellen Frankel Paul, Fred D. Miller, Jr. and Jeffrey Paul (eds), *Liberalism and the Economic Order*, Cambridge: Cambridge University Press, pp. 51–64. Chapter 13, (1993), 'Consumption without Production: The Impossible Idyll of Socialism', Freiburg, Germany: Haufe, pp. 49–75; *Konsum ohne Produktion: Die unmögliche Idylle des Sozialismus*, pp. 17–47. Chapter 17, (1993), 'The Individual as Participant in Political Exchange', in Aage B. Sorensen and Seymour Spilerman (eds), *Social Theory and Social Policy: Essays in Honor of James Coleman*, Westport, Ct.: Praeger, pp. 11–21, an imprint of Greenwood Publishing Group, Inc., Westport, Ct.. Chapter 18, (1994), 'Democracy within Constitutional Limits', in Hendrikus J. Blommestein and Bernard Steunenberg (eds), *Government and Markets: Establishing a Democratic Constitutional Order and a Market Economy in Former Socialist Countries*, Dordrecht: Kluwer, pp. 39–47. Chapter 20, (1991), 'The Minimal Politics of Market Order', *Cato Journal*, **11** (2), 215–26. Chapter 21, (1994), *Politicized Economies in Limbo: America, Europe and the World, 1994*, Catania, Italy: Università degli studi di Catania, p. 20; *Economie Politicizzate nel Limbo: L'America, l'Europa e il mondo, 1994*, p. 20. Chapter 22, (1996), 'Society and Democracy', in Nick Kuenssberg and Gillian Lomas (eds), *The David Hume Institute, the First*

Decade, Edinburgh: The David Hume Institute, pp. 25–33. Chapter 23, (1994), 'Notes on the Liberal Constitution', *Cato Journal*, **14** (1), 1–9. Chapter 26, Fraser Institute and the Instituto Cultural Ludwig von Mises conference volume forthcoming. Also published (1995), 'Federalism as an Ideal Political Order and an Objective for Constitutional Reform', *Publius* **25** (2), 19–27.

1. Introduction

The separate chapters in this book were not written with the idea of inclusion in an integrated volume. They are separately prepared papers, some of which incorporate responses to events that occurred during the years after the revolutions of 1989–91, and all of which were surely influenced, even if indirectly, by those events. Summary evaluation of the volume's content suggests that there is relatively little treatment of what is, perhaps, the most relevant post-revolutionary fact: the apparent minimal influence exerted by the revolutions on the 'ordinary politics' of Western welfare states, notably, including the United States. Is our politics, as observed, really much different from that which described the setting in the mid-1980s, well before the momentous and unpredicted events at decade's end?

As the separate chapters indicate, my efforts are not readily identified by dating or by location. My inquiries do not reflect responses to the current topics of this or that year or to this or that country or region. The chapters in Part I are foundational in the sense that they address the role for the economist as scientist, and particularly in the socio-political settings that have emerged after the revolutions. This subject matter is critically important because, for many economists, their imagined roles as putative advisers to a benevolent and monolithic political authority stand exposed by the historically observed failure of command-control systems. If, then, economists have lost some of their legitimacy as advisers to governments, how can their scientific knowledge be brought to bear on the political economy of reality? Can the economist be anything other than advocate for particular interests, and, if not, how can the claim be made that economics, as such, has advanced over the three centuries since those heady years of mercantilist follies?

In the several chapters contained in Part I, I accept the challenge posed in these questions, and I lay out my own understanding of just what the economist-as-scientist can and cannot do in the intellectual environment at century's end. As the title of the first chapter in Part I suggests (Chapter 2 in the book), I claim that there is, indeed, a science of economics, and that the economist, as practitioner, can make productive contributions to the ongoing dialogue, even if the sometimes extensive margins of ambition must be tempered. Chapters 3 and 4 were written directly in response to specific invitations by journal editors to make personal predictions about future developments in economics (for the

Economic Journal) and in public choice (for *Public Choice)* over ensuing decades. Chapter 6 was also written in response to an invitation to speculate about the locational-institutional specification of the basic discipline. Chapter 7 was written as an invited response to the question: how should economists do economics? The whole set of complementary chapters in Part I, provides my own current interpretation and understanding of what the role of the political economist must be at the turn of the century.

The chapters included in Part II are more specifically focused on the momentous events of 1989–91 and some of their predicted consequences. None of this material is topical, however, in the sense that the differentiation in time and place renders the analysis now irrelevant. The events surrounding the revolutions did, indeed, stimulate the analyses, but the findings do not have half-lives by which their validity may be measured.

Let me, both along with and for fellow political economists and social philosophers, acknowledge that we failed fully to understand the vulnerability and fragility of socialist institutions in the presence of incentive incompatibilities. And let us further agree that only as we observed the failures of command-control systems did we begin to offer 'explanations' and 'understandings' as belated excuses for our failures to advance earlier predictions that our claims to scientific knowledge should have made possible. Even the few among us, notably von Mises and Hayek, who did partially expose the structural implausibilities of socialism, and who thereby deserve full recognition, *ex post,* did not themselves feel sufficiently self-confident to await the predicted collapse. Hayek, in particular, fought a life-long battle against the ideas of socialism, the fatal conceit grounded in philosophical error, and, despite his own late-career emphasis on the importance of evolutionary forces, he did not, for a moment, include the demise of socialism among the detritus of history.

For myself, I advance no claims at all for either historical insight or earlier evaluation of institutional structures. With the one exception of Chapter 13, which is itself a post-revolution 'explanation', the separate essays in Part II are concentrated on analysis of post-revolutionary reactions, including those experienced by citizens toward observed happenings. How is 'the market' viewed by those who participate in the production-exchange-distribution nexus, summarized under this terminology, and, especially how does this view relate to comparative institutional heritage? How is 'the market' understood by those persons who have never lived in a regime described by the absence of controlled prices and regulated entry and exit? In a limited sense, several of the chapters in Part II discuss the culture of the market economy and carry the implication that the absence of this culture may be a critically important element in the failures of post-socialist economies to achieve the miracles that were hurriedly and naively predicted.

In his provocative book, *The End of History and the Last Man* (1992), Francis Fukuyama confidently predicted that economies everywhere would be organized on market principles and that liberal democracy would describe their political complement. Fukuyama may have been off target, as may now be perceived. Markets do not, and cannot, emerge full blown without an understanding and appreciating culture, at least in such fashion as to achieve tolerable efficiency standards. And politicians calling themselves 'democratic' may mask many variants of corruption, oppression and coercion. The 1989–91 revolutions did not, in themselves, serve to remove from public consciousness, once and for all, the notion that the state, as idealized, remains categorically equivalent to the state, as politically realizable. The benevolent and omniscient state, which can be imagined and within which man achieves his ultimate realization, has existed as an idea and ideal from the ancient Greeks through to the modern Hegelians. The elementary fact that this ideal state is infeasible and that its espousal is identical to the application of science fiction has never informed political discourse. This fact should have been, but was not, conclusively demonstrated by the grand historical experiments of this century. Fukuyama to the contrary notwithstanding, the scientific truths of political economy have not yet carried the political day, in the East, Centre or West.

The title for Chapter 10, 'Socialism is dead, but Leviathan lives on', is accurately descriptive of much of the world at the turn of the century. In this chapter, the focus shifts more directly towards analysis of post-socialist attitudes and institutions in nonsocialist Western societies. And here I do address what continues to remain for me the most puzzling and disturbing question: why have the politics of these Western countries been so little influenced by the events of 1989–91? Why have the spillovers been so negligible? Why do we live with 'socialism in the small' as if it is expected to work effectively, when 'socialism in the large' so demonstrably failed? Perhaps in 1996 we are still too close to the events either for influences to have worked themselves out or for us to have observed currents that are present. Perhaps the politics of the new century will incorporate an appreciation of this century's socialist experiments – an appreciation that we cannot as yet discern.

The separate chapters in Part III were also written in the post-socialist years of the early 1990s and, for that reason alone, must reflect some influence of events. But, in subject matter, these chapters are directed more towards developments in the research programme that has described my own efforts for four decades – a programme summarized under the rubric 'Constitutional political economy'. I have entitled Part III 'Constitutional understanding' by way of emphasizing that a key to political reform, in all countries, is located in public attitudes towards the institutional structures through which political decisions are made and implemented.

The material discussed in these chapters represents extensions and applications rather than foundational treatment of the overriding constitutionalist argument. I have more or less presumed that this normative argument, at least in this book, requires no renewed articulation. I acknowledge that, in this sense, the separate chapters in the book are indeed integrated by the inclusive or comprehensive vision of a social order in which members can simultaneously achieve the shared objectives of liberty, peace, economic prosperity and justice. Those who may not share such vision, and who think that the achievement of these objectives is simply beyond feasibility limits, may not find my discussion of much interest or value.

The 'constitutional understanding' upon which the discussion in the chapters of Part III is grounded is an essential ingredient for any institutional or structural reform that may be contemplated. Attention must be drawn to the structures within which public and private interactions take place, that is to the rules that become the parameters that constrain actions affecting others than the isolated actor. By methodological necessity, any analysis of rules as compared with analysis of outcome patterns is more process oriented, thereby invoking the familiar process versus end-state distinction. Care must be taken, however, to differentiate between the objects that may be evaluated and the objects that may be chosen. To suggest that the objects upon which social or collective choices are, and must be, exercised, are themselves rules, structures or institutions rather than end-states or outcomes is not to suggest that personalized evaluations cannot be applied to outcomes and that the evaluations of processes cannot be instrumentally derived. Evaluations may, of course, be applied directly to end-states, or, in formal parlance, to 'social states', and rules may be evaluated teleologically, strictly in terms of their predicted efficacy in generating preferred patterns of results. A constitutionalist perspective may also be consequentialist.

The situation cannot, however, be reversed. Exclusive attention to end-states or outcomes, as if these were objects both for evaluation and choice, can scarcely be other than teleological or consequentialist. Elsewhere (Buchanan, 1993a) I have advanced the positive proposition that collective choices can only be made among rules. So long as individuals retain liberty of action along *any* dimension of behavioural adjustment, there can be no choice of a 'social state', regardless of the rule or procedure through which choices are made. A 'social state' is, and must be, always an *emergent* outcome, one that may be evaluated but never chosen.

Rules themselves may be evaluated both instrumentally, in terms of their predicted efficacy in facilitating the generation of preferred patterns of end-states, and noninstrumentally, in terms of directly valued properties that they embody. It seems reasonable to suggest that such dual evaluation of the basic structural elements of social order may be required for the maintenance of social stability. Persons may acquiesce in the coercive impact of rules that produce nonpreferred end-states provided that the rules, in themselves, incorporate valued characteristics such as generality in application and fairness in promulgation.

The structural institutions for political order summarized under the term, 'federalism' (the subject matter of the chapters in Part IV), may be discussed as an application of this dual evaluation. Analysis suggests that preferred patterns of outcomes may be generated in a political structure in which authority is divided between a central government and separate but less inclusive units which, in their turn, compete one with another. For a polity with a large membership, a structure best described as a 'competitive federalism' could be predicted to produce outcomes, over a sequence, and measured by the value of economic product, and by maintenance of individual liberties of entry and exit in the market nexus, that are, generally, superior to those emergent under alternative political arrangements. Even apart from such an instrumental evaluation of federal structures, however, there remains the prospect that decentralized political authority may command evaluative support for its own sake and regardless of its efficiency in facilitating the achievement of the familiar shared objectives. In this particular respect, only a political structure that embodies devolution of genuine authority into units sufficiently small may be able to exploit fully the moral capacities of members (see Buchanan, 1978).

Can Europe fulfill its twenty-first century destiny by putting in place the effectively competitive federalism that seems still to remain within its opportunity set? Or will the residual and offsetting pressures of left-over socialism and resurgent nationalism prevent any realization of the federalist ideal? Can the United States devolve political authority from its over-extended central government? Is a viable federalism still within the feasible? These questions must remain unanswered. The discussions in Part IV are little more than preliminary explorations.

I have entitled the book *Post-Socialist Political Economy,* but there should be no inference that any of the analysis and interpretation is other than provisional. To a large extent, the political economy of the post-Cold War epoch remains to be determined, by the forces of historical development, by social and cultural evolution, by directed political change and by exogenous shocks that remain in the unknowable future. We have, indeed, entered a new century, well ahead of the calendar.

This new century cannot match the record of its predecessor, along many dimensions, many of which measure retrogression rather than its opposite. The world did not necessarily become a better place in the twentieth century, despite technological explosion and dramatic growth in levels of personal incomes and wealth. Personal liberties and lives were everywhere surrendered to collectively imposed coercion.

What does the post-socialist century promise? And how can the preferred features of this promise be realized while the undesirable features are avoided? Where are the political leaders who must emerge to implement the constitutional reforms without which social chaos must substitute for reasoned choice? Where and who is the new James Madison, and in what setting can she or he exhibit the wisdom of the Founder, persuade the modern sceptic and, perhaps most importantly, temper the compassion of the short-sighted among us?

The baling-wire syndrome that so accurately describes American pragmatism in political practice, and which has now extended to the world at large, must somehow be replaced as our dominant metaphor. Both personal and political horizons must be lengthened. Ronald Reagan was fond of saying that politics is part of the problem not the solution. He should have said that short-run solutions (fixes), whether political or private, create and exacerbate long-run problems.

We must accept the ultimate responsibility that is inherent in our own ability to choose. We create the future by the actions we take now. Generalized free-ridership along with overreaching constituency politics produces the future that no one wants. Each of us has a personal moral obligation to think and to act as if this future is not inevitable.

PART I

Scientific Vistas

A11 A10

2.   There *is* a science of economics[1]

all the sciences have a relation, greater or less, to human nature; and that, however wide any of them seem to run from it, they still return back by one passage or another. Even Mathematics, Natural Philosophy, and Natural Religion, are in some measure dependent on the science of man, since they lie under the cognisance of men, and are judged by their power and faculties (David Hume, 1888, p. xix).

The title of this chapter stems from reflection on the content of a possible introduction to a volume of Karl Brunner's nonmonetary papers. I was asked to write such an introduction, and the editor suggested concentration on the Interlaken conferences on 'Analysis and Ideology'. When Karl Brunner initiated this series of conferences in 1974, his stated purpose was that of introducing (exposing) European, and especially German-speaking, economists to their American counterparts who allegedly brought along analytical baggage that was more 'scientific' (hard-nosed) than that which described much of the Marxist-inspired rhetoric then encountered in Europe's academies. In taking this entrepreneurial step, he was motivated by the conviction that economics does, indeed, have scientific content, analogous to, even if quite different from, that of the natural sciences. And this conviction was accompanied by the belief that genuinely scientific argument, along with the empirical evidence that could be marshalled in support, was both necessary and sufficient to overcome the temptation of scholars to indulge in ideological romance.

My concern here is not about whether Karl Brunner succeeded in accomplishing what he sought with the Interlaken conferences. My purpose is to examine the nature of the alleged scientific content of whatever it is that economists, as professionally trained, bring to problems of social organization. How does the economist differ in this respect from the philosopher (Posner, 1993)? Is economics more than either a part of contractarian political philosophy or a branch of mathematics (Rosenberg, 1992)?

Even if we recognize that the propositions of positive economics are scientific in the modern sense of terms here, how can we expect that demonstration of these propositions will affect the choices among institutional-organizational alternatives faced by members of a political community? What, precisely, did Karl Brunner have in mind when he predicted that a wider exposure of German social scientists to 'scientific economics' would ultimately exert an impact on the direction of change in political regimes?

I suggest that we think of the role of the economist, and of economic science, in terms analogous to that of the ordinary natural scientist, and of natural science. Think then of the natural scientist not as a discoverer of new laws of nature and the universe, not as someone who is continually expanding the boundaries of what we know about the natural environment, but, instead, as a human repository of knowledge about the natural environment, as it is now known to exist. Think, that is, of the noncreative natural scientist, and of the role of such a person, and of science, in society.

What does such a scientist do? As a rough cut of an answer, consider the definition of the natural or physical feasibility space. The scientist draws the boundaries between what is and what is not feasible given the known constraints of the physical universe. Ragnar Frisch (1959) referred to these constraints as *obligative*, which he contrasted with constraints that are *facultative*. The predictions of natural science tell us what we can and cannot do with the materials and potential forces that exist. The scientist does not go beyond a positive stance; no advice is offered to members of the body politic, in either private or public spheres of action, as to what should be done within the parametric limits of the feasibility space. And no critics accuse the natural scientist of committing a naturalist fallacy when the propositions of science are observed to affect the choice behaviour of nonscientists. The propositions of ordinary natural science are simply incorporated into the considerations of the choice alternatives that we face.

If economics is to be compared with natural science, economists should be able to define what can and cannot be done with the *human* materials and potential that exist. Economists, and economic science, should generate a feasibility space, fully analogous to that generated for the physical universe by natural science. But what laws of human nature become the analogues of natural laws? This question is addressed in the second section. The third section introduces the critical difference between the natural sciences and the human sciences; the difference summarized by the artifactual features of the environment within which humans confront choices and take action. The fourth section discusses the role of economic science in restricting the domain of feasible outcomes or social states. A highly abstract illustration of the whole argument is presented in the fifth section. The final section summarizes the chapter.

HUMAN NATURE

Post-medieval social philosophers – from Thomas Hobbes down to David Hume and Adam Smith – were excited about the prospects for developing the sciences of man alongside those of the natural world. The base point for this judgment was the conviction that there were uniformities in human nature that allowed for systematic inquiry. For Adam Smith, each person's drive to better his own position provided a uniform motivational element from which all understanding of economic interaction emerges. It is important to note that betterment was implicitly defined to be objectively measurable. Each person's effort to better his own position is observed as a striving to secure command and use of a larger share of goods that are commonly valued. This elementary insight is often overlooked, and it is obscured by the utilitarian rhetoric that has continued to dominate economists' thinking for two centuries. If a person's effort to better his own position is made equivalent to a person's attempt to maximize his utility, and if, in turn, utility is defined as that which is maximized, the predictive content of any genuinely economic model of human behaviour is emptied. What remains is the science of rational choice, which, although formally operational, does not perform the function previously specified. Until and unless the domain for human choice behaviour is restricted further than the minimal limits imposed by rationality criteria, the economists' enterprise warrants little respect.

The exchange relationship is, of course, central to economic interaction, but a concentration on the surface characteristics of exchange itself may add to the confusion here. At the point of trade, parties differ in their evaluation of the goods traded, and this difference motivates the trade itself. But the goods that are traded are mutually valued by both parties to exchange, and if either party could, somehow, secure more of *either* 'good' without giving up some of the other, behaviour would be observed to occur along such a nontrading dimension. Trade involves giving up less-valued goods for more-valued goods, by both parties to the transaction. Both of the goods that enter into the trading process remain as positively valued arguments in the utility functions of both traders, before, during and after trade takes place.

An alternative, if somewhat more complex, way of putting the point made here is to state that each good that enters into the trading relationship embodies potential distributional conflict. No trades are observed to take place in goods that are in sufficiently abundant supply to sate all demands, or in goods that are technologically nontradeable, no matter how highly valued (for example, sunshine in Alaska in January), or in goods that meet full Samuelsonian requirements for publicness, as technologically defined.

The economist's first step towards restricting the domain of attainable positions lies in postulating that human nature is such that persons seek larger shares of those goods that are commonly and positively valued and seek smaller shares of those goods that are commonly and negatively valued. That is to say, signs need to be attached to 'goods' (or 'bads'). Note that this step is classificatory only; it does not require any postulate to the effect that the trade-offs among goods be identical over separate persons. The classification requires only that the set of goods that is commonly valued to be positive be identical over all potential traders. In more familiar terms, the set of arguments in individual utility or preference functions, as identified by signs of the partial derivatives, must be the same.

HUMAN BEHAVIOUR WITHIN RULES

A categorical difference between the enterprise of the natural scientist and that of the economist emerges as the latter tries to move toward delineation of the boundaries of behavioural feasibility – a difference that makes the economist's task enormously more difficult in some relative sense. The natural scientist is able to, and indeed must, take the universe as it is found and without the overlay of a complex institutional structure that has evolved, in part constructively, and that operates to channel and to facilitate patterns of behaviour that cannot be classified to be 'natural' in any primitivist sense. Furthermore, the institutional structure is not unique; distinctly different sets of rules may describe separate historical and locational settings. How can the economist, as scientist, even so much as commence to establish boundary marks between the attainable and the unattainable?

One means of reducing the task to manageable proportions is to drop any claim for generality and to introduce historical-institutional specificity. With a postulated set of structural parameters, that is, within a defined set of legal rules or facultative constraints, the economist can proceed with the basic classificatory exercise without advancing any claim to generalizability to other institutional settings. For my primary purposes in this chapter, examination and elaboration of this reduced-claim procedure is sufficient, although I shall refer briefly to the problem of generalization at a later point in the argument.

Consider, then, the basic institutional framework for the regime that facilitates the emergence and the operation of a market economy. Persons, individually or as members of organizations, are assigned enforceable rights and claims to both human and nonhuman endowments – rights that allow these endowments to be used as the assigned owners desire, within certain legal limits. Persons, again individually or as members of organizations, possess rights to enter into and complete exchanges one with another and to transfer rights on reciprocally agreed terms. As persons exercise their assigned rights by choosing and acting along the dimensions within their authority, a network of production, exchange and distributional relationships emerges, and from this network there will be generated an outcome, or patterns of outcomes, that may be described by vectors of prices, allocations of resource inputs and distributions of final outputs.

All of this summary description is, of course, familiar territory to the economist. But let me make the connection to the classificatory exercise mentioned above. Recall Adam Smith's most famous passage where he states that the butcher offers the supper's meat for sale, not from benevolence, but from his own self-interest. Economics is widely, and correctly, interpreted as providing understanding-explanation of Smith's statement. My argument here is that Smith's seemingly elementary proposition has genuine scientific content and in the following way. The imagined 'social state' in which there are no persons offering meat for sale is nonfeasible, given the institutional parameters that define the rights or liberties of potential sellers and buyers and given the motivational postulate of the science. An even more romanticized alternative would be a setting in which sellers offer meat to those who desire this good, but without demanding payment in return. This result, too, may be imagined, as a social state that would be most highly preferred by meat consumers, but few would fail to incorporate the elementary elements of economics in thinking that this result could never be realized.

The principle to be emphasized is the necessity of making the distinction between those states of the world, those 'social states', that can be imagined to exist and those states that can be realized, given the inclusive rules within which economic interaction must take place. The set of imagined positions is, of course, much larger than the set of potentially realizable positions, even within the limits imposed by the acknowledged natural or physical constraints. Within any given institutional structure, the difference between the set of imagined positions and the set of attainable positions stems exclusively from the operation of the motivational postulate that is central to the science of economics itself.

RESTRICTIONS ON THE DOMAIN

It may be helpful to clarify the process through which the science of economics restricts the domain of outcomes or end-states of human interaction. Individual preferences are not simply taken as data. Instead, preferences are restricted by the two-part postulate to the effect that (1) persons seek their own betterment and (2) betterment is objectively measurable in goods that are defined to be commonly valued, whether positively or negatively.

Consider an individual's ordering of two social states, both of which are technologically feasible, but one of which imputes to that individual a larger quantity of a positively valued good, with the same quantities of others' goods. The individual's preferences must be such as to produce a ranking of such a state relatively higher than that accorded to the alternative. Given such an ordering, the individual cannot select the less-preferred to the more-preferred alternative if he or she is assigned rights of choices along the relevant dimension of behaviour.

In application to the last variant of the Smithian example discussed above, where sellers are imagined to offer goods without payment, such a state is to be classified as nonfeasible, so long as sellers retain rights of entry into and exit from the exchange relationship. One-sided, or nonreciprocal, 'exchanges' in goods, valued by both parties, are not permissible way-stations along the road to emergent market outcomes classifiable as feasible.

This conclusion may be accepted, but the critic may immediately resort to the institutional specificity imposed initially on the whole discussion. The offer of goods without return payment, that is, trade without reciprocation, may be acknowledged to be beyond the limits of feasible economic interaction, under the standard rules of the market, in which sellers and buyers retain rights of entry to and exit from potential exchanges. But, as noted earlier, these rules are not, themselves, natural, at least in the ordinary sense. Instead, rules of the market may be considered to be artifactual, having themselves evolved historically or been constructively put in place. Is it possible, therefore, both to imagine a social state where goods are offered without a requirement of payment and to classify such a state as potentially realizable under some alternative nonmarket assignment of rights?

Consider, again, the supply-demand of meat, classified as a commonly valued good. Suppose that the rules of the market are abrogated, and that these rules are superseded by politicization-bureaucratization of this sector of the economy. Some persons are directed to produce and supply meat to those who are authorized to receive the product, and there is no reciprocal exchange. Relatively little reflection is required to suggest that the situation attained under this regime is *not* likely to be that which might have been imagined to be possible as an alternative to the market counterpart. The producer-supplier will not be observed to respond to the preferences of consumers-demanders; the product itself will not be descriptively equivalent to that traded in markets. By replacing the set of market rules, there will be, of course, a change in the set of attainable or feasible positions. But these positions will differ from those reached under in-market behaviour along many more dimensions of adjustment than economically illiterate imagination could suggest.

Nonromanticized analysis suggests that the economist's classificatory exercise is more general in scope and applicability than might initially seem to be the case. Those social states or positions that can be imagined but never realized by behaviour within the rules of the market cannot necessarily be realized under any alternative set of rules, or assignments of rights. Care must be taken to avoid the comparison of false alternatives. That which might be imagined but not realized under one regime cannot necessarily be brought into being by a shift in regime. Given a regime change, the set of imagined social states may, once again, be subjected to the economist's classificatory scrutiny, with the distinction between the feasible and nonfeasible subsets being defined.

The point to be emphasized is that many, indeed the overwhelming majority, of the technologically feasible positions cannot be behaviourally realized, *under any regime.* Most of those positions or social states that are romantically imagined to be possible are inconsistent with the motivational postulate of economics, with human nature as it exhibits its uniformities. Economics need not be the dismal science, but it can scarcely avoid being labelled as the nonromantic science. The setting in which producers-sellers offer high-quality goods for nothing while showing interests in the desires of consumers is nonfeasible in a generalized sense. There is no regime, no set of rules, no assignments of rights to choose and to act that will generate such a social state and remain consistent with the central proposition of economic science.

AN EXAGGERATED ILLUSTRATION

I can present the basic argument with an illustration (Figure 2.1) which, although it is admittedly exaggerated in some respects, conveys the counter-conventional message effectively. Consider the familiar PD matrix, depicting the interaction of two players, each of whom has two available choice-action alternatives. My concern here is with the generalization properties of the interdependence rather than with particular two-person strategic aspects. Assume, first, that the two persons are assigned rights to act along the dimensions indicated. *A* chooses between rows; *B* chooses between columns. Assume, further, that the ordinal payoffs reflect objectively measurable quantities of a commonly-valued good, rather than utilities.

First, note that the outcome in each cell of the matrix is a 'social state', but that these states, as such, are not within the choice set of either participant. These states or positions emerge from the interaction process, given the choice of each person along the dimension assigned. To this point, nothing has been claimed about the relation of the payoffs to individual utilities. If the domain of choice

		B		
		b_1		b_2
A	a_1	I (3, 3) **3, 3**		II (4, 4) **1, 4**
	a_2	III (1, 1) **4, 1**		IV (2, 2) **2, 2**

Figure 2.1

is not restricted, the utility payoffs might be such as to generate any one of the four outcomes, without violating the postulates of rational choice behaviour for the players. Suppose, for example, that the ordinal utility payoffs are those indicated in the parentheses. In this case, the outcome is in Cell II. Until and unless there is some specification that relates objectified payoffs to utilities, there is no means to predict the emergent outcome or solution to the interaction.

If we generalize the model to allow for interaction among large numbers of persons, each one of whom is assigned rights to choose and to act along many separate dimensions, we can remain within the postulates of rational choice while still generating *any* outcome consistent with the obligative or technological constraints. Any social state that can be imagined may emerge, given the requirement that preference orderings over states cannot be restricted.

The economist is, however, more than a rational choice theorist. The economist, as scientist, specifies the relationships between the utility payoffs that describe human choices and the objectifiably measurable payoffs in the interdependence. In Figure 2.1, the basic economic hypothesis is that persons must act so as to maximize objective payoffs. Persons seek to get more rather than less, as measured in some denominator of common value. This proposition is central to the economist's scientific enterprise. Given this hypothesis, the economist can make falsifiable predictions about the effects of changes in facultative constraints and, in the process, classify all imagined social states into feasible and nonfeasible sets, both specifically to a given regime and generally to all regimes.

Consider, again, the simple interaction in Figure 2.1. If individuals are modelled as maximizing the payoffs indicated, the outcome in Cell IV is predicted to emerge, provided only that the participants are presumed to behave separately and independently. Given the structure of the model, no other outcome is possible (see Binmore, 1994.) If enforceable exchange contracts are possible, the Pareto-superior outcome in Cell I may be reached, but note that this result requires that the payoffs in Cells II and III be modified so as to eliminate the temptation to renege.

What my argument suggests is that the outcomes depicted in Cells II and III, those in the off-diagonal cells of the matrix, are to be classified as nonfeasible. These describe social states that can be imagined and ordinally ranked by both players, but that cannot be attained, given the rights to choose as assigned and given the central proposition of economics. These states are beyond feasibility limits, not because they are technologically impossible, but because they can never be behaviourally produced by the choices and actions of the human beings involved.

As noted in the more general discussion of the previous section, however, the assignments of rights need not be immutable. Suppose, for example, that *A* is the dictator. Cannot A, quite simply, command B to behave, to do b_1, so as to generate A's most preferred result in Cell III? And, vice versa, with Cell II if B should be dictator?

This question is critical, and my argument involves the claim that it must be answered negatively, at least in any generalizable form. The behaviour of B, when coerced by A, is not equivalent to that behaviour that is voluntarily undertaken, either as an independently acting party or as a participant in an exchange relationship, in which reciprocation is forthcoming from another party or parties. At this point, attempts to formalize, mathematize and simplify the interaction process may be dangerously misleading and serve to obscure the elementary reality.

If all of the technologically possible choice alternatives can be fully specific in each and every descriptive feature, and for all actors, then the assignment of control to a single authority can coercively achieve any state. There is no behavioural space which allows any participant to adjust along any dimension. Each person, other than the single dictator, must be a total slave, and there is no *inter*action, as such. This wholly unreal setting tends to seem analytically useful, in some reductionist way, when illustrations such as that introduced here are employed. If the course of action for B, defined by b_1, is set out in such a form as in the matrix, it seems to follow that b_1 is b_1 is b_1, and that this course of action remains invariant whether it is voluntarily chosen by B or is forced upon B by A. If, however, B is acknowledged to retain some residual liberties from control, in any regime, then such simple illustrations must be used with caution. And, if so used, the logic through which the off-diagonal positions may be classified to be nonfeasible become convincing.[2]

A SUMMING UP

I am fully aware of the fact that I have restated long familiar arguments in this chapter and that few practising economists, especially those of the Chicago tradition, will find much to criticize. In a real sense, I have done little more than to repackage the economists' positive and scientific proposition to the effect that demand curves are downsloping. I should suggest, nonetheless, that packaging can on occasion matter, and that perhaps the somewhat different rhetoric of my argument will prove more convincing than the familiar postures.

In part, the manner of putting the argument in this paper stems from reconsideration of some of the analyses of social-choice theorists, who have insisted for a half-century that preferences of individuals over social states cannot and should not be restricted. I have continued to be highly critical of this research programme, both in its search for some meaning of social welfare and for its presumption that social states are possible objects of social choice. The very language of social-choice theory has, however, allowed me to develop the argument of this chapter in a manner that may prove didactically useful. Armed with such an argument, economists may just be able to man their scientific defences more adequately than heretofore.

Economists are frequently accused of committing the naturalist fallacy, the derivation of an 'ought' from an 'is'. The approach taken in this chapter should help us avoid such a charge. If the economists can observe politically motivated action aimed quite explicitly at the achievement of results that are clearly beyond the boundaries of feasibility, given the existing regime, no norms are violated when and if they call attention to this as scientific fact.

When the economists suggest that 'the market works', no normatively positive charge need be attached to such a claim. Reference is properly limited to the proposition that, if persons are assigned rights of disposition over their own activities (and uses of their endowments) an outcome will emerge from the interaction that falls within the feasibility space. It may well be the case that alternative outcomes or social states may be imagined and ranked ordinally to be more desirable than those outcomes predicted to emerge from markets. But such alternatives may or may not be feasible, and it falls to the economist, as scientist, to carry out the classification that is required. And it is in this role as scientist that the economist should be able to prevent ill-fated efforts to organize political action aimed at achieving results that are beyond the boundaries of behavioural feasibility.[3]

The discussion of minimum wage legislation offers a practical example. In a regime where firms and individuals retain rights to hire and to fire employees, the economist can make a scientific statement to the effect that an increase in the legal minimum wage must reduce employment of relatively less-skilled workers. The imagined social state in which there is a higher minimum wage accompanied by no decline in employment is nonfeasible and must be so classified. And with particular reference to such an example, we can only look with misgiving on the modern urges toward empirical verification. Statistical inquiry may reveal the existence of parallel increases in minimum wages and in employment. But to rely on such empiricism to invalidate the economists' scientific enterprise is equivalent to making the observation that Peter Pan really does fly because one's vision does not disclose the existence of the supporting wires from the rafters.

Finally, I share what I think was Karl Brunner's belief that many of the errors in political economy stem from the failure of political decision makers to separate feasible from nonfeasible states of the economy. Scientific ignorance, when combined with informed self-seeking on the part of sectional interests, has prevented the attainment of results that might have proved to be beneficial to everyone in the economic nexus. The intense 1993 opposition to NAFTA in the United States was fuelled only in part by the informed self-interests of protected groups fearing damage from any opening-up of markets. The opposition was also grounded on economic ignorance that generated a fear of imagined consequences that could never be brought into reality.

As scientists, economists have an important social role to play. There is a repository of knowledge that remains within their unique responsibility. They default on their role when they, too, become romantic dreamers and try to assist misguided politicians in the search for nonattainable and imaginary worlds. We can only hope that Francis Fukuyama (1992) is correct when he suggests that the demise of socialism will mark the triumph of economic science.

NOTES

1. A version of this chapter was presented at the University of Texas, Dallas, Texas, March 1994.
2. For elaboration of the argument of this paragraph, see Buchanan (1995).
3. The role of the economist as scientist presented in this paper is different from, but not necessarily inconsistent with, the role of the political economist sketched out in my early 1959 paper. In that effort, I was concerned with how the economist, armed with the propositions of positive economics, might participate in the social discussion of policy alternatives. I suggested that the political economist's role should be that of presenting proposals as *hypotheses*, with the ultimate test being the achievement of unanimous agreement on change. In the context of the analysis here, my earlier concern was with the potential role of the political economist in the discussion of social choices among alternatives, all of which are within the set of attainable or feasible positions. See Buchanan (1959).

3. Economics in the post-socialist century

This chapter's title specifically suggests that the focus of scientific inquiry in our discipline is not independent of history. Nor are the events of history independent of developments in economics. Both in our roles as citizens (public choosers) and as economic analysts, we have learned from this century's experiments in politicized direction of economic activity, and this learning must, itself, affect both socio-political processes and the shape of further scientific inquiry. In both of these symbiotically related capacities, we simultaneously learn from and make our history.

The verb 'make' deserves emphasis, because it points to the basic difference between the subject matter of the social and the natural sciences. There is no set of relationships among persons that we can label to be 'natural' in the definitional sense of independence from human agency. The political economy is *artifactual*; it has been constructed by human choices, whether or not these have been purposeful in any structural sense. And the political economy that exists is acknowledged to be subject to 'unnatural' change. As the great experiments of this century demonstrate, attempts can be made to *reform* social structures, in the proper meaning of the term. By comparison and by contrast, it would be misleading to use the word 'reform' with reference to the natural world even with the dramatic advances in our scientific understandings. From the artifactual quality of that which is the subject of inquiry in economics, we infer, first, the necessary interdependence between science and history and, second, the relatively more direct linkage between science and purposive design.

In the next section of this chapter, I shall argue that the post-socialist century will be marked by a convergence of scientific understanding among those who profess to be economists. This convergence will contrast starkly with the sometimes acrimonious controversy that described discourse in the century past. This relatively clear difference in the economics of the two centuries will, itself, prompt inquiry into the sources of the earlier conflict. The third section previews the possible re-evaluative enterprise that may take place in ensuing decades and introduces the suggestion that in such an enterprise, profound methodological transformation may be accomplished. The convergence of understanding will also modify the relevance of the positive–normative distinction that became familiar only in this century. The fourth section elaborates the argument, and here I suggest that the political economy of the next century will indeed become more normative in the now conventional meaning of this term. But the normative focus will necessarily be quite different from that which seemed appropriate in the setting where all economies, to greater or lesser degrees, were subjected to politicized direction and control. The revised normative focus will be on the constraints within which economic actors, individually or corporately, make choices among alternatives. And the accompanying, and indeed prior, positive analysis will involve comparisons among alternative sets of constraints, or rules. As the fifth section suggests, 'constitutional economics' will command increasing scientific attention in the upcoming century, whether or not the relevant research programmes are explicitly classified under this particular rubric. The final section adds a postscript.

TOWARDS A SCIENTIFIC CONSENSUS

Consider the following statement by a widely respected observer:

> They (the diverse parties in Eastern Europe in 1990) are also saying – and for the left this is perhaps the most important statement – there is no 'socialist economics,' there is only economics. And economics means not a socialist market economy, but a social market economy (Timothy Garton Ash, 1990, p. 21).

In the 1990s, few who profess to call themselves economists in East or West will challenge the elementary proposition to the effect that economies that are described by individual (private) ownership of the means of production work better than economies where individual ownership is absent. And there exists widespread agreement on what is meant by the descriptive predicate 'work better'. More goods and services are produced, with 'more' being measured in terms of the values placed on such goods and services by individual participants. This convergence of scientific judgment within economics has already been evident for three decades. Since the 1960s, there have been relatively few claims advanced by economists concerning the superiority of centrally planned economies. And, indeed, few modern economists are either old enough or honest enough to recall the frequency of such claims during the middle decades of the century. This still-emerging consensus on the relative efficiency of market and socialist systems of economic order will characterize the first several decades of the post-socialist century.

Since the emergence of economics as an independent discipline, there has been near-unanimity in analysis of the effects of particularized constraints on voluntary exchange. The destruction of potential value generated by tariffs, price floors or ceilings or prohibitions on entry and exit – the demonstration of this result has remained a central emphasis over two centuries and can be predicted to remain in place over a third. But scientific advances have been made in understanding why collectivities impose such value-reducing constraints, and, in addition, economists can now measure the opportunity losses more accurately. Differences will continue as analysis comes to be applied, and especially if policy alternatives are presented in piecemeal fashion. But emerging scientific consensus will be indicated by the crossing of the intellectual-analytical bridge between the acknowledged failure of socialist organization in the large and the inefficacy of politicization in the small (market by market).

Predictions of convergence seem more uncertain when attention shifts to macroeconomics, the domain of inquiry opened by the Keynesian revolution. Market organization works, but within what set of parameters? And how detailed need political direction be in determining the values of the relevant parameters here? Controversy rather than consensus describes the state of play in the 1990s. What might be projected for the 2000s?

Convergence here will occur in what might seem a reverse order. Economists will attain broad consensus on choices among policy options *before* observed agreement on underlying analytical models of macroeconomic interaction. The lasting Keynesian contribution will be the emphasis on the dominance of man's 'animal spirits' in the subjectively-derived definitions of the expectational environment within which entrepreneurs, in particular, make future-oriented choices. The attempted extension of rational choice models to intertemporal and interdependent choices within an equilibrating adjustment framework will, ultimately, be deemed a failure. Both strands of inquiry here will converge early in application to policy. Those economists who stress expectational instability will move toward recognition that only structural reform can serve the implied macroeconomic purpose. And those who extended rationality precepts have already restricted reform efficacy to structural parameters.

Ultimately, this convergence on policy norms will be matched by broader consensus in the underlying analytical exercise. And here the Keynesian heritage will win the day even if, in yet another sense, the implied results may seem non-Keynesian. The limits on man's capacity to choose rationally in any operationally meaningful way must, finally, be reckoned with and the scope for subjectively determined choice behaviour acknowledged. At the same time, however, those and additional limits on the choice behaviour of political agents, and the interaction of these agents within the institutions of politics, will be incorporated into the whole macro-analysis.

RE-EVALUATION OF THE ECONOMICS OF THE SOCIALIST CENTURY

If my central prediction proves accurate, economists must, increasingly, begin to raise – and try to answer – the following set of questions: Why did economists share in the 'fatal conceit' (Hayek, 1988) that socialism represented? How were economists, who claimed scientific competence in analysis of human choice behaviour and the interdependent interactions of choices within institutional structures, duped or lulled into the neglect of elementary principles? Why did economists, who model man as *homo economicus* in analysing markets, fail to recognize that incentives remain relevant in all choice settings? Why did economists forget so completely the simple Aristotelian defence of private property? Why did so many economists overlook the psychology of value, which locates evaluation in persons not in goods? Why did so many professionals in choice analysis fail to recognize the informational requirements of a centrally controlled economy in both the logical and empirical dimensions? Why was there near total failure to incorporate the creative potential of human choice in models of economic interaction?

These and similar questions will occupy many man-years of effort in the century ahead. In the examination of the flaws in economics over the socialist century, the perspective of the discipline itself will be challenged and perhaps changed in dramatic fashion. Economists may come to recognize, finally, that the dominance of the implicitly collectivist allocationist paradigm, elaborated in a setting characterized by developing mathematical sophistication, lies at the root of much of the intellectual confusion. The alternative perspective that conceives of the economy as an *order* of social interaction (see my essay in Sichel, 1989) should gradually gain adherents. The accompanying mathematical representations will shift, and game theory's search for solutions to complex interactions under complex sets of rules will surely replace extensions of general equilibrium analysis at the frontiers of formalism.

The shift toward emergent order as a central perspective will be paralleled by a corollary, even if not necessary, reduction of emphasis on equilibrium models. The properties of systems in dynamic disequilibrium will come to centre stage, and especially as economics incorporates influences of the post-Prigogine developments in the theory of self-organizing systems of spontaneous order – developments that can be integrated much more readily into the catallactic than into the maximizing perspective.

A RECOVERY IN NORMATIVE RELEVANCE

A predictable by-product of the ideologically-driven controversy that characterized the socialist century was concerted effort to separate positive from normative elements of the economists' enterprise. Methodologists variously reiterated the is–ought and fact–value distinctions. With controversy receding, we can predict some increase in reasoned discourse in defence of normative standards. Such a return to respectability of normative argument applying economic analysis can serve to reinvigorate the discipline for aspiring young scholars who have been turned away by the antiseptic aridity of a science without heat. A bit of the excitement that described the zeniths of both classical political economy and early Keynesian macroeconomics seems well within the possible.

No direct challenge to the logic of the naturalistic fallacy need be invoked in the recognition that the very definition of the 'is', which itself depends critically on the perspective adopted in looking at the subject matter, will influence the shape of the 'ought', which emerges when a value ordering is applied to the analysis of the 'is'. The possible 'deconversion' of economists away from the allocationist-maximization-equilibrium paradigm and towards some vision of the economic process in subjectivist-catallactic-disequilibrium terms must, in itself, have implications for the sort of institutional change that *any* ultimate value stance might suggest as appropriate. The complementary shift in the perspective on politics and political process – a shift that has already occurred – will force normative evaluation to incorporate comparisons among institutional alternatives that remain within the possible. From this evaluation there must emerge, even at the level of practical proposals for reform, a much wider range of agreement among economists than that which described the past century.

TOWARDS A REVISED NORMATIVE FOCUS ON INSTITUTIONAL CONSTRAINTS: THE EMERGENCE OF 'CONSTITUTIONAL POLITICAL ECONOMY'

The predicted convergence of attitudes among economists at the level of normative evaluation will only take place within, and in part because of, a dramatically revised focus of the whole of the enterprise. A century ago, Knut Wicksell warned his fellow economists against the proffering of normative policy advice to government implicitly modelled as a benevolent despot (Wicksell, 1896). He suggested that improvements in policy results could emerge only from changes in the structure of political decision making. The normative attention of the economists must be shifted from choices among alternative policy options within given sets of rules to choices among alternative sets of rules.

As we know, Wicksell's advice was totally ignored for two-thirds of a century. Only since the middle of this century have economists increasingly come to appreciate the force of his message. In several research programmes, economists have commenced to turn some of their attention to *choices among constraints* and away from the exclusive focus on the familiar *choices within constraints*. At the level of individual behaviour, the economics of self-control has emerged as a viable research programme on its own. And at the much more important level of collective action, constitutional economics or political economy has come to command increasing scientific interest, especially in the 1970s and 1980s. These research programmes, along with the closely related programmes in the 'new institutional economics', broadly defined, seem almost certain to become more dominant in the next century.

The extension in the range of possible agreement on the ranking of alternatives, whether treated at the level of the analysts' normative discourse or at the level of direct choices by participating and affected persons, is a logical consequence of the shift of focus away from in-period or within-rules choices to choices among constraints or sets of rules. The necessary increase in uncertainty over the predicted sequences of outcomes generated by the workings of differing rules will force any rational chooser to adopt more generalizable criteria for choices among rules than for choices among outcomes. Any attenuation of identifiable interest produces this convergence effect; the conceptual model need not extend to the limits of the familiar Rawlsian veil of ignorance.

Wicksell was the most important precursor of the public choice 'revolution' in the analysis of politics and political process. His call for attention to structure, to constitutional rules, reflected an early recognition of interest-motivated choice behaviour in politics that might be incompatible with ideally preferred results. By contrast, the normative economics of both the classical and the ordinal utilitarians incorporated comparisons between imperfect markets and idealized politics. Almost in tandem with the development of public choice, which in its positive analysis simply extends the behavioural models of economics to persons in varying roles as public choosers, the events of history during the last decades of the century have offered observers demonstrable evidence of the failure of politicized direction of economic activity.

As the century's end approaches, economists in their normative capacities must, by necessity, compare institutional alternatives on a pragmatic basis, as informed by an understanding of organizational principles in the large. They will be unable to rely on the crutch of an idealized political order which seemed to make the task of their predecessors, the theoretical welfare economists, so easy and, in consequence, made their arguments so damaging to the standards of discourse. Increasingly, the economists will find, because of the emerging consensus in both positive and normative elements of their task and in both micro and macro applications, a greater role to play in political dialogue.

Economists, almost alone, understand the notion of choice itself, and the simple intrusion of opportunity cost logic into continuing debates provides, on its own, sufficient *raison d'être* for the profession's existence. And, having got their intellectual house in order after the internal confusion that described almost the whole of the socialist century, with a renewed inner-disciplinary confidence economists can expose the arguments of the intellectuals who discuss policy alternatives as if there are no limits on the possible.

POSTSCRIPT

I acknowledge that my predictions are tinged with hope. I sense some moral obligation to believe that preferred developments remain within the set of possibles. Little would be gained by speculation about worst-case scenarios, especially when I do not consider myself to be issuing precautionary warnings.

One caveat: I have limited discussion to possible developments that retain at least some relevance to economic reality. I have not speculated about the intellectualized irrelevancies that will continue to command some 'economists' attention so long as the discipline's ultimate *raison d'être* fails to exert positive feedbacks on the structure of inquiry.

A more significant qualification to projections here, and to those advanced by my peers, stems from the necessary limits imposed by temporal constraints. We can, perhaps, speculate meaningfully about developments in research programmes that have emerged or are emerging, and we may offer up descriptive narratives that extend over three or possibly four decades. But even to imagine developments over a full century must reckon on the emergence of research programmes that remain now within the unthinkable.

An instructive exercise is one in which we imagine ourselves to be transported back to the 1890s, and to suppose that we were then asked to speculate about developments in economics over the new century. The record would tend to confirm the hypothesis set out earlier; the subject matter of our discipline was, indeed, influenced strongly by the events of history, and, to some much lesser extent, these events were themselves influenced by the scientific inquiry of economists. But history, inclusively considered, also embodies technological change. And who could question the critical importance of the information-processing revolution in shaping the very questions that economists ask and attempt to answer? The veritable rage for empirical falsifiability of the ordinary sort may be near to running its course. But the still-developing technological frontier has enhanced economists' ability to simulate interactive behavioural results in complex institutional arrangements. Experimental economics, and especially as applied to imaginative game-like settings, seems to be a research programme in its ascendancy.

As an end note, let me suggest that prediction, in any strict sense, is impossible. Rational expectations models have re-emphasized the point that all information we can have about the future is contained in the data that we now observe. Any prediction will, therefore, be nothing more than an articulation of that which already exists. But, if 'the future', as embodied in such predictions, exists 'now', we are frozen in the time-space of the present. If we accept real time, we must acknowledge that the real future remains unknowable for the simple reason that it does not yet exist, (Shackle, 1972).

4.   Public choice after socialism

'Public choice' was born during a period of time of intense ideological conflict and grew to maturity more or less in parallel with the decline of the Marxian-socialist-collectivist ideal for the organization of socio-political-economic interaction. Public choice, as a set of ideas about politics, was not a causal influence in the demise of Marxian socialism, which would have taken place even if there had been no such emergence of a subdiscipline. On the other hand, public choice has been influential through its ability to offer an understanding-explanation of the observed failures of political processes, whether these are socialist efforts to control whole societies by command or particularized efforts at sector-by-sector politicization. The consequences of public choice will presumably by reflected in the increased difficulty that collectivist-control advocates will face in restoring the *status quo ante* in non-Western regimes and in expanding the range of politicization in Western settings.

With relatively few exceptions (for example, George Stigler), dealers in ideas, whether first or second hand, agree with the summary statement that 'ideas have consequences'. And most of us, even if we totally reject Marxian monocausality, also accept the obverse statement that 'consequences generate ideas'. Especially with reference to ideas relevant to socio-economic-political orders of human interaction, the events of history must surely be allowed to affect both the models that social scientists advance in explanation and the normative models that are suggested by reformers. History is the only laboratory available for social science, even if its limitations in such a role are fully recognized. Indeed, we may suggest that the lags and gaps in the feedback loops between consequences and ideas allow the regular occurrence of phenomena analogous to the speculative bubbles familiar to theorists of financial markets.

Both the lags and the gaps are important here. The lags refer, of course, to the temporal dimension; participants in social interaction may be slow to recognize the accumulating results of changes in institutional structures. 'Failures' may not be sensed for years, decades or possibly even centuries, especially in the absence of data from competing societies.

The gaps in the effective operation of the loops are perhaps even more significant than the lags. Because of the inability of the social scientist to conduct experiments in closed and controlled laboratories, there is little prospect of generating results that are convincing to sceptics, at least as compared with the enterprise of natural science. In social science, there is nothing akin to 'failure to fall off the edge', as might have once convinced the flat-earther. Any particular set of historical results, as observed, may be explained or interpreted by more than a single theoretical framework: falsification in Popper's sense may seldom be possible. Discrimination among alternative hypotheses may require prior agreement on the imagination of an experiment.

EXPANDING THE EXPLANATORY DOMAIN

What, then, can we make of the current and prospective state of 'public choice', as an inclusive research programme, in the post-revolutionary, post-socialist moment? We live now in a setting where genuine 'public' choice, that is, the set of attitudes held by the citizenry about the behavioural motivation of political actors, may have extended beyond any of the models that have been carefully introduced by the academic theorists. The venality that is widely imputed to politicians and bureaucrats is surely misplaced in many instances, and concentration on overt misbehaviour distracts attention from the organizational structure that allows the observed results to emerge. There is, in this respect, an important educational role for public choice to play, in its constitutional economics variant, in shifting the focus of discussion and understanding to the institutional-constitutional structure within which politics takes place.

I have addressed the issues of constitutional emphasis elsewhere (Buchanan, 1991a). Beyond this constitutional emphasis, however, is it time that positive public choice theorists make efforts to expand their domain of inquiry by moving beyond the relatively narrow behavioural limits that seem to be imposed by the economic model for behaviour? Should we begin to examine the effects of other motivational postulates on political outcomes?

Consider an example, one that comes naturally to any neoclassical economist. There is a meaningful economic content in the notion of overall economic efficiency, provided that care is taken to place all of the definitions inside the necessary qualifiers. And economists know that any restriction on freedom of persons to exchange, domestic or foreign, tends to reduce efficiency. A smaller-valued bundle of goods is made available to citizens in the economy than would be available in the absence of the restriction.

Let us now allow some members of the legislature to act as if overall efficiency in the national economy matters. These legislators vote against any and all restrictions on trade. But how many members so motivated would be required to ensure political support for a general policy of free trade, as opposed to a regime of 'black hole tariffs'? (Buchanan and Lee, 1991; Magee, Brock and Young, 1989).

The results suggested by this particular example, and by others that might be introduced, are not encouraging for those who want to challenge orthodox public choice models. The single legislator who voted for the 'public interest' and, hence, against any and all proposals to restrict trade would find his or her own constituency interests forced to sell competitively while buying from monopolists (Buchanan and Lee, 1991). The distributive game that modern democratic politics represents forces the individual legislator to act contrary to any meaningfully defined 'public interest'. If the legislator does not so act, he or she will not survive in the competitive electoral process.

Introduction of the example into the discussion of the question initially posed as to the motivational postulates for political actors suggests that at least a part of the traditional public choice emphasis, as well as the criticism, has been wrongly placed. Political actors are not necessarily motivated to depart from public interest motivational postulates because they initially are propelled by other objectives. Instead, the structure of the politics in which they act requires them to act contrary to public interests if they are to survive at all. We do not necessarily get the results we see because politicians, like the rest of us, are sometimes motivated by self-interest. We get the results we see because the incentive structures of politics ensure the survival of those politicians who do depart from public interest norms. Politicians are forced to seek private interest objectives for much the same reason that private sector entrepreneurs are forced to seek maximal profits. The seminal Alchian (1950) analysis of the market's analogue to evolutionary selection can be extended to politics in relatively straightforward fashion. The difference between the two evolutionary models lies in the compatibility with overall efficiency. The profit seeking of the private entrepreneur produces results that tend, when extended over the whole market and particularly to its dynamic growth, to maximize total economic value in the economy. By contrast, the private interest seeking of the elected politician, that is equally necessary with entrepreneurial profit seeking for survival, when extended over the whole political process, tends to shift results away from rather than towards any meaningful conception of 'public interest', whether this be economic value or any other generalized objective.

The comparison between the evolutionary forces in market processes and in political processes that is suggested here may be extended generally. Economists have discussed at some length the spontaneous coordination that takes place in an operative market economy, even if there remain aspects of the process that warrant further attention. Public choice analysts, or indeed other political science theorists, have not, to my knowledge, examined in detail the 'spontaneous coordination or discoordination' properties of political interaction structures. In both market and political orders, the mathematics of game theory offers a useful beginning, but this mathematics has not been exploited fully in either case. Beyond game theory, however, the insights offered by some of the analyses of spontaneous orders that occur outside of equilibrium settings may prove useful in application to politics as well as to economics. (See Buchanan and Vanberg, 1991.)

VEILS THAT ALLOW THE CROSSING OF BRIDGES

How can the bridge between individual pursuit of private or special group interest and promotion of the general interest be crossed? Starting from the orthodox economic model of behaviour in which persons are modelled as rational utility maximizers, the only readily available response involves the argument for the design of a choice setting in which the possibly diverging interests coincide, that is, a setting in which pursuit of private or special interest also promotes the general interest. Within a well-structured legal order, the operative market economy accomplishes this feat, provided only that the general interest is defined to be overall economic efficiency. But what is the political analogue that might accomplish the same purpose? Clearly, such an analogue cannot exist so long as politics is conceived as a distributive game among persons and groups in a community.

The distributional elements in politics must be eliminated if private or special interests are to be brought into line with the general interest. And these elements disappear only if the individuals who choose are placed in settings where their own positions (or those of the groups that they represent) are not identified. Such a setting is present if the individual is placed behind a veil of ignorance and/or uncertainty (Buchanan and Tullock, 1962; Harsanyi, 1953; Rawls, 1971). The individual's own interest becomes equivalent to that of the inclusive group that claims him or her as a member. That which is in the interest of the group, generally, defines the interest of the individual.

The discussion in the preceding section suggests that a somewhat different interpretation and usage of the veil of ignorance and/or uncertainty is possible. In the standard interpretation-usage, as noted, the question is how to design choice settings so as to exploit individual self-interest motivation. The motivation is, in itself, postulated for the whole exercise. The alternative interpretation-usage drops such a postulate. The individual, whether he or she acts privately or as an agent for a special group, may not be 'selfishly' motivated; he or she may seek to promote the general or public interest for the inclusive membership of the community. But if the structure that defines the conditions for choice contains distributional features, the person who tries to further the general interest does not survive. In this formulation of the problem, something like a veil of ignorance and/or uncertainty becomes a necessary characteristic of the choice setting if individual participants who may seek to promote the generalized interests are to remain as effective players in the political game.

In this alternative formulation, the veil of ignorance and/or uncertainty offers a bridge that allows for the political survival of those who try to act in furtherance of the general interest, which only coincidentally involves action that promotes their own interests or those of the special group represented. The evolutionary perspective surely tempers considerably the criticism of public choice that has been directed at the underlying economic model for individual behaviour in politics.

PUBLIC CHOICE AND A RULE OF LAW

The suggested evolutionary perspective also allows a relationship to be established between the veil of ignorance and/or uncertainty and the rule of law. Critics of the veil, as a practicable device in the design of constitutions as opposed to a Rawls-like derivation of normative principles, have pointed to the difficulty if not the impossibility of reducing the identifiability of political actors to any extent dictated to be useful in the choice-making exercise. But, if participants, whether at the constitutional or ordinary politics level, cannot fail to identify their own, or their group's, interests, how can the choice setting be modified so as to approximate as closely as possible the conditions provided by the thick veil?

Generalization in the objects for political choice is immediately suggested. If 'players' in the political game are required to choose only among options that, if agreed upon by the required coalition of players, must apply to *all* participants, a major source of distributional conflict is removed. (In a simple two-person game, the requirement here removes all off-diagonal cells from the set of possible solutions; choice is reduced to one from among positions along the diagonal itself.) In this construction, any player would continue to have an identifiable distributional interest in securing a solution that will ensure differentially advantageous benefit. But a generalization rule would serve effectively to prevent the realization of any such solution, to the differential benefits of anyone or any group.

Return to the free trade example introduced earlier. In the distributive game in which representatives vie for politically enforceable differential restrictions (or differential subsidies) for their constituent industries (or regions, professions, ethnic groups, gender categories, age groups and so on), any efforts toward promoting a general interest result must be predicted to founder. If, however, a generalized constitutional rule should be in effect that would legally guarantee *equal* treatment for all contending parties (industries, regions, groups and so on), no such outcome need be observed. If a particular industry should succeed in getting, say, tariff or quota protection that shuts out, say 20 per cent of foreign supply, the general rule would indicate that all imports be cut in like amounts.

In this setting, the political choice reduces to the selection of one from among the several *general* alternatives (one from the several cells along the diagonal). While distributional elements are not totally eliminated, the sources of distributional conflict are very substantially reduced, so much so that the elements that remain can be taken to reflect genuinely differing conceptions of what might be the genuine public interest. At the least, in such a choice setting, the political agent who seeks to further the general interest is not faced with a survival threat. In a very real sense, the arguments reduce to those involving alternative visions of what the public interest is.

Modern US jurisprudence has extended an enforceable rule of law in application to many personal rights; differential or discriminatory treatment by any political authority is prohibited. By dramatic contrast, constitutional interpretation has allowed a progressive narrowing of the rule of law in application to the economic treatment of persons and groups. Political authority may discriminate in treatment with little or no appeal to the violation of generality, as principle. As a result, modern politics, as it is observed, has become increasingly a politics of redistribution. The results follow the patterns predicted by the public choice models. Politicians are required by the nature of the choice settings that they face to act strictly in their own or in their constituents' interests. The politician who tries to do otherwise, who tries to further the public interest, is, at first, ineffective in the game that is played, and, second, is soon eliminated from the ranks of the players. Modern politics selects for those traits that succeed in the distributive game.

BEYOND SCIENCE

In this final section, I propose to relate the discussion of the second, third and fourth sections to the intent of the chapter, as indicated both in its title and in the introduction. I suggested that the disfavour towards politics and politicians that describes public attitudes in the post-revolutionary post-socialist moment may have been extended beyond the limits supportable from either analytical or empirical science. The economic models for the behaviour of public choosers that have informed public choice do offer highly useful insights into the political reality that can be observed. And, in this sense, these models produce an explanation-understanding of political failure, generally, and of the grand socialist experiments in particular. But in the post-revolutionary moment more is needed than this science-based understanding of what has happened in history. Extended positive analysis can also prove helpful in suggesting feasible means of achieving reform or moving beyond science into 'better' political order.

Public choice, as a predictive-descriptive social science, is vulnerable to the charge that the whole exercise is, at best, amoral, and, at worst, immoral (see

Brennan and Buchanan, 1988; Kelman, 1987.) There is no space for genuinely public-spirited behaviour in public choice, as an all-inclusive explanatory model of politics.

I have, first of all, suggested that public choice scholars should be sensitive to such criticisms, and that efforts should be made to examine carefully how changes in the basic motivational postulates might affect results. As I initially opened up discussion in this respect, an evolutionary perspective seemed to offer promise. What happens when and if a political representative, or a group of representatives, tries to act in furtherance of the general interest? Within the incentive parameters that describe modern politics, the response seems clear; such a person or group does not survive, as the game is played.

Once this point is recognized, the focus shifts *from* the motivational postulate for the behaviour of political actors *to* the characteristics of structure within which the choices are made. (And I acknowledge that orthodox public choice theorists have perhaps been overly defensive of the economic motivational bases for analysis.) The directional effect upon research effort seems clear enough. More attention should be placed on the incentive structure of the politics-as-observed, on the institutions as they are, as opposed to the stylized and sometimes empty models that are driven primarily by the motivational postulate.

Consider two familiar and traditional examples. First, an organized political community, with a long established, predictable and stable tax-sharing system confronts a genuine public goods decision, say, how much mosquito abatement to finance. The publicness characteristic of the good ensures that there will be relatively minor differences among the separate legislative constituencies in benefits received from the programme. The orthodox public-goods, public-choice model is helpful here, but there is nothing in the structure, as such, that makes it either difficult or impossible for a legislator to act in terms of his or her own assessment of the whole community's interest.

Second, a politically organized community without a stable and predictable tax sharing system faces a collective choice as to the location of one or more special benefit projects – projects that yield rewards only to identified constituencies. The legislative representative for any constituency must, in such a choice setting, act as an agent for the constituency's members. There is incentive incompatibility with any promotion of the overall general interest – an incompatibility that is not present at all in the first example. In sum, the publicly spirited politicians can thrive in the political regime that adheres to general standards of publicness. The privately spirited politicians necessarily emerge in the regime that departs from publicness or generality. Which of these two examples comes closest to the descriptive reality of politics in modern welfare states?

The evolutionary perspective is helpful to the extent that it allows concentration on the survival traits under alternative regimes. More generally, however, an evolutionary perspective must be used with caution lest it be extended too readily to the evolution of regimes, as such, and be taken to imply acquiescence before the forces of history. As the observed politics of Western welfare states demonstrate, there is no assurance that the regimes that evolve are such as to satisfy criteria that include compatibility with the survival of publicly spirited political leaders. Both modern Western regimes and those in transition from socialist structures must be treated as institutional variables subject to reform and change through deliberatively motivated action.

I have considered possible developments in 'public choice' in the new century. I have made no effort to be comprehensive, nor have I tried to advance either general or specific predictions. I have, instead, outlined the prospects for a research programme that seem to offer considerable promise – a programme that does parallel developments in applied economic theory and that does have a potential contribution for those who are trying to design the institutions for those societies in post-revolutionary transition.

5.   Post-socialist political economy[1]

In this chapter, I shall speculate about prospective developments in 'political economy', by which I shall mean the generalized application of the lessons from economic science, as well as those to be drawn from the historical experiences of this century, to the understanding of and the possible reform in the institutions of human interaction.

I want to discuss the demise of socialism *as an idea*, as opposed to the demise of socialism as historical fact. In the 1990s, we are in a period where intellectual discourse is best described by the presence of a generalized acknowledgement that socialism in its historical meaning is dead, but also by a generalized unwillingness (on the part of many participants in the discourse) to allow the spirit to depart in peace. We seem to be caught up in a setting closely analogous to that which describes any religion that incorporates the immortality of the human soul, where death of the body does not imply death of the spirit. We can say, with considerable accuracy, that socialism is dead in body but not (for many) in spirit or soul; and my central theme in this chapter is that the political economy of the next decades, in both West and East, will be described by the struggle of socialism's spirit, or idea, to find embodiment in varying institutional forms, against the continuing forces of Western liberalism (individualism) as an idea, within the developing scientific consensus that defines the feasible opportunity set of social-economic-political arrangements. The outcome of this struggle is not predictable, at least in any of its institutionalized particulars. Individual independence, or *liberty*, will always be valued, both directly and instrumentally, but individuals will also seek to exercise collective control over some of the resources at their disposal. It is much easier to imagine institutional utopias that will simultaneously satisfy these conflicting values than it is to suggest practicable means to get there from here. But more serious research, examination and discussion of federal, confederal and other relationships that combine autonomy with interdependence are more or less dictated by the urgency of events.

SOCIALISM, THE ECONOMY AND THE NATION-STATE

In its classically received definition, *socialism*, as an organizational system, is described by *collective*, as opposed to *private*, ownership of the means of production, by which reference is to the ownership of capital in all of its productive forms, including land and natural resources (Nove, 1987). More generally, we may define socialism to be characterized by *collective* control over the allocation of productive resources and the distribution of the final product. Note that, in this second definition, collective control is not contrasted with private or individual control over resource allocation and product distribution. The proper contrast here is that between collective control and the absence of control. In the nonsocialist or market economy no one controls either the allocation of resources or the distribution of product. Allocations and distributions emerge from the workings of the economy in which many persons and groups make interdependent but separated choices, not as among final allocations or distributions, but as among the alternatives that they separately confront. The ideological urge toward socialism, or collectivism generally, has, and does, stem in part from a failure to understand and to appreciate that, in the absence of collective control, it is not necessary that someone – some person or group – must, indeed, control allocation and distribution. Such understanding of spontaneous order will surely not emerge full blown from the generalized observation that, in practice, socialism failed to work as it was supposed to work by the romanticized models of its early proponents.

But let me return to the relationship between socialism and collective control. If allocation and distribution are to be collectively controlled, the collective entity or unit must be specified, in terms of membership, territorial boundaries, extent of authority and other relevant characteristics. If 'the economy' is to be collectivized, what does 'the economy' mean? This question, and similar ones, cannot be answered independently of historical experience, which yields an empirical record that describes the development of culture, technology, economic institutions and political structure. And, although the linkages must be recognized, the emergence of socialism, as an organizational ideal, coincided with the apogee of the nation-state as the dominating political unit in a culture of nationalism. Despite the internationalist rhetoric of early Marxism, socialism (defined as 'collective control') would have carried significantly differing implications for any attempts at application either globally or locally. In historical fact, the nation-state defined the unit for the collectivization of national economies that took place under socialist ideological impetus. It is important to emphasize that the failures of socialism commonly discussed after the events of 1989, especially those of the USSR and the countries of Eastern Europe, are, strictly defined, failures of the collectivization of the economies of nation-states.

FAILURES OF SOCIALISM IDENTIFIED

There are, generally, four bases for failure of collective controls over economic interaction, whether these controls be attempted at the national, the international or the local community level. There is, first, the information or *knowledge* gap between any controller, or control group, and that level of information that might be available to the many participants in the economic nexus, each of whom necessarily confronts knowledge that is localized to his own situation. This argument was the basis upon which von Mises (1932) and Hayek (1935) projected their early diagnoses of socialism's collapse. There is, second, the *incentive* incompatibility as between the objectives sought by the controllers, whatever these might be, and those sought by individuals who participate variously in the economy. This argument is, in one sense, as ancient as Aristotle's defence of private property, but it has been introduced into modern discourse primarily by the property rights and public choice strands of political economy. Third, and an argument that is an amalgam of sorts between the first and the second arguments, there is the stifling of the *creative* potential for individual entrepreneurship under collective control. Finally, and an argument that is not often explicitly listed as a basis for socialism's failure, there is the impossibility of taking advantage of *scale* in a collectivized economy, which must, in order to carry out its central objective, be closed to extensions of the economic nexus.

The failures of the attempts at collectivized control over the economies of the large nation-states in this century, and notably in the Soviet Union, are attributed to the first three of the bases noted above. Large national economies, for the most part, are presumed to be sufficiently large to internalize many of the scale advantages. As the size of the collectivized economy diminishes, however, scale elements may emerge to become important. (In 1989, Albania still made its own tractors.) It is also important to note that the scale factor exerts its influence in a direction that is opposed to the first three factors. As the size of the collective units falls, scale does become increasingly significant, but both the knowledge and the incentive problems become less important. A small socialist community, existing in isolation from economic interaction with others, may effectively exploit most information and may not face enormous incentive difficulties, but it must, by its smallness, remain grossly inefficient due to its failure to capture scale advantages.

SOCIALISM IN MARKET ECONOMIES

I think that it is appropriate to label the epoch that we are now entering as 'post-socialist', because, for the reasons noted, socialism, as a general organizing principle, is acknowledged to have failed demonstrably. In all countries that previously identified their economies to be socialist, there exist reform efforts aimed at introducing markets and market institutions. As noted earlier, however, these efforts are often accompanied by redefinitions of 'socialism' so as to eliminate reference to centralized collective control institutions and to substitute reference to collective objectives independently of organizational forms.

It is important to recognize that nowhere, either in those countries previously calling themselves socialist or in those that carry the label 'mixed' or even 'capitalist', is there strong public or political support for elimination of socialist sectors, that is, for a pure market economy. We are not, surely, entering what we might call the 'capitalist market epoch'. There has been little or no spillover from the observed failures of socialism, in the large, to the possible failures of socialist organization, in the small, as applied to sectors of those national economies that remain organized broadly on market or capitalist principles. This absence of transference in ideas deserves examination. How is it possible to acknowledge the failure of socialism as a principle for the organization of the total economy and, at the same time, continue to lend ideological as well as practicable support for collective control over relatively large shares of production and distribution in an economy – control which, in many countries, extends to include more than one-half valued product as measured?

The categories of production and distribution that are socialized in economies that are often classified to be nonsocialist are familiar: national defence, police, education, health, transport, communication, radio and television, housing, external trade, insurance, energy. Some or all of the broad industry groupings listed are socialized in all countries. And we can use the term 'socialism' in its classical sense here – the means of production are collectively owned and managed. For example, educational services are provided through collectively organized, collectively operated and collectively financed schools, the physical facilities of which are owned collectively. The investment in providing educational services is determined collectively, and the distribution of these services among potential demanders-users is settled through collectivized-bureaucratic channels. The same, or closely similar, institutionalized description could be applied to the other socialized categories. Significant variations could, of course, be observed in the usage of direct pricing both as a means of rationing the distribution and of financing total outlay.

My concern here is neither with such variations in the use of direct pricing of collectively produced services nor with the precise boundaries between the socialist and market sectors of mixed economies. My concern is with the possible spillovers, in assessment and in practice, between the acknowledged failures of socialism, as an inclusive or quasi-inclusive system of organization, and the viability of socialist sectors that may exist alongside private or market sectors of modern mixed economies. The first point to be made is one of classification and distinction. The appropriate distinction is not that between 'collective', in some generic sense, and 'private' ownership and control, but rather it is that between patterns of ownership and control that allow competitive discipline to exercise an influence and those that do not. And here reference to the relationship between socialism and the nation-state, as previously discussed, is again necessary. To the extent that productive sectors are collectivized by communities that compete, one with another, within the larger economy defined by the boundaries of the nation-state, it is inappropriate to classify these sectors to be 'socialist' for the purpose at hand.

As an example, we may return to education. If the provision of educational services is organized and financed by local units, by localized collectives, that exist alongside each other in a more extensive national economy, the educational services industry is surely closer, descriptively, to the market pole than to that of centralized, monolithic socialism. In a real sense, the separate local units simply replace individuals (families) or firms as units in the working of market organization. And the total investment in, and final distribution of, educational services in the national economy is *not* collectively determined at all; these are, instead, emergent outcomes of the many locally collectivized but decentralized choices that are made separately and independently of each other. The competition with other units must, of course, severely constrain the operation of the activity or enterprise that is locally collectivized, even to the extent of eliminating the semblance of collective control, as such. There may be, however, institutional arrangements that will, simultaneously, allow for some exploitation of competitive forces and some satisfaction of collectivist urges.

The failures of centralized socialism should carry a message for reformers who would shift toward more centralized organization and control of locally collectivized or socialized productive sectors. In the United States, we should beware of efforts to nationalize the educational industry, along with other parts of the public sector that remain largely, if not totally, under localized collective control. Standardization will almost surely reduce, if not eliminate, the competition among localized collectives, thereby exacerbating the informational and incentive problems, with little or no gain in scale economies.

I propose, now, to concentrate attention on those sectors that are centrally socialized, by which I mean that the collective unit is coincident in authority with the broadly inclusive national economy or economic nexus. What lessons can be drawn from the failures of socialism, as a general principle of organization, for these centrally socialized industries, and what reforms might we expect to see proposed and possibly implemented?

The response to this question depends on the extent to which the demise of socialism, as fact, carries with it the demise of socialism, as an idea – the distinction mentioned earlier. If the failures of socialism, in practice, have served to undermine the intellectual-ideological bases that have served to legitimize the institutions of socialist organization, we might, indeed, predict such carryover. Those socialized sectors of mixed economies will, in this case, be subjected to increasing critical scrutiny in the decades ahead, and reforms that are summarized under the 'privatization' rubric will become even more frequently observed to become potentially effective. If, however, the intellectual-ideological foundations for socialist order are able substantially to withstand the events of 1989, we may predict minimal carryover impact on the operation and support of socialist sectors of Western economies. Is socialism now rejected as an ideal or does its failure refer only to attempted practical implementation of an ideal that remains?

What is the socialist ideal? And to what is it counterposed in ideological argument? As noted earlier, the central normative thesis is that the allocation of resources and the distribution of product should be controlled collectively – that allocation and distribution should not be left to emerge from the coordination processes of the market in which individuals, separately, make choices without consideration of economy-wide allocative or distributive consequences. In this definition of the central normative thrust of socialism, so-called 'market socialism' appears to be an aberration. An organization of the economy that would serve to satisfy the separate demands of individuals, as expressed in some artificially constructed institutional analogues to markets, would totally fail to advance the socialist ideal, which is precisely that of replacing the spontaneity of decentralized individual choice with explicit collective control.

My own assessment is that, despite the events of 1989, there has been little flagging in intellectual support for socialism as an ideal. The demonstrable failures have produced a begrudging recognition that informational, incentive and entrepreneurial difficulties encountered in efforts collectively to control whole economies are overwhelming, and that decollectivization is dictated in many sectors. But the necessary trade-off is seen to be that between the sacrifice of collective control – a sacrifice that is intrinsically undesirable – and the promised gains in productivity, an objective that is valued. The liberal position that rejects the desirability of collective control, quite apart from its efficacy, has not informed the thinking of more than a very small number of the participants in the post-1989 discourse.

If my interpretation is correct here, we should not expect dramatic shifts in the organization of currently-socialized sectors of those countries whose economies have not been described to be within the explicitly socialist group. Reform movements that include privatization have been and will be observed, but these movements will be motivated primarily by pragmatic objectives of internal efficiency rather than by a reversal of the underlying socialist ideal. There will, of course, be a greater awareness of the efficiency-damaging features of collectivized control, wherever exercised. But there will also be increasing recognition that the presence of a substantially large market sector, alongside the socialist one, must, in itself, place limits on the inefficiency of collectivist organization.

So long as resources, and especially labour, are allowed to move between the market and socialist sectors, while, at the same time, persons are allowed to enter into private production of close substitutes for goods and services that are produced collectively, there are 'inefficiency boundaries' that socialized or nationalized industries cannot go beyond. If collectivized industries are open to market competition, both in input and output markets, both domestic and foreign, there could be little or no basis for depoliticization *per se*. The critical element is, of course, that collectivization, as it operates, tends to carry with it monopolistic restriction that allows for the exploitation of resource suppliers and product demanders. (An example is the US Postal Service which could scarcely be viable except for its legally protected monopoly position.) As noted earlier, it is the absence of competition that is crucial here, and it is competition, as the embodiment of the spontaneous forces of the market, that the socialist ideology categorically rejects.

WELFARE TRANSFERS IN MARKET ECONOMIES

I have defined socialism, generally, as collective control of the allocation of resources among separate uses and the distribution of products among persons in the political community. This definition has the advantage of facilitating a categorical distinction between socialism, so defined, and the welfare or transfer state. By the latter, as a generalized organizational structure, I refer to an economy-polity in which individuals are allowed to determine the allocation of resources through decentralized markets, both for inputs and for outputs. Consumers are the ultimate sovereigns, as in the idealized market economy of the classical liberals. In its idealization the welfare state embodies no collective control over allocation, but it does claim collective authority and control over the *distribution* of economic value among persons of the community.

The distinction between socialism and the welfare state, as idealized forms of organization, may be illustrated by reference to Bentham's famous utilitarian comparison between pushpin and poetry. The socialist position requires a collective evaluation as between these two uses of scarce resources, presumably with a bias toward elevating poetry to priority status. The position of the welfarist would not, ideally, allow for a judgment as between such uses of resources; rather, the position would imply that, if the distribution of economic value is arranged to meet collectively determined norms, any allocation as between pushpin and poetry might be indirectly legitimized. Again by comparison, and in its idealized form, the classical liberal position would legitimize any allocation and any distribution that emerges from the free play of market forces.

Of course, we should rarely expect to find personal representatives for either of these ideal-type positions. Many of those who are classified as classical liberals, myself included, may assign normative legitimacy to limited collective redistribution and may also recognize that collective allocation is necessary in technologically-defined public goods interactions. Similarly, many supporters of modern welfare transfers, although they place their primary normative emphasis on distribution, may extend collective norms to the allocation of basic goods such as education and medical care. Some mixture of ideal types may be anticipated, but the distinction made here between socialism and welfare statism is important because, post-1989, many of those who espoused socialism have made efforts to shift the meaning of this term so as to make it apply primarily to the welfare state idealization of collectivized distribution. In the face of this apparently determined effort to capture terminological ground, the categorical distinction between socialist allocation and welfarist distribution deserves emphasis.

What elements in socialism's failure extend, at least in principle, to the organization and operation of the redistributionist welfare or transfer state? Listed above as sources for socialism's failure were: knowledge, incentives, entrepreneurship and scale. Because allocation is not explicitly collectivized in the welfare state, problems of knowledge, incentive incompatibility and entrepreneurship are substantially attenuated by comparison with the socialist order, despite the collectivization of distribution. Individuals, in their capacities as producers, organizers of firms, entrepreneurs and input suppliers, are at liberty to respond to the demands of individuals, as demanders of outputs. They can take advantage of localized information, and they face incentives that are ultimately consistent with the demands of consumers. Indirectly, the distortions induced by the tax-transfer mechanism must, of course, reduce efficiency in some ways comparable to full-scale collectivization. But there remains a difference in kind as between socialism and the transfer state.

The welfare-transfer state encounters its own difficulties, however, in the form of *motivational*, as opposed to *directional*, incentives. The worker-investor-producer-entrepreneur in the redistributionist state may face proper directional signals, but these signals are weak by comparison with those present in the liberal order. For example, an investment or profit opportunity may promise a differential return of $100 over alternative prospects, pre-tax and pre-transfer. But, with a relatively large transfer sector, this differential may be reduced to, say, $40, post-tax and post-transfer. Clearly, the effect is to make the response more sluggish and to make the aggregate economy less flexible in adjusting to changes in technology as well as to other exogenous shifts in the environment.

Closely related to, but different from, the generalized motivational problem, the welfare-oriented collectivity also finds it impossible to levy charges and pass out transfers in a nondiscriminatory manner. Some producers of economic value will be taxed heavily, some lightly and some not at all. Some claimants for transfers will secure large stipends, some small stipends and some no stipends at all. And the existence, and the persistence, of such differentials in treatment will, in turn, offer incentives for persons, as producers and as claimants, to shift from disfavoured to favoured positions. The result is allocational distortion by comparison with the efficiency norms of the ideally neutral structure. These 'excess burden' costs may become large in the large welfare state, and they are over and beyond those identified to emerge under the generalized motivational rubric above. I shall discuss still a further incentive related basis for partial failure of the welfare state in the section following.

The welfare-transfer state, like the socialist state, can only with difficulty remain open to the necessary competitiveness of international markets. The incentive difficulties noted above ensure that the country that attempts relatively more comprehensive redistribution than its trading counterparts must suffer the consequences in its rate of economic growth. Recognition of this elementary fact exerts dual pressures; towards limits on the size of the transfer sector internally and towards national autonomy. If the second of these influences predominates in policy direction, there must be losses from the failure to exploit the scale advantages that are captured only in the international trading nexus.

POLITICAL ECONOMY AND DEMOCRATIC GOVERNANCE

This book, as well as this chapter, is entitled, 'Post-Socialist Political Economy', which suggests that the political and economic elements of social organization cannot be readily disentangled. The demise of socialism involves both the acknowledged economic failures of collective control of resource allocation and product distribution and the accompanying failures of governance processes to secure individual rights and liberties. Socialism, as a totalitarian political regime, has been rejected by the regime's members, almost independently of its economic record. Unfortunately, it is also the case that many persons remain under the delusion that the introduction of democratic governance will, as if by some magic, ensure the satisfactory resolution of all problems of economic organization. This view imputes the failures in historical experience to those of politics rather than economics, and the romanticized contradiction of 'democratic socialism' is still encountered in quasi-serious argument. In terms of current ideological impetus, the thrust toward democratization of the politics of the socialist bloc countries seems more powerful than that toward decollectivization of the economies. And the painful transition of these countries toward some post-socialist political economy will surely be marked by some shattering of the roseate dreams of democratic deliverance.

The post-socialist political economies of Western countries will be democratic, in both form and substance. The demise of communism as the socialist embodiment has substantially eliminated any threat of totalitarianism. But democratic governance creates its own problems, and especially democratic governance that operates without satisfactory constitutional constraints. These problems ensure that those sectors that are socialist in organizational form are not operated at levels of efficiency that would be attainable, even given the standard incentive and knowledge constraints. Over and beyond these familiar efficiency-reducing elements inherent in socialist organization as such, there are particular constraints that emerge in democratic settings. Employees in socialized industries make up a natural interest group that is able to bring pressure on democratically elected legislators. The socialist equivalent to bankruptcy in the market does not exist. Producing interests, whether in socialized or market sectors, will always seek differential protection. But a major transactions cost barrier is supervened by the monopolistic structure of socialized industries. A private industry must first bear the costs of internal cartelization before seeking legislative protection. A socialized industry is effectively cartelized from the moment of its establishment.

The interactions between the institutions of democratic governance and the welfare-transfer sector of modern states accentuate one efficiency-reducing feature of any collective intrusion into market order. If a substantial share of the total economic value produced in an economy is coercively transferred from those who initially receive payments as pre-tax distributive shares to those who qualify as claimants or recipients, there arise incentives, not only to avoid assigned tax liabilities and to qualify for claims, but, in addition, to change the structure of the tax-transfer system through the political process. Investment in rent seeking seems to offer profit opportunities. Individuals and groups will seek not only to capture the rents that any existing tax-transfer system makes possible, but also to modify directly the structure of the system itself. This sort of rent seeking activity is 'socially wasteful' in a way that differs from the more familiar excess-burden destruction of potential economic value. The interest group that secures favourable tax or transfer treatment for its members may find its investment profitable, but other competing groups make losses. And the total investment may far exceed the politically created gains that seem to be promised.[2]

Overt exploitation of democratic politics as a means to further differential advantages by particular groups in the economy will increase as the ideological 'temperature' falls from that level that described the long socialist epoch. To the extent that individuals considered themselves to be members of an inclusive, economy-wide collectivity, as opposed to identification with separated interest groups, there was less motivation to seek gains at the expense of others within the larger nexus. If, and to the extent that, this collective mind-set becomes weaker, separate groups will try to use institutions of democratic politics along with those of markets to secure differential advantages. The 'end of ideology', whether total or partial, is not without major costs. This effect is perhaps especially important in those countries that previously organized their economies on socialist principles, but the spillovers will also apply to any countries that contain large socialist and/or transfer sectors.

UTOPIAN SPECULATIONS

To this point, I have confined discussion largely to positive analysis of the political economy of the post-socialist epoch that we are now entering. In sum, I have suggested that this period will be described as one in which the socialist-collectivist mind-set will not have disappeared, although it must exert a significantly reduced influence on events. There will be general, although begrudging, acknowledgement that market organization is superior in the generation of economic value. But this attitude will have minor spillover effects on the socialized or transfer sectors of nonsocialist economies. A genuinely revolutionary establishment of the ideal structure of political economy as envisaged by the classical liberals will not take place. Individuals remain unwilling to jettison romanticized notions of collective control over economic processes. Economic understanding, in itself, does not produce ideological conversion to *laissez-faire*.

Effective reform must incorporate both the advances in economic understanding, based on the experiences of history and on progress in analysis, and the inner collectivist-communitarian urges that motivate the behaviour of many individuals. These two elements carry implications that are directly contradictory only in those institutional settings that are described by a precise correspondence or mapping between the political and the economic nexus – a correspondence that was rarely questioned in the epoch of the political nation-state and the attempted socialist organization of national economies. Reform that is aimed towards some breaking of this correspondence offers the genuine opportunity of the coming decades.

Markets succeed in producing higher-valued bundles of goods and services because they exploit the forces of *competition*; socialism fails because these forces are not allowed to operate. The emphasis here is on the presence or absence of competition rather than upon the presence or absence of collective organization, as such. The implication is that, if the collective unit that might be organized to meet the collectivist urges can be placed in competitive settings, the limits to inefficient operation are built into the system. To the extent that the economy of a nation-state can be opened up to the competitive forces of international markets, the potential failures of internalized collective controls, even if attempted, are severe. Further, if, a devolution of activities to locally organized collective units can generate competitive forces within the nation-state as among these units, that will ensure at least tolerable efficiency in operation. Federal, confederal and consociational structures, both within existing nation-states and between and among such nation-states, surely become the subject matter of research programmes of increasing importance. The European community of nations offers perhaps the critical testing ground here. Will the historical nation-states of Western Europe move toward a common market economy that will exploit the forces of competition among the separate national units, or will these nation-states try to implement Europe-wide collective control over the whole economy? In the first case, Europe will, indeed, become the dominant economy of the next few decades. In the second case, Europe will stagnate.

Technology may be important in shaping the events of history. The information-communication revolution has served to bring all parts of the world closer one to another. In an optimistic projection, this technology might guarantee that the economies of the world will become more open, and that the increased competitiveness, on many levels, will act to constrain severely the efficiency-reducing effects of attempted collective controls.[3] The utopian realist, by comparison, will not rely on technology to produce deliverance, but will, instead, advance and support constitutional-institutional change in both the internal political structures of nation-states and the external relationships among these units. Three decades ago, Michael Polanyi, the distinguished chemist turned philosopher-political economist, gave a series of lectures at the University of Virginia under the title, 'History and Hope' (Polanyi, 1962). Let me end by using this combination of words to suggest that the history of this century does offer hope for the post-socialist century that will follow. But hope alone is not enough; hard-headed recognition of both the potential and the limits of man's ability to control his destiny is required. And such recognition must replace the romance, or in Hayek's terms (1988), we must shed the 'fatal conceit' that described the socialist century.

NOTES

1. A version of this chapter was presented at the Jerusalem Center for Public Affairs, Jerusalem, Israel, in June 1991.
2. The rent seeking research programme dates from the seminal paper by Gordon Tullock (1967a). Most of the early contributions are contained in Buchanan, Tollison and Tullock (1980).
3. For a presentation of this optimistic projection, see McKenzie and Lee (1991).

6.   Economic science and cultural diversity

This chapter offers an outsider's response to the question: 'Is there a European economics'? I propose to broaden the issue by asking: 'Does the scientific content of economics depend on cultural parameters'?[1] This reformulation of the question recalls the central issue of the nineteenth-century *Methodenstreit* between members of the German historical school and the early Austrian economists, notably Carl Menger, as well as the early twentieth-century disputes between the American institutionalists and their neoclassical peers.

My response is predictably ambivalent. There is, indeed, a universalizable science of 'economics', made up of a core set of propositions that apply to human behaviour in any and all environments, transcending boundaries of time and space. There is also, however, a more inclusive economics that allows the derivation of propositions about the workings of organizational alternatives that are meaningful only within particular historical and cultural settings. The answer to the question need not be a categorical 'No' or 'Yes'.[2]

BEHAVIOUR WITHIN CONSTRAINTS

Economics is a science of human behaviour – a behaviour that is more complex than that of nonhuman animals. Genetic determinants remain central to any explanatory enterprise, but human behaviour is also influenced by norms that act as internal constraints. And such constraints may differ as among separate interaction environments that may be temporally, geographically, culturally and institutionally classified. Behaviour is, of course, also influenced directly by external constraints that may operate on basic propensities to act that may be uniform over all members of the species, quite independently of time and space. The distinction between internal and external constraints on behaviour is not at all easy to make, but it remains central to any resolution of the question concerning the provinciality of economics as a scientific enterprise.

How is economics, a science of human behaviour, different from a science of the behaviour of another animal species or subspecies, say, smooth-haired fox terriers? In the second of these undertakings, the practising scientist would recognize that any observed experimental results depend on the constraints imposed on behaviour, including those that may be informally programmed by prior training. However, under uniform conditions that may be objectively specified, the scientist would predict that similar patterns of behaviour would emerge among all members of the subspecies. All else being equal, European fox terriers in the 1990s would not be predicted to behave differently from Asian fox terriers of the nineteenth century.

How is the first undertaking different? How is economics, defined as a human behavioural science, to be methodologically distinguished from that applicable to any animal species? To be sure, the constraints within which behaviour takes place may be observed to vary systematically with geographical location due to the territorial dimensionality of political organization, but would it not remain appropriate to hypothesize that uniform constraints generate uniform patterns of behaviour?

Many economists may be unwilling to extend the claims of their science so far. They will recognize the difficulties involved in separating, even as a conceptual exercise, behaviour that may be observed from the institutional setting within which such behaviour takes place. Observed behaviour reflects the presence of both internal and external constraints, and, to the extent that internal constraints influence choices at all, there are historical, geographical and cultural dimensions to be placed on the derivation of a scientific proposition (Buchanan, 1994a).

Several developments in economics, inclusively defined, over the half-century following World War II may be summarized in the statement that 'institutions matter'.[3] But the 'institutions matter' claim may be narrowly interpreted as nothing more than a call for economists to examine more carefully the structural constraints within which behaviour takes place – constraints that are implicitly assumed to be subject to exogenous change. Such an interpretation prompts ideas to the effect that reform limited to modifications in formal institutional structures may be all that is required to ensure progress towards the achievement of agreed upon end-state objectives. (In this attitude, we may locate some of the early post-1992 expectations that the introduction of formal legal reforms facilitating the emergence of markets would in itself ensure economic growth and stability in former communist regimes.)

The economist who does not extend his or her scientific claims so far and who acknowledges the influence of internal constraints on behaviour may, nonetheless, agree on the directional efficiency of institutional reform. But any claim for the efficacy of such reform may be placed squarely within a temporal and spatial dimension.

CULTURAL EVOLUTION AND THE UNIVERSALITIES OF ECONOMIC SCIENCE

If the reality of cultural evolution as an influence on human behaviour is acknowledged, it follows that differences in cultural history must exert behavioural consequences. Even if uniformity in basic genetic characteristics is postulated for all members of the human species independently of time and place, any particular person or group whose behaviour may be isolated for examination is described extragenetically by a cultural history that cannot be stripped away to reveal some common behavioural generator within. The technology of modern science is unable to show us 'the naked ape' as an analytical tool in any operationally useful sense. But to say that behaviour cannot be fully explained by postulated genetic uniformities is not, of course, the same as saying that genetic determinants are absent altogether or even that they remain unimportant relative to nongenetic elements.

As noted earlier, there is a universalizable scientific economics, even if limited in scope – an economics that allows for the derivation of some falsifiable hypotheses that may be tested quite independently of historical and cultural context. The resolution of any apparent paradox here lies in the distinction that must be made among separate levels and directions of inquiry defined in terms of the specificity of the predictions sought. There are propositions in economics that transcend history and culture. Persons seek their own betterment – a state that can be objectively identified in measures of the availability of commonly valued 'goods'. With respect to these basic propositions, there is no 'European' or 'twentieth century' economics, as such. As we move much beyond these basic propositions, however, and as we try to predict behavioural responses to constraint changes more specifically, the influence of history and culture becomes increasingly relevant.

Adam Smith's understanding and explanation of a market order was conditioned by the parameters that described the 'laws and institutions' of eighteenth-century Scotland, which included the morality of the traders he observed. Much of what Smith said was generalizable, as indeed the timeless and spaceless repute of *The Wealth of Nations* (Smith, 1776) attests. But economists have perhaps been careless in their relative neglect of the cultural provinciality of the behaviour that Smith implicitly postulated. The butcher acts in his own self-interest when he supplies meat for purchase, but the butcher is presumed to act within the moral norms that impose internal limits on opportunistic cheating.

The 'discipline of continuous dealings' may, of course, be invoked to explain why norms for behaviour that seem internal may be externally imposed. But, as Hayek (1976) has stressed, the achievement of the extended market order must have depended, historically, on the evolution of codes of personal conduct that restrict opportunistic behaviour even in dealings with strangers. These aspects of behaviour are culturally determined, and they cannot be universalized so as to apply comparably in settings described by categorically divergent temporal and spatial dimensions (Buchanan, 1994b).

If the object of inquiry is sufficiently specific to require predictions as to the efficacy of self-enforcing norms in constraining the opportunistic behaviour of market participants (predictions that would, of course, be needed if alternative political-collective rules are considered), the cultural environment must be relevant. And, in such a context there is surely a 'Western' economics, even if not specifically 'European', that must be different from 'Non-Western' economics.

THE LIMITS OF MARKET AND POLITICS

Let me return to Adam Smith. He used the eighteenth-century postulate that persons uniformly seek their own advantages to construct his analysis of the efficiency of the simple system of natural liberty and, finally, to demonstrate that the wealth of the citizens of nations is furthered by removing political controls on market behaviour. In its largest sense, Smith's message can be interpreted as telling us that there are mutual gains from trade, and that these gains will be exploited if persons are allowed voluntarily to enter into and exit from exchange relationships. From this seminal source, the normative argument for *laissez-faire* seems to follow directly. Why should personal behaviour be restricted in any way if, left unrestricted, it operates to the general advantage of all parties?

The enthusiasts for *laissez-faire*, early and late, failed to recognize that there are two distinct parts to Smith's message: (1) There are mutual gains from trade and (2) these gains will tend to be exploited by voluntary behaviour of the prospective traders. The validity of the first proposition depends only on the identification of 'goods' and the existence of differences in preferences and/or endowments (capacities) among potential traders; there is no direct behavioural content. The second proposition, by contrast, implies that potential traders are predicted to behave so as to secure the *mutual* gains guaranteed by the validity of the first statement. Note, in particular, the relationship of the second proposition to the more general hypothesis that persons seek to maximize the satisfaction of their own preferences. The two hypotheses correspond only if trade or exchange is the unique behavioural alternative to the *status quo* or pretrade status of either of the two traders, in the finally factored down two-party exchange confrontation.

The familiar PD matrix (Figure 6.1), with ordinal payoffs is illustrative (see Mueller, 1979). Consider the options that face each of the two players, *A* and

B. Each may cooperate (*c*) by reciprocally entering into the exchange relationship and may defect (*d*) by attempting to exploit differentially the trading opportunity that exists. Each player secures higher payoffs in the solution *cc* than *dd*. But note that, as depicted, one or the other of the two players secures the differentially highest payoff in the off-diagonal cells. To hypothesize that mutual gains from exchange will be exploited is to suggest that either (1) the PD setting does not describe the pre-trade situation or (2) the players are internally constrained from maximizing the objectively defined ordinal payoffs. (If payoffs are defined as utility or expected utility indicators, the exercise becomes tautological.)

		B	
		c	d
A	c	3, 3	1, 4
	d	4, 1	2, 2

Figure 6.1

Economists who claim universality for the basic behavioural propositions of their science and who seek to ground normative inferences strictly on these propositions may fall back on the first of these two escape routes. That is to say, the claim may be that the properly estimated expected payoffs are not such as to place players in the dominance setting indicated. In practical terms, potential traders must always and everywhere confront penalties (in expected value terms) for unilateral efforts to capture differential advantages. Stealing, cheating, default, defraud and breach are never privately advantageous.

This generalized argument advanced in support of the *laissez-faire* norm seems illegitimate. It is surely more convincing to argue that internal constraints may modify behaviour in certain cultural temporal environments so as to cause potential traders to shun patterns of behaviour that involve the seeking of differential advantage at the explicit expense of trading partners. But the obverse possibility must also be reckoned with. In some cultural settings, such internal constraints may not be present, in which case Smith's second proposition concerning the exploitation of the mutuality of gains may not be valid. In this case, the normative defence of *laissez-faire* does not carry through, at least at the initial stage of discourse. Market organization, characterized by freedom of entry into and exit from exchange, will not necessarily ensure 'the wealth of nations', at least in the sense of the achievement of the economic value that the resource potential might ideally make possible.

Recognition of the limits of *laissez-faire* as the normative principle for organizing the economy of a society owing to the possible absence of operative internal constraints does not, however, carry the twentieth-century romantic inference that political or collective organization is necessarily more effective. In the absence of internal behavioural constraints that limit personal behaviour in seeking differential advantage, markets do not work well. But neither do the political correctives that the romantic model of 'public interest' motivation seems to generate. As the modern theory of public choice has demonstrated, politics fail, along with markets, when observed results are set alongside ideally attainable alternatives.

ECONOMICS AND MORAL PHILOSOPHY

My discussion has already digressed too much towards political philosophy and away from the central focus of the chapter which is aimed at answering the question about the universalizability of economic science in the face of temporal-cultural diversity. Nonetheless, the primary result seems clear. If the propositions of economic science are to be useful in drawing normative inferences concerning the constitutional-organizational structure of society, cultural parameters that describe the behavioural attitudes of participants must be taken into account. In this sense, there is indeed an economics that must be culture bound. But if, by contrast, the propositions of economic science are limited exclusively to the derivation of empirically testable hypotheses about the effects of changes in externally imposed constraints, there need be no cultural identification. Demand curves do slope downward, independently of time, place and culture, although particular response patterns may be quite divergent in different settings.

As suggested earlier, there are important political implications to be drawn from a recognition that cultural differences can affect economic behaviour. Although his particular identification of its sources may in part have been empirically and historically inaccurate, Max Weber's emphasis on 'the spirit of capitalism', as related to an underlying ethos was surely relevant to any understanding of economic development in Western Europe (Weber, 1930). Transferences of formalized institutional structures, including the privatization of property, to environments with substantially different ethical standards in the expectation of *Wirtschaftswunder* were foredoomed to disappoint such hope.

Even more significant may be the cumulative changes in the ethos of the West. The overreaching of the modern welfare state has exerted dual effects on the taxing and spending sides of the ethical as well as the fiscal account. In the large number settings of Western nation-states, ethical norms for voluntary tax compliance necessarily erode as revenue exactions increase. Similarly, the moral acceptability of dependency status is enhanced as increasing numbers of citizens qualify for transfers. The widely observable features of modern society cannot fail to exert indirect influences on the behavioural attitudes of persons engaged in market interactions. How long can tax cheaters remain honest traders? And how long can persons supply 'honest days' work' when take-home wages move ever closer to the levels of nonreciprocated welfare payments?

It is coming increasingly to be recognized that the welfare economics of the 2000s will not be the welfare economics of the 1950s. The nongenetic behavioural uniformities of the members of the species will have been modified. Perhaps economists should stick to their lasts and continue to use their universalizable propositions to assist in the formulation of institutional-constitutional change that will at least be directionally efficacious. But they must do so in the full knowledge that economic prosperity and social tranquillity may require reconstructive change in the ethical-moral constitutions within which behaviour is also constrained.

NOTES

1. When I mentioned the initially assigned question to three colleagues, separately, each of them responded with immediate reference to 'economics', as produced by the academic-scientific establishment and noted the possible influence of incentives operative within the European establishment. Interestingly, this interpretation of the question did not occur to me at all.
2. In an interesting recent paper, Michael D. White (1994) examines the position of Jevons on the relevance of cultural determinants in economic science.
3. Such research programmes as law-and-economics, the new economic history, public choice, property rights economics, constitutional economics and the new political economy deserve mention.

A13   A10

7.   Economics as a public science

For Knight, the primary role of economic theory is ... to contribute to an understanding of how by consensus based on rational discussion we can fashion liberal society in which individual freedom is preserved and a satisfactory economic performance achieved (George J. Stigler, 1987, p. 58).

How should economists do economics? This opportunity allows me to develop propositions about peculiar features of economics and the implications for activity that stem therefrom. My position is essentially that imputed to my professor, Frank Knight, in the frontispiece citation from George Stigler's *Palgrave* entry. But the implications of this position require some articulation.

In a summary sense, I use the word 'public' as an adjective in the chapter's title to describe what there is about 'economics' that makes it distinct from other inquiries. All science is public in the familiar sense summarized in the second section. But there is a 'publicness' to economics that goes well beyond the familiar, and it is this public aspect that makes those of us who claim to be professionals behave (or so should behave) quite differently from our hard science counterparts. In making the argument here, I call on the theory of public goods in application to the science itself.

Not surprisingly, attention must be paid to the role of teaching, which should be different (but often is not) from that which describes other scientific disciplines. Also, not surprisingly, some indirect reference must be made to the practical applications of the science.

SCIENCE AS A PUBLIC GOOD

The knowledge component of any science is recognized to meet the classificatory definition of a public or collective 'good' in the sense laid out by Paul A. Samuelson in his seminal paper (Samuelson, 1954). Once generated, knowledge can be made available to everyone as easily as to anyone. And there are no readily available means through which persons may be denied access to knowledge that is valued.

The implications familiar from welfare theory follow directly. Because knowledge qualifies as a public good, persons, acting separately or organized as through firms, cannot be predicted to produce genuinely scientific knowledge in the amount that might be judged to be 'efficient', as determined by the preferences of all members of the politically organized community. There is a publicness-externality justification for some collective subsidization of the production of basic scientific knowledge.

The generalized understanding of the working of an organized economy that is generated by the activity of economists is not different from the understanding of the physical universe generated by the activity of natural scientists. In either case, such understanding is not likely to be advanced sufficiently, either quantitatively or qualitatively, in the absence of some collective support, as appropriately institutionalized. Economists, like physicists, chemists or biologists, would be relatively unrewarded in the operation of a wholly decollectivized society.

In the United States, the sciences are institutionally subsidized, directly or indirectly, through publicly supported academic structures. In these structures, scientists are rewarded only in small part for their direct contributions to knowledge. Instead they are recompensed for the instruction and training of others, only a small fraction of whom are themselves expected to become practising scientists. The scientists-instructors are engaged by collectively-financed institutions to provide a generalized understanding of their areas of specialized knowledge to those members of the community who are expected to be its leaders. Such understanding of science is alleged to be central to general education. In this sense, a knowledge of science, including economics, is a necessary qualification for literacy.

ECONOMICS IN PUBLIC APPLICATION

It is only in the application of its scientific content that economics comes to be categorically distinct from its scientific neighbours. And it is at this point that the 'public science' appellation becomes relevant. With relatively few exceptions, the applications of natural science can be, and are, organized through noncollective or private institutional structures. For example, the scientific discovery of a synthetic drug is preliminary to subsequent research, testing, development, production and marketing of a final product, each stage of which may be organized by privately-owned, profit-seeking firms. These stages toward the ultimate application of the scientific findings do not embody the characteristic publicness features that describe the activity of basic science. Rivalry replaces nonrivalry in potential usage, and exclusion offers a means of linking costs and promised benefits for those who place the differentially higher values on the final product.

With economics, properly defined, there is no comparable shift from 'publicness' to 'privateness' as the move from pure to applied science takes place.

Applied physics becomes engineering, and those who do engineering, as such, command and secure compensation in the ordinary marketplace. The engineer applies the laws of physics and chemistry to enable him to instruct clients as to how to achieve whatever objective is designated to be desired. Applied economics, if interpreted analogously, would become 'social engineering', but confusion emerges when it is recognized that there is no external client that dictates the objective to be sought. The 'economist as social engineer' is too often placed in the roles both of the engineer, as applied scientist, and the philosopher-king, as the ultimate social chooser among end objectives. The professionally trained scientist who sets himself up as an 'applied economist' cannot readily market his knowledge in the private sector. The reason is that the scientific knowledge, even at this level of application, remains 'public' in the sense that there is no partitionable product upon which users may separately place value. Another way of putting this point is to say that access to applied economic knowledge does not provide persons with privileged claims to sources of market value.

What, then, is the 'product' of economic science? If we accept the existence of a body of scientific knowledge that contributes to an understanding of the social interaction process, it is surely incumbent on us to have some idea as to how this knowledge may be applied in furtherance of some preferred objectives. It is here that the peculiar status of economics emerges on to centre stage. The 'product' of genuine economic science can only be described as the enactment, or repeal, of 'laws' or 'rules' that act to constrain or channel behaviour so as to allow persons to produce more effectively those goods and services that they themselves value. Note that this definition of the 'product' of economic science is fully consistent with the Knight position summarized in the Stigler frontispiece citation and with Adam Smith's statement to the effect that political economy is the science of legislation.

There are two distinct features of the 'product' here that make the publicness attribution appropriate. First of all, any general law becomes public in the Samuelsonion sense for all members of the group of persons who are subject to its application and enforcement. A law that limits the activity of one person also limits the activities of others within the relevant jurisdiction. The essential meaning of law itself is subverted if arbitrary differentiation or discrimination in application is introduced. Hence, if economic science has, as its final product, better laws, rules or institutions, the public science appellation is valid.

There is, however, quite a different sense of 'publicness' that is involved here. If, indeed, we acknowledge that economic science makes possible an understanding of social interaction, why do we not defer to the scientific authority of those who are professionally trained? Why do members of the citizenry reject the efforts of economic scientists to assume roles as 'engineers'? The response is straightforward. We may acknowledge the superior understanding of the economic scientist while, at the same time, we do not accept that this science can be decisively important in informing us about the choices we must make in choosing among the laws and rules that we are to impose upon ourselves. Differently from natural science, the applications of economics cannot be separately and independently tried out for particular persons in separated markets. With economics, the publicness feature of law guarantees that only one experiment can be conducted at a time and an experiment that necessarily involves all members of the community as its subjects. And only on rare occasions will everyone volunteer to become a guinea pig. It is scarcely credible to think that the authority of economic science could ever be such as to command such universal assent. (See Hutt, 1936.)

What to do? It is as if the application of scientific knowledge in, say, physics could not be introduced until and unless generalized public agreement is achieved. What would the physicist try to do under such circumstances? It would seem necessary to try to instruct everyone in the elementary principles of the science, thereby providing a basis for general agreement on various practical applications. Persons would need to be informed about the science, at least sufficiently to be able to know how to discriminate among authorities who claim scientific status. Needless to say, the teaching of physics would be, and should be, quite different in such a setting from that which is observed. Teaching would necessarily be extended well beyond the contributions toward minimal literacy contained in general education.

In its application, therefore, economics is public in a sense that is quite distinct from natural science. And there are profound implications to be drawn for the activity of scientists that stem directly from these differences. Teaching must involve a transmission of the basic principles of the science itself with the objective of placing the student in a potential role as a participant in the ongoing 'public choice' process in which the parametric constraints for economic interaction are selected. Economists often complain about the observed fact that 'everyone is his own economist', in an expression of the view that scientific counsel fails to command the deference it seems to warrant. In the absence of an effective exit option, however, everyone will continue to be, and should be, his own economist, at least to the extent of participating in the selection of constraints that are to be imposed collectively – constraints that affect the actions of everyone simultaneously.[1] The effective scientific community in economics is, therefore, necessarily inclusive in a sense that is not applicable in natural science.

'Doing economics', as the specialized activity of economists, should reflect a different emphasis on the transmission of basic knowledge relative to the discovery of new knowledge at the scientific frontiers. Because of the public features of economics noted, the activity of doing economics must be more akin to that observed in the behaviour of the ordinary scientist who rarely makes discoveries. In modern practice too much talented intellectual capital is used up in searches for the solutions of stylized puzzles with little or no relevance for the ongoing necessarily repetitive, and sometimes boring, activity of 'teaching' the long-accepted principles of the science.

ECONOMICS APPLIED IN POLITICS

Over and beyond the generalized publicness features that make the application of economic science so different from that of natural science, the elementary logic of 'democracy' intrudes to introduce even a more insurmountable barrier to the translation of scientific principles into political reality. Even if *all* participants in a community are sufficiently informed about how an economy works and, therefore, also about what changes in constraints might result in the generation of a more highly-valued bundle of 'goods', implementation of such changes may be impossible because the *subset* of participants who make up the dominant political majority may impose alternative changes that promise to yield higher benefits to that subset, even at the possible sacrifice of potentially higher gains for all members.

In a very real sense, the operation of majoritarian democracy acts to 'undo' the publicness characteristic of applied economics by endogenously introducing discrimination between members of dominant political coalitions and those persons who remain outside. The 'economist as engineer' who acts as if he or she is proffering advice to the inclusive membership of the polity finds no purchase for his or her wares. And the 'economist as engineer' who proffers advice that is useful in advancing the interests of a politically dominant coalition, in part at the expense of other members of the polity, may feel uncomfortable with the conscious violation of ethical-moral neutrality.

WHAT IS, WHAT MIGHT BE AND WHAT OUGHT TO BE

As the discussion indicates, the political economist is allowed to treat the set of structural parameters (the laws or constitution) as variables and to apply the principles of the science in generating predictions about the working properties of alternative sets of constraints, both those to be observed and those to be imagined. This sets economics apart from other disciplines in which the scientist simply accepts the constraints of the universe to be invariant.

This peculiar feature of the science of political economy becomes the source of much confusion when attempts are made to extend the simpler precepts of scientific method derived from concentration on the activity of natural scientists.

Consider the familiar is–ought distinction traceable to David Hume. For the natural scientist there is an 'is'. For the economist there is an 'is', but there is, also, a whole set of 'might be's' that are feasible. This sometimes fuzzy set of 'might be's' is bounded by the constraints imposed by the uniformities of human nature – uniformities that are acknowledged to exist, but which are not hard-wired in any sense analogous to those encountered in the natural world. A substantial share of the economists' scientific effort is devoted to delineating the institutionally feasible constraints on behaviour that may be predicted to generate generally preferred outcomes or social states.

It is this extension of economic science to the analyses of the 'might be's', that seems to fuzz up the sometimes forced positive–normative distinction, so beloved by the unsophisticated methodologists. The economist may, in fact, be saying no more than that 'water runs down hill' while being accused of committing the naturalistic fallacy.

That which is observed as economic reality may, indeed, be modified by changes in the rules within which human behaviour is allowed to take place. But that which is romantically imagined is no more possible in economics than in the more clearly restricted realms of the natural world. Economics, and economists, must make the categorical distinction between science fiction and potentially attainable reality. Failure to do so can produce results both exemplified by and experienced in the human tragedy of this century's failed pursuit of the impossible socialist idyll.

NOTE

1. 'Exit' and 'voice' (Hirschman, 1970) are substitutes in their ability to ensure protection against exploitation. If an individual has available multiple exit options, and faces relatively low cost in switching among them (as in the stylized competitive market), the exercise of voice may not be highly valued. By contrast, when exit options are nonexistent or prohibitively costly, the individual may, rightly or wrongly, perceive participation (voice) as one means of limiting collective coercion.

PART II

Post-revolutionary Interpretation

8. Economic theory in the post-revolutionary moment of the 1990s

Economic theory offers an explanation of the relationships between the interactive behaviour of persons and patterns of social outcomes on the presupposition that individual action is motivated by economically meaningful and conceptually measurable self-interest. Economic theory, as such, does not embody the behavioural hypothesis that persons do, in empirical reality, act so as to further measurable self-interest. To the extent that they do so, economics offers the source of hypotheses that often withstand the falsifiability test. But such falsification, if it occurs, should not be interpreted as refutation of the underlying theoretical construction, although it would suggest limits of practical usefulness.

In this elementary sense, economic theory has been vindicated by the events of this century, culminating in the revolution that has signalled the failure of the great socialist experiments. Socialism, as an inclusive system of organizing economic activity, did not achieve the objectives that its advocates defined at its inception. Socialism did not produce the goods, defined as the economic values that can only emerge ultimately from the preferences of individual participants. Economic theory explains the failure of socialism through its focus of attention on incentive structures, on informational requirements and on the necessary uncertainties in the linkage between choices and consequences. The *ex post* explanation does not, however, excuse economists, generally, from their apparent failure to predict the consequences that did, in fact, occur. Why did the revolutions that marked socialism's death take place before more than a tiny minority of practising, professional economic theorists made predictions of systemic failure?

I suggest that this woeful record of economists' performance stems from a set of scientific errors that must be put right before economic theory can begin to exert a productive influence on the hard problems of transition from socialism to alternative structures. We know, of course, that these scientific errors were, in part, driven by the ideological bias that economists shared with intellectuals generally. But the errors in scientific understanding can be divorced from the ideological setting. It is possible to discuss the role of economic theory, as such: first in its failure to predict socialism's demise; second, in its widely accepted explanation for the antisocialist revolution, *ex post*, and third, in its potential contribution to problems of transition in the post-revolutionary moment of the 1990s and beyond.

It first is necessary to lay out the general domain for discussion. I define my own understanding of economic theory in the sense used in this chapter and sketch out familiar territory in the history of ideas, with emphasis on the eighteenth-century discovery of the spontaneous order of market interaction – the discovery that sparked the genuine intellectual excitement of the classical political economists. Then I discuss, briefly, the classical economists' presuppositions for the constitutional framework necessary for an effective functioning of economic order and trace out the collapse of the classical-neoclassical understanding of the working of an economy – a collapse that was influenced by the challenge of Marxian socialism, by the implicit acceptance of political idealism and by the loss of systemic evaluation and analysis. I note the emergence of the maximization or allocationist paradigm, as aided and abetted by the particular mathematics of the calculus, at the expense of emphasis on the catallactic subject matter of market organization and the effect of game theory as a complement to a catallactic approach. Finally, I examine the elementary, but essential, contribution that economic theory can bring to participants, academic and lay alike, who have not experienced the history of market institutions. The genuine 'miracle of the market' that did, indeed, excite the classical economists can offer a basis for an enthusiastic public philosophy in post-revolutionary societies – a philosophy that the cynical, jaded and intellectually soft citizens in Western nations may have lost forever. As economists in the West, we, too, must recover our *raison d'être* as political economists-cum-political philosophers, and not as social engineers. Our science has much to answer for but also much to contribute.

THE RELEVANT DOMAIN

As the definition in the first sentence of the introduction implies, the subject matter of economic theory is a set of relationships among choosing and acting persons and the patterns of results or outcomes that these relationships generate. An alternative way of placing the emphasis here is to say that economics offers a theory of organizational-institutional *order*. The theory tells in a generalized and pattern-predictive sense 'what will tend to emerge' under this and that set of circumstances, conditions and constraints. We use economic theory in precisely the same way that we use much other knowledge. We explain why there is tropical fruit – say, bananas – on the supermarket shelves a thousand miles from the location where the fruit is grown. We use economic theory here just as we use physics to tell us why water runs down hill. We do not, of course, claim that theory enables us, in advance, to predict that bananas, as identified, will be on the market's shelves. Nor would we use physics to predict that the liquid substance to run down that ravine will be water. Economics allows us to predict that whatever people want to purchase will be available for purchase. Economic value will tend to be created in the form that people prefer, as driven by the same persons in their dual role as producers. The grower, the shipper, the distributor, the market manager, the shelf stocker, the cashier, all these put bananas on the shelves because they expect that, in so doing, they can exchange bananas for money, which will, in turn, allow for their own purchases of the goods that they desire – goods that will, in further turn, be put on the store shelves by those of us who purchase the bananas.

My purpose here is not to bore you with a summary of first-week elementary economics. But I should insist that those of us who are professionals in the discipline often neglect these elementary principles at our peril, and especially when we recognize that only a very small minority of nonprofessionals possesses even a generalized understanding of how the economic order works.

If my summary seems perhaps too elementary as well as too conventional, let me contrast my definition of the subject matter with more familiar claims. Economics or economic theory is *not* about 'the allocation of scarce means among alternative ends' (Robbins, 1932). This familiar means-end formulation draws attention, first, away from the creation of value as opposed to some allocation or utilization of value that is presumed to be in existence, and, second, from the interactive relationships among persons that define the order of an economy. Biblical mythology is helpful with reference to the first point. After the expulsion from the Garden, the lot of humans requires that they create economic value if they are to survive at all. Absent such creation, or production, there are no resources, no means, to allocate among ends or purposes. And, if man moves beyond self-subsistent existence, production as a means of securing ultimate consumption must involve the establishment of exchange relationships with others. Economics allows us to construct a generalized understanding of the complex set of exchange relationships.

As noted earlier, economic theory in its essential respects is no different from other scientific knowledge, within the appropriate limits of its enterprise. These limits are transgressed, however, when attempts are made to move outside the constraints imposed by the human subject matter and to objectify economic reality on some presupposition that values can be divorced from the subjective consciousness of participants in the order. To recall Gertrude Stein's comment about Oakland, 'there is no there there' in the sense of an objectifiable economic universe that lends itself to scientific observation and evaluation – a universe that exists separately and apart from the interlinked set of human choices and actions that bring 'the economy' into being. At best, therefore, the economist as scientist is restricted to potential explanation of patterns of results, and especially when noneconomic motivations for human actors are necessarily incorporated in what may be observed.

The enterprise of economics is, however, sufficiently open-ended to allow the potential for genuinely exciting scientific advances, which will be influenced, in part, by the events of history. The unexpected and dramatic collapse of communist totalitarian regimes has renewed and reinforced the attention of economists in incentive compatibility in varying institutional structures, in the informational characteristics of choices made under uncertainty.

ORDER WITHOUT DIRECTION

Economic theory, as such, was born with the scientific discovery of the spontaneous coordination that emerges from the separated, locally directed and self-interested actions of participants in a nexus of exchanges. Prior to this breakthrough in the eighteenth century, there could scarcely have existed an 'economic science', properly understood, since there was no reasoned understanding of the observed patterns of the order that resulted from human behaviour directed toward economic purpose. Production, exchange and consumption could, of course, be observed, but there was no integrating vision that allowed the separated actions to be related.

At this point, we confront etymological confusion that has plagued the discipline from its beginnings – a confusion that is not, to my knowledge, matched in any other science. *Economics* as a term, finds its origins in Greek and refers to management or to economizing, yes, to the utilization of scarce means *by a decision-making unit*. In this accurately derived etymological use of the term, economics was, of course, always with us, and there were preclassical theories of economic management in which the direction of the national household by the king, the prince, the bishop or some other sovereign became the subject matter for learned discourse. German cameralism provided a set of precepts for the prince to follow in arranging the economic affairs of the principality, and the economizing on the use of scarce resources was central to any such exercise. Although *mercantilism*, as a descriptive term applicable to systems, was coined by Adam Smith, we find this term useful to refer to those sets of policy directed principles that offered guidance to those who 'managed' the national economy, who established specific objectives such as national accumulation of treasure, national rates of growth and national levels of employment.

It is not surprising that Keynes found the mercantilist writers to be kindred souls, since in his attempt to shift the emphasis of economics back to macroaggregative management, Keynes necessarily moved away from the central thrust of the whole explanatory enterprise. The macroeconomic theory of midcentury was strictly within the management tradition and consistent with the etymological origins of 'economics' as a term.

Adam Smith himself perhaps added to the ultimate confusion by the selection of the title for his treatise. *The Wealth of Nations*, read descriptively from the title's words alone, suggests that nations are the units that are wealthy or poor and, by inference, that increases in nations' wealth are desirable. Smith did not, of course, have such a reading of his title in mind, since the whole thrust of his argument is that individuals, not nations, are the relevant units and that wealth consists in whatever it is that individuals desire. And Adam Smith's work was the channel through which economic theory in the sense used in this chapter was established – a theory of the spontaneous coordination achievable through an interlinked network of market exchanges and a theory that demonstrates the inefficacy of attempted economic management for a whole society.

Throughout the two and a quarter centuries of its history, economics, as a theoretical science, has been burdened with its two-track and mutually contradictory analytical cores. More than mere bifurcation is involved here. The approaches required for analysis in the two research programmes are categorically different. A theory that offers an explanation or understanding of the coordinating properties of an exchange network cannot be harnessed into 'economizing' service in any strict managerial sense, although, of course, such a theory becomes an essential component in any design and construction of the framework of rules like constitutions within which economic interaction is allowed to operate.

My own resolution of the confusion in economics is clear from my discussion. Economic theory, properly defined, is limited to the domain of exchange relationships, and the behaviour within those relationships, along with the institutional structures that emerge or are constructed to constrain those who are participants. If progress is to be made, economics must, once and for all, throw off its etymologically influenced interpretation. Ideally, we should replace the very name; *catallaxy* or *catallactics* is etymologically descriptive (see Buchanan, 1979a.)

THE CONSTITUTIONAL FRAMEWORK

As people in the former Soviet republics are finding out in the 1990s, the free market does not accomplish the coordination promised by some of its naive advocates in the absence of a set of constraints that may be considered to be the rules or the constitution for the market game. The classical discoverers of the coordinating properties of markets did not sufficiently emphasize the necessary presence of such rules or institutions. If no such rules exist, the chaos that the nonsophisticate in economics more or less naturally imagines may, indeed, become descriptive of reality.

The elements of the constitutional framework are familiar, and these need not be discussed in any detail here, but a summary statement is required in order to ensure that there are some common bounds for subsequent analysis. The political-legal order must embody security of person and property, and the basic rights that define such security cannot, in themselves, emerge from an exchange-like process, despite the pronouncements of the libertarian anarchists. Without some prior agreement on or acknowledgement of what is mine and thine, how could you and I even commence a trading or exchange relationship (see Buchanan, 1975)? Once we are secure in rights of ownership, we are free to make exchanges in rights, in the expectation that those received in trade will themselves be genuinely owned, once possessed. A regime in which rights are severally assigned, mutually acknowledged and legally protected defines the broad boundaries of the playing field for the inclusive economic interaction process.

A corollary of the ownership and control of person and possession is the enforcement of voluntary contracts of exchange, once made. The political-legal order must operate so as to ensure that individual contractors abide by the terms of agreed upon, but not fully implemented, exchanges of rights. And, as with the initial assignments, we could scarcely expect effective contract enforcement to emerge, itself, from contractual foundations, although the libertarian argument here is somewhat more persuasive than in the former case.

There are additional, and supplementary, elements in a constitutional framework that allow a market order of an economy to function effectively. These elements, some of which remain subject to ongoing scientific debate (for example, monetary arrangements), need not be treated in this summary. My point here is to emphasize only that it is the constitutional framework (the laws and institutions, the constraint set) that becomes the appropriate focus for those who seek to reform or to improve the operation of the social process in its economic aspects.

The eighteenth-century discovery of the ordering properties of market exchange was a discovery of such properties *within*, rather than independently from, the political-legal structure. And classical political economy, the emerging science that elaborated this discovery, at least in early form, was interpreted as a challenge to the whole enterprise of economic management. *Laissez-faire* – to leave alone – applied negatively to politicized effort to interfere with, and to improve upon, the workings of markets. It should never have been extended to the criticism of the necessary political effort aimed at establishing and maintaining the constitutional framework. The categorical distinction between these two levels or stages of politicization was never clearly articulated, and this ambiguity compounded that discussed earlier that involved the meaning of terms.

THE LOSS OF WISDOM

What happened to economics after the fourth decade of the nineteenth century? We know that the excitement of scientific discovery that characterized classical political economy did not survive. Somehow the basic theoretical understanding of market order seemed to slip away, at least partially, and we observed a peculiar melange of scientific progress and scientific retrogression.

Several sources of difficulty can be identified. The classical economists' understanding of market coordination was seriously incomplete. There was no plausibly acceptable theory for the pricing of productive inputs. The cost-of-production theory for the pricing of outputs offered the basis for the Ricardian-Marxian backward extension to input pricing and notably to labour. The theory of surplus value, allegedly produced by, but not fully received by, labour, was used effectively by Marx to undermine the efficacy of markets, even within the mind-set that embodied the earlier discoveries. The distributional implications of market coordination were moved to centre stage, providing grounds for revolutionary political proposals that were well beyond any mercantilist schemes for political management of national economies. The Marxist argument tended to weaken economists' normative evaluation of their whole scientific enterprise.

In this respect, it is singularly unfortunate that the theory of input pricing that emerged as a consequence of the 1870s marginalist revolution in economic theory could not have been developed a mere half-century earlier. Such a time shift might have forestalled the Marxist critique, which was clearly based on straightforward scientific error, and the consequences that we all know might not have occurred at all.

Quite apart from the Marxist extension of classical principles that indirectly caused economists to lose confidence in their own *raison d'être,* developments in moral philosophy were also of major importance. Influenced by the ideas of Hegel, philosophers lost the eighteenth-century scepticism about the operations of political-collective institutions – a scepticism that we can interpret to have been squarely based on both analytical and empirical hypotheses. As a substitute, there emerged a romantic model of the state – a model that came to be increasingly dominant, an idealist vision of an omniscient and benevolent collective entity. Both common-sense observation and theoretical understanding were lost. Alongside idealism in political philosophy, and especially in Great Britain, classical utilitarianism provided the framework for normative evaluation of alternative policy propositions, with the effect of drawing attention away from problems of implementation through the realities of politics.

Political idealism and utilitarianism are important because, even in those societies that were not so directly influenced by the Marxian challenges, the romantic model of the state became the source for totally unwarranted comparisons between the market order, as observed in operation, and the state, as idealized. Developments in economic theory did identify and classify institutional and operational failures in the workings of markets, as against the *laissez-faire* idealizations, but no comparable failures of politicized corrections were brought within the canon of political science until the public-choice revolution of the last half of this century.

MAXIMIZATION, MATHEMATIZATION AND THE THEORY OF GAMES

Genuine scientific progress has been made in economic theory since the moment of its eighteenth-century origins in discovery. The marginalist revolution, and particularly the theory of input pricing that emerged in consequence, tended to complete, in broad basic outline, the theory of market coordination. Even in this respect, however, the contributions of axiomatic general equilibrium theory midway through this century were necessary to round off the whole enterprise. But, as I also noted, the management or economizing conception of subject matter, and applied at the level of the national economy, has never been absent from economists' professional tool kit.

The potential for intellectual confusion was enhanced by some of the methodological implications of the marginalist revolution itself. In voluntary market choices made by participating individuals, values are determined at the relevant margins of adjustment, and the very idea of marginal comparison of values stems from mathematics, the central logic of the calculus. It is not then at all surprising that economic theory, as developed throughout this century should have use of more and more sophisticated mathematical tools. And, as applied to the decision making of individuals, the calculus of utility maximization is helpfully explanatory. But the availability of the applied mathematics surely generated a bias toward artificially forced and unwarranted extension beyond individual choice to collectivities, to macrounits, to society, to the economy. Social engineering became one of the several post-marginalist versions of mercantilist economic management. As also noted, the Depression inspired shift of attention to movement among economy-wide macroaggregates, a shift that Keynes and the Keynesians provided with quasi-scientific status, added powerful complementary force to economic management as the ultimate motive impulse for the formulation of economic theory itself.

Even without macroeconomics, however, the increasingly rigorous efforts to define the hard core of economic theory would have ensured an emerging economizing framework, as readily mathematized through the maximization paradigm. Post-Marshall economics became the theory of allocation of scarce resources or means among competing ends – a formulation that lends itself more or less directly to a marginalizing calculus. Emphasis was shifted away from the coordinating properties of interlinked markets, in which the separate participants may, indeed, be modelled as utility maximizers, and towards properties of markets conceptualized as if they were alternatives to or substitutes for economic management schemes for inclusively defined aggregations.

A major change of direction in economic theory may have occurred in midcentury when the theory of games provided an alternative mathematics to the marginalist calculus – a mathematics that carries important implications for the very way that economists conceive what their enterprise is all about (von Neumann and Morgenstern, 1944). In the theory of games, attention is immediately focused on the interaction process as such, with participants modelled as taking separate actions within specified rules (the constitution), and out of which some solution emerges that is chosen by no one, either individually or collectively. During the second third of the century, the ongoing dominance of the maximization paradigm tended to obscure the potential contribution that game theory's elegance can make toward restoring, indirectly as it were, the catallactic focus of economic theory, a focus that was never totally absent. Only within the last three decades of the century did game theory's economic emphasis shift from the choices of strategies of separate players to the search for solutions and to properties of alternative solutions and then, by inference, to the effects of alternative sets of rules on solutions, the domain of constitutional economics.

THE MIRACLE OF THE MARKET

I have found it useful to organize this chapter as a history-of-ideas narrative of the development of economic theory, as personalized through my own definition of the science as stated at the outset. In one sense, therefore, the whole discussion to this point becomes prefatory to the main purpose of the assignment, as suggested in the title of the chapter itself. What role can economic theory play in those societies that have experienced genuine revolutions, in which socialist organizational structures have been explicitly rejected, both in practice and in idea, but in which market-like institutions have not emerged, at least in forms similar to those observed in Western mixed economies? What role should economic theory play in the necessary transition from socialism? The 1990s are properly classified as a post-revolutionary moment in history. Will economic theory be of value in this moment?

I suggest that we can look for an answer in the historical epoch that describes economic theory's finest hours – the few decades that span the turn between the eighteenth and the nineteenth centuries, the period of classical political economy. The ideas of Adam Smith may or may not have themselves influenced events directly as initiating causes of political changes. (I do not engage George Stigler on this point here.) But we cannot deny the role that these ideas played in the undermining of the intellectual foundations, the putative legitimacy, of the eroding mercantilist structure of national economic management. The economists were effective in convincing political leaders, and a sufficiently large number of citizens, that an economic order without politicized direction could not only be imagined but could also be expected to increase the well-being of the economy's participants generally. The central role played by economic theory during this whole epoch seems clear enough. Persons had to be, and were, convinced that a market economy would work, and work with tolerable efficiency, before they would begin to feel comfortable in unstrapping the complex harness of politically controlled economic management.

The eighteenth-century scepticism about the motivation as well as the predicted efficacy of political-collective action in furthering the interests of citizens provided fertile ground for the acceptance of the economists' ideas. The potential constitutional function of market arrangements was for the first time understood, separate and apart from any concern with any prospect for efficiency in generating valued product. In retrospect, we can understand why the classical economists, along with their media and lay supporters, were so enthusiastic about the potential value of the newly emergent science of political economy.

The setting in the post-revolutionary societies in the 1990s is in many respects similar to that of the emerging industrial economies in the late-eighteenth and early-nineteenth centuries, at least similar enough to warrant speculation about the positive role that might be played by the more sophisticated, and more complete, modern theory or science of economic order. To the citizenry generally, to the intelligentsia, to newly enfranchised political leaders, all of whose history has dispelled any and all of the romance that collectivism-politicization might once have held, the miracle of the market, warts and all, offers promise. The observable consequences of socialism leave little space for the motivation of strictly distributional criticisms of market capitalism.

The timing seems ripe for an emergent and new found enthusiasm for a Central and Eastern European *Wirtschaftswunder* – an enthusiasm that can be jointly grounded in a loss of faith in politicized economic management and a generalized understanding of economic theory in its most basic, and elementary, sense. The highly sophisticated analyses of potential market failures, as evaluated against nonattainable perfection, can be put on the shelf for those who understand the current relevance of the hard-core principles. To citizens in this post-revolutionary moment, simple analyses of market successes offer the essential components of attainable dreams. Vaclav Klaus, Prime Minister of the Czech Republic, is reported to have called for a 'market without adjectives', and it is perhaps only in a post-socialist setting that we might have expected such comment from a highly successful political leader. Can we even imagine a US counterpart making such a statement?

As noted, economic theory can provide post-revolutionary intellectuals with a much more sophisticated understanding and explanation of a market order than that which effectively energized the followers of classical political economy two centuries ago. And the body of doctrine incorporated in modern economic theory is sufficiently inclusive to offer continuing challenge to those scientists attracted by the aesthetics of new ideas. The hard-core can excite the intelligentsia while the several research programmes around the periphery offer promise to the practising scientists.

For those who seek to use economic theory for more specific reform purposes, the critical distinction between adjustments in the constitutional framework, the constraints within which economic activity takes place, and attempted politicized interferences with market results remain of critical importance. The post-revolutionary institutional settings are in flux; rights have not been fully assigned and acknowledged; legal rules and norms of behaviour have not been fully established; contracts among traders have not evolved through a commercial history. And, significantly, a culture of reciprocal exchange is not descriptive of social reality – a culture that is embedded in our subconscious in Western economies (see Chapter 11). The most elementary of all economic principles – 'there exist mutual gains from trade' – remains to be absorbed by people in post-socialist societies. The teaching of economics becomes socially productive in these societies in ways that we can scarcely appreciate in Western cultures.

In my definitional introduction to this chapter, I stated that economic theory, as such, is not itself an empirical science but that it does provide the source for hypotheses that may be subjected to falsifiability tests. The dramatic events that have taken place, and others that will follow, in post-revolutionary economics must surely offer empirically minded economists wonderful opportunities for examining the implications of simple hypotheses. Never in history have economists been offered such near laboratory conditions and on so enormous a scale. Almost regardless of methodological preferences, the economist who concentrates on post-revolutionary societies must be excited about his or her scientific enterprise.

I should acknowledge that my interpretation and prediction of the role that economics and economic theory will play in the post-revolutionary moment are tinged with hope. My response is really to the question 'What role can economic theory play?' rather than to the more neutral question 'What role will economic theory play?'.

The management-economizing conception of economics, and especially as extended normatively to policy prescription, may not have been sufficiently exorcized, and I am concerned that economists in post-revolutionary societies will import many of the 'wrong' or misguided research thrusts of Western economics, rather than select carefully for potentially helpful research directions. Without attempts to be exhaustive here, I can list (alphabetically) several research programmes that would seem to offer productive insights to professionals in the new post-revolutionary economies: Austrian economics, catallaxy, constitutional economics, game theory, general equilibrium theory, experimental economics, law and economics, new institutional economics, property rights economics, public choice. By comparison and by contrast, the following programmes would seem to offer little or no promise and, indeed, may be distracting elements: input–output analysis, industrial policy, linear and quadratic programming, optimal control theory, optimal growth theory, optimal taxation, social choice theory, social welfare functions, theories of planning.

ECONOMIC THEORY IN THE WEST

As an end note to the chapter, it is appropriate to ask the question 'What is the role for economic theory in the mixed economies of Western countries that have not experienced revolutionary changes in institutional structures'? I am much less sanguine here than in response to the same question posed earlier for post-revolutionary societies. Western economists, as practising scientists, tend to take the elementary principles of their discipline too much for granted, and they devote far too much effort, interesting though it may be, to esoteric intellectual puzzles that often have little relevant content, even in some remote sense. (The exception, as noted, may be in modern game theory, where the intricacies of the analytics may be required to force belated recognition of the foundational shift in approach to economic process.)

Economists forget that, quite unlike the other sciences where professionally agreed-upon principles command authority beyond the scientific community boundaries, economics must be made convincing to the public and its political leaders – a task that requires continued teaching of the elementary verities. 'Every man his own economist' is a plague that has been with economics since its inception as an independent body of thought. As a result, the failure of the theory's professionals to renew the principles allows interest-driven politicization to intrude continuously into the operations of the market order.

We observe little enthusiasm for the principles of markets based on a widening understanding of the market's efficacy in producing and delivering valued product. And, despite the impact of modern public-choice theory in offering a partial explanation or understanding of political failures, we do not observe an intellectual rejection of 'socialism in the small' that is anywhere remotely comparable to the near universal rejection of 'socialism in the large' in the post-revolutionary settings.

The relatively pessimistic conclusion is that the future role of economics and economic theory lies with the post-revolutionary societies rather than in the sometimes tired science that is academically established in the West, and, merely by way of such establishment itself, will devote resources to the maintenance of whatever role serves its own interests.

9. Analysis, ideology and the events of 1989[1]

We have all been challenged to think about the consequences of the momentous events of 1989. My initial comment here is by way of confession; I continue to feel a sense of inadequacy in confrontation of the current history that we have observed. I find it difficult to think clearly, to organize analysis, to model reality so that it makes sense, even in an abstracted structure that only those of us who deal mainly in ideas would find helpfully explanatory. It is no excuse to suggest that our mind-set is appropriate only for relatively stable nonrevolutionary circumstances, and that the revolutionary events of 1989 must, necessarily, remain outside the limits of current interpretation. For me, reliance on such an excuse would undermine the legitimacy of the whole academic-intellectual enterprise. If those of us who earn our keep by thinking are confused by the onrush of events, how can we expect others, who work while we philosophize, to accord us the respect that we sometimes claim?

An American political scientist, Francis Fukuyama, provoked a spirited discussion in 1989 and 1990 with an article entitled, 'The End of History' (Fukuyama, 1989). For the most part, Fukuyama's critics failed to acknowledge the central challenge that was contained in his article. We may, of course, suggest that 'history' was the wrong term to deploy, but we may restate the challenge in a set of questions: What was it that ended in 1989 and the years immediately preceding? Can we deny that something has, indeed, ended? Can we think about the world in the same way as we did before 1989? Are we not now required to look, not merely through a different window, but at a different world?

That which has ended is a vision of socio-economic-political reality, a vision that was itself an integral part of the world, if for no other reason than the fact that individuals made choices on the basis of that vision. The set of ideas from which that vision was constructed, which we may label 'collectivist-socialist', which derived initial inspiration from Hegel and which was converted into revolutionary reality by Marx, no longer exists as a meaningful intellectual-emotional foundation for social organization, either as an idealized alternative to that which is observed or as an idealized description of any system of socio-political order in existence. That is to say, we must now look at the complexities of social interaction among persons and associations of persons without resort to the collectivist-socialist utopia or dystopia as a helpmate in our analysis, interpretation and evaluation.

If we accept the proposition that 'ideas have consequences', then we must predict that the unanticipated disappearance of the collectivist-socialist vision of socio-political order will ultimately generate profound changes in the course of history. But what form will these changes take? Will some new dialectic emerge, and, if so, what conflicts in principle will describe it?

It is here that I feel most embarrassed intellectually. I think, along with Keynes, that ideas do exert influences on events. But I find it difficult to get handles on an analysis of possible futures in the post-socialist epoch. Are we poised on the verge of some as yet undiscovered and unexploited motivating idea that will excite individuals sufficiently to generate political action?

In what follows, I want to advance some speculations on a theme, which should be taken as little more than that. They surely do not deserve to be called predictions; possibly they might qualify as conjectures.

POLITICS IN THE LARGE AND IN THE SMALL

For another purpose I have used the title, 'Socialism Is Dead, But Leviathan Lives On' (Buchanan, 1990a; Chapter 10). The collectivist-socialist vision that has lost all of its appeal is that of the centrally planned and controlled economy, with individuals finding their own realization as integral components in a socialist community. It is now universally acknowledged that this sort of economy does not work; it does not produce goods. And, further, the experience of the century indicates that individuals do not shed their individuality in artificially collectivized communities. Politicization in the large has, in this sense, been almost totally discredited.

That which has not been discredited by the demise of socialism is politics in the small, by which I mean piece-by-piece interference with market processes. The economies of the nations that have not been subjected to centralized planning and control are described by literally hundreds of politically imposed controls, regulations and restrictions in the form of quotas, tariffs, price, wage and rent floors or ceilings, prohibitions on investment, on entry, exit, occupational mobility and so on – the list could be extended. There has been no crossing of the bridge between the rejection of socialism (that is, politicization in the large) and politicization in the small. Individuals, as members of the body politic, or their intellectual and/or political leaders-agents, have not, generally, come to any acceptance of the notion that, if politicization does not work when applied over all markets, it will not work when applied for particular markets, taken one at a time.

The crossing of this particular intellectual-evaluative bridge will be difficult for reasons that are well known to those who have followed developments in modern public choice theory. Economists, since Adam Smith, have been almost unanimous in their scientific judgement that politicized interference with single markets, one at a time, destroys potential economic value. Throughout the two centuries of its existence as a body of scientific discourse, political economy has provided the positive basis for the normative condemnation of piecemeal intervention with the workings of markets. There have been precious few economists who have claimed that price controls, tariffs, entry barriers and so on increase economic value. By contrast with the fundamental intellectual oversight that characterized economists' attitudes toward socialist organization (the oversight that Hayek [1988] has aptly called the fatal conceit), there has been no epistemological failure represented by a misunderstanding of the effects of politicized piecemeal controls over markets.

Over many decades, economists have experienced frustration as they observed politicians and political forces continue to impose and implement restrictions, controls and regulations, market by market, with apparent total disregard for the acknowledged effect of destroying potential economic value. Why have, and why do, politicians, and especially those directly responsive to electoral constituencies, seem so uninterested in the generation of value? Why does economic efficiency carry so little political weight?

Public choice theory supplies a relatively easy answer to these questions. Politicians are indeed responsive to the evaluations of those constituents whom they represent. But a characteristic feature of any single market intervention, taken in isolation, lies in the concentration of benefits and the dispersal of costs. The costs of the market restriction, taken overall and measured inclusively, may exceed the benefits and, by the theorems of economics, will normally do so, but so long as there is a disparity in the distribution, as between the two sides of the account, political response is likely to be favourable to the more concentrated set of persons affected – the beneficiaries. The relative concentration of benefits prompts investment in information about the consequences of political action, and this is matched by investment in efforts to influence political agents. At the same time, and in parallel with this, the larger number of potential losers, each of whom is affected slightly, remains rationally ignorant and invests neither in information nor in political influence.

This elementary 'logic of collective action', to use Mancur Olson's (1965) terminology here, applies, however, only if the destruction of potential value can be organized and implemented on a piecemeal basis, that is, by interfering with one market at a time. If politicized interventions are extended simultaneously over many markets, the shortfall in value will become evident for all to see – both constituents and leaders. In this case, we should predict some rough equivalent, politically, to the reaction against centralized planning and socialist organization that we now observe.

THE FUTURE FOR *LAISSEZ-FAIRE*

We should not, of course, expect to observe any simultaneous extension of politicized control to all or even to many markets in an economy. The politics of constituency response will proceed in steps, as political entrepreneurs build up interest group support, not necessarily one group at a time, but in minimal coalitions as required by logrolling within the allowable decision rules. And even if the effects, overall, may be the destruction of a major share of the value potential of an economy, any simultaneous dismantling of the politicized control network, as extended over many markets, will prove exceedingly difficult to organize.

But let us return to the possible relationship between ideas and events. The eighteenth century was marked by the genuine discovery that depoliticized and decentralized markets allowed to operate within a framework of law produce more wealth than the mercantilist organizational alternative. This discovery, by Adam Smith and his peers, excited the minds of those who came to the new understanding, and classical political economy provided the intellectual-analytical basis for major political reforms that embodied the dismantling of much of the mercantilist apparatus.

The situation in the 1990s is, in some respects, comparable to that of the late-eighteenth and early nineteenth century. We have discovered (rediscovered) that socialism as an economy-organizing principle does not work, that efforts at politicized displacement of a market economy must fail to produce the goods and services that citizens desire. And we share in a broad understanding of this observed failure. Major reforms have taken, and are taking, place that involve the privatization-marketization of previously socialised economies.

As I have noted, however, piece-by-piece politicization of those national economies that were never explicitly socialist in either a structural or an ideological sense has proceeded apace. And there has been little or no idea-generated feedback that motivates political reform here, because the controls in these economies were put in place in the face of a ruling scientific consensus to the effect that potential value was thereby being destroyed. Hence, there is no discovery, or rediscovery, waiting to be made, no newfound understanding of the simple principle that free markets do, indeed, produce more highly valued bundles of goods and services.

Nonetheless, the standard arguments for the extension of politicized control over particular markets may prove less persuasive in the post-socialist epoch. The claim that 'politics works better' as applied to a single market or group of markets may seem more questionable with the widening recognition that 'politics works worse', in the large, as applied over all markets. But it would be naive to expect something akin to public renewal, of the general principle of *laissez-faire*, except possibly in those economies that were formerly under socialist organization. In Western welfare states, there will be no recapture of the imagination that could be even remotely comparable to the understanding and enlightenment that followed on the teachings of the classical economists. The intellectual leaders have understood how markets work; and they have rejected markets, almost universally, in favour of the socialist alternative, on the false notion that socialism 'works better'. Now that they must, however reluctantly, acknowledge socialism's failure, in both a relative and an absolute sense, where will they turn?

LEGITIMACY AND LIBERTY

My speculation (and I insist that it is no more than this) leaves the intellectuals in the Western welfare states out of account, more or less as the Marxists were allowed to lapse into irrelevancy during the last decades of socialism's effective life. I am able to think about a post-socialist future in which significant political change emerges from a shift in the attitudes of ordinary citizens, from, as it were, a genuine revolution in 'public philosophy', and one that the intellectuals can only follow and very reluctantly at that.

Return to the events of the 1980s. By 1989, there came to be a near universal acknowledgement that socialist organization of an economy fails to produce goods and services, as desired by citizens. In short, socialism has been proven to be grossly inefficient in producing value. A second, and equally important, feature of socialist organization was also widely acknowledged, and particularly by those who were direct participants; the socialist economy maximizes the control of the bureaucracy over the lives of ordinary citizens, while most persons share in the normative precept that dictates minimization. The excessive bureaucratization of life under socialism was as significant in causing the system's collapse as the deficiency in generating valued output.

The public reaction against bureaucratization had been working its way throughout the structure of social interaction long before any formalized reform in the socialist structure took place. Persons in socialist regimes learned to seek out and find ways and means to subvert the ubiquitous bureaucratic restrictions. 'Free markets' emerged, even if these were variously described as 'shadow', 'black' and 'underground' and in all cases remained formally illegal. As socialism came to be formally supplanted, nominally on grounds of efficiency, there was a carryover of attitudes to the effect that the bureaucratic intrusions characteristic of socialism were 'illegitimate' as well as inefficient. Politicization of economic life in the large was universally seen to fail on efficiency grounds, but politicization, as bureaucratization, was also seen to be illegitimate on fundamental moral principle. Persons claimed the rights to trade when, as, if and with whom they chose. 'Free to choose' assumed moral force.

This reference to the shift in attitudes in formerly socialist economies may exert important spillover effects on attitudes in Western welfare states. I have already suggested that the arguments from efficiency alone will offer relatively little assistance in the depoliticization of particularized restrictions on the separate workings of markets. There are gainers as well as losers from each such restriction, and the concentrated gains are more likely to stimulate political response than the dispersed losses, despite the preponderance of losses over gains, in the aggregate. But the argument from legitimacy cannot be countered so easily. To the extent that citizens claim that they possess moral rights to participate in voluntary market exchanges, free of politicized interferences, those who would deny such claims are forced into a defence of political-bureaucratic coercion, with the failed socialist experiments of the century standing omnipresent in the background.

Might we not expect that attitudes towards the politically orchestrated coercion of the Western welfare states will undergo major shifts as the philosophical grounding of collectivism is discredited? Why should the politicians and bureaucrats who act for the welfare states be accorded a degree of public respect and honour that is so totally at variance with the status of their counterparts in the now despised institutional residues of socialism? (There may be, of course, some difference in public attitudes when democratic procedures themselves lend legitimacy to the actions of bureaucratic agents.)

I suggest that the argument from liberty, the argument that advances the claim of the individual to freedom from state coercion in voluntary economic transactions, may provide the emotional-evaluative source for the breakdown and erosion of the 'legitimacy' of Western regulatory politics. And it is important to recognize that legitimacy matters. The bureaucratized regulatory intrusions in the market economy in Western welfare states require widespread voluntary acquiescence. A simple shift in perception, in attitudes, followed by action, on the part of a relatively small number of market participants would, very quickly, lead to an erosion of the effectiveness of the political control apparatus. How long could a price ceiling imposed on the sale of a standard commodity remain effective in a setting where persons almost universally deny the legitimacy of majoritarian politics to interfere in market pricing?

I am not, of course, imagining a scenario that is nonexistent, even in the best ordered Western societies. Secondary and nominally illegal markets are present wherever and whenever political control establishes artificial scarcities. Illegal drugs are produced, supplied, demanded and consumed; prostitution persists; 'key' prices supplement controlled rents; persons are employed at subminimal wages; street vendors peddle contraband goods; currency transactions replace traceable funded exchanges. And, as attempts at politicized regulation of markets extends further, the share in total economic value originated in and processed through the underground sector increases, as witness experience in Latin America and, for Europe, in Italy.

This discernible erosion of the control apparatus in the welfare state may, prior to the late 1980s, be attributable largely to those in the citizenry who have little or no respect for law generally. What I am suggesting here is that these persons will be joined in increasing numbers by others who gradually come to the realization that political restrictions on their voluntary choices, imposed for the explicit benefit of specialized interests, no longer command legitimacy. Once the bloom is off the romance that was collectivism – a romance that captured public imagination in all parts of the world for more than a century – politicized restrictions on individual liberties must meet a much more severe standard in order to be accepted.

THE POLITICS, LAW AND ECONOMICS OF DISORDER

The socio-political-economic setting that may emerge, in both Western and Eastern countries, is perhaps equidistant from George Orwell's totalitarian dystopia and the ideally ordered utopia of the classical liberal followers of Adam Smith. Centralized collectivist controls over the economic interactions of citizens may be less extensive than might have been predicted in 1980. And, even where such controls nominally exist, they may be treated with more disdain and contempt, even to the extent that fully effective enforcement becomes impossible. This side of the equation in the post-socialist epoch may seem, taken alone, to gladden the heart of the classical liberal whose idealized polity is described by a state that is constrained constitutionally while remaining powerful within its authorized limits. But the predicted loosening-removal of collectivist controls, and public attitudes towards politics generally, may also extend to those institutions of political order that the classical liberal judges to be minimally necessary for viable social interaction.

Having rejoiced in the destruction of the collectivist myth that the 'state knows best', the classical liberal may also observe a weakening and erosion of the 'civic religion' that embodies general agreement that 'on some matters, the state, as reflecting a set of shared values, indeed, does know best'. It seems at least within the possible that the collectivist-socialist mystique that has provided one source legitimacy to politics generally will, like a ball of yarn, unravel so rapidly that fully legitimate, and indeed necessary, political processes will be undermined, in which case libertarian anarchy may offer perhaps a useful descriptive analytical model for the post-socialist epoch.

In this sense, disorder rather than order might be characteristic of the societies in the next decades. The university campuses of the 1960s may prove to be the demonstration models for the inclusive communities of the upcoming century. Agitators in the streets, subject to crowd psychology and highly vulnerable to demagogic persuasion, may become even more commonplace than today. Governments, manned by responsive political agents, will be unable to act because there will be no moral force behind a will to govern. Citizens may increasingly refuse to pay taxes, both in their private capacities as evaders and avoiders and in their public choice capacities as potential voting supporters of tax-proposing parties and politicians. Governments may come to rely, increasingly, on the residually remaining power to levy taxation through inflation. Public goods, even within the narrowly defined limits of conservative argument, may not be provided, or, if financed at all, may be minimally extended, accompanying services badly performed and facilities poorly maintained.

Crime, against both persons and property, may continue to increase as the legitimacy of basic enforcement is reduced as a necessary complement to the erosion of the legitimacy of politics. The public image of the policeman as the agent of the state, the potential enforcer of law that may itself not be legitimate, may further encourage citizenry into collusion with criminals. And those who are themselves policemen may come to fear the prospects for citizens' reaction against possible overzealous enforcement more than they value the law that they exist to enforce.

The individual may find himself or herself relatively free from bureaucratic restriction imposed through political agency, but an alternative source of inefficiency may be present in the form of vulnerability to opportunistic behaviour on the part of other persons with whom mutually advantageous economic interchange might seem possible. Contracts for delivery of services may be difficult to enforce, and agreed terms of exchange may lose meaning in the absence of well-defined legal rules. Economic transactions may, necessarily, come to be based more on personal relationships of trust, surely a retrogressive step in the historical evolution of markets in Western countries.

The courts of law in Western countries will, themselves, have aided and abetted in the emergence of the disorder that I have sketched briefly here. Lawyers, and judges, were, like their peers in other leadership roles, caught up in the romantic vision of politics that described the socialist epoch. They justified, and formally legitimized, discretionary bureaucratic restrictions on the economic liberties of persons, regardless of the consistency of such restrictions either with the letter or the spirit of the historical constitutional structures.

In contradistinction with the politically subservient courts in socialist regimes, courts in Western democracies (particularly in the United States) attempted to erect and to maintain wholly arbitrary and artificial differences between the economic and the noneconomic liberties of persons in terms of protection from political intrusion. The noneconomic liberties, such as those of speech, press, assembly, religion and franchise were zealously protected, while the economic liberties of trade, location, entry, exit, occupation and so on were held to be subject to the dictates of majoritarian politics and its accompanying bureaucracy. The situation in the United States has reached absurd limits; it is unconstitutional for the government to restrict an individual's liberty to burn the flag of the country, but fully constitutional for the government, central or local, to restrict an individual's liberty to make a mutually advantageous and voluntary exchange with another person, on terms of their own choosing. Such absurdities in the law cannot, of course, find any justification in ideas, and, ultimately, individuals must be allowed the simple economic liberties.

Again, if treated in isolation, this possible spillover from the demise of the socialist vision must be applauded. But if economic liberties are defined to include exchanges in rental housing, what is to prevent them being defined to include exchanges in addictive drugs, body parts and babies? The answer must, of course, lie in a generalized public understanding of the differences between those politically imposed constraints that are 'constitutionally legitimate' and those that are not.

ORDER WITHIN CONSTITUTIONAL LIMITS

I have labelled my remarks as speculative rather than predictive (and a respected critic has suggested that the preceding section is wholly out of place). I should stress that the symptoms of disorder described above need not emerge in the decades ahead when the citizenry must, in some fashion, learn to live with post-socialist reality. Hayek has stated that he wrote his great polemical essay, *The Road to Serfdom* (1944), not so much as prediction but as warning. He sought to tell his temporal peers that, unless counterposing ideas were promulgated and actions taken, the serfdom that was socialism was indeed the likely future. For Western countries his warning may, in small measure, have prevented the future that he feared. My speculations here should be taken in the same spirit. The constitutional-legal-political-economic anarchy that I have sketchily outlined to be within the possible need not occur, in Eastern or Western societies, if the central ideas of classical liberalism can be rediscovered and understood, and if the political choices made by individual citizens come to reflect these ideas.

As I indicated by the subtitle of one of my own books (Buchanan, 1975), the society within which we can live in peace, prosperity and liberty lies 'between anarchy and Leviathan'. For well over a century, social scientists and social philosophers have failed in their task of providing the public with a general understanding of the ordering principles of viable social order. We now have the totally unanticipated opportunity to move into the intellectual vacuum that the demise of socialism has created. There will be no rebirth of socialism as an intellectually respectable ideology; of that we can be certain. But some modern variant of the Hobbesian war of 'each against all', defined over groups, may find its own persuasive ideological advocates, with the result that we may, once again, find ourselves in a disordered 'solution' that ensures minimal rather than maximal benefits to all.

Citizens, either in single polities or as combined, have a common purpose in organizing politics to allow persons to get on with their lives, while at the same time living with some assurance that politics will not get beyond its duly constituted limits. The voluntary interactions among persons in sets of interlinked markets generate social order, even if the results, as such, are not within the grand design of any person, party or state. But the social order of the market can degenerate into the disorder of anarchy unless market relationships are embedded within a constitutional-legal framework where individual rights of person and property are well-defined, mutually respected and enforced. This constitutional framework that is necessary for the functioning order of the market must also contain well-defined and enforceable limits on the range and scope for political action. The legitimacy of politics must track the constitutional limits.

NOTE

1. A version of this chapter was published as a monograph (Buchanan, 1991a); a lecture version was presented in Zurich in September 1990.

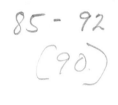

H11
P26
P27

10. Socialism is dead but Leviathan lives on[1]

More than a century ago, Nietzsche announced the death of God. Behind the drama of its presentation, this statement was intended to suggest that the omnipresence of God no longer served as an organizing principle for the lives of individuals or for the rules of their association, one with another. If we can disregard the revival of fundamentalism, notably in Islam, we can refer to this century as one 'without God'. And, indeed, many of the horrors that we have witnessed find at least some part of their explanation in the absence of human fear of a deity's wrath.

I want to suggest here that, since Nietzsche, we have now passed through an interim period of history (roughly a century) during which, in one form or another, the God pronounced dead was replaced in man's consciousness by 'socialism', which seemed to provide, variously, the principle upon which individuals organized their lives in civil society. And I want to match Nietzsche's announcement with the comparable one that 'socialism is dead'. This statement seems much less shocking than the earlier one because it has been and is being heard throughout the world. I suggest, further, that the gap left by the loss of faith in socialism may, in some respects, be equally significant in effects to that which was described by the loss of faith in the deity. In a very real sense, the loss of faith in socialism is more dramatic because it is at least traceable to the accumulation of quasi-scientific evidence. The god that was socialism took on forms that were directly observable; there were no continuing unknowns waiting to be revealed only in another life. And the promised realization of the socialist ideal could not be infinitely postponed in time. In other words, the god that was socialism is *demonstrably dead*; there could have been no comparable statement made subsequent to Nietzsche's announcement.

These are strong claims, and I intend them as such. Socialism promised quite specific results; it did not deliver. It failed in the straightforward meaning of the word. And, those of us who are in positions to think about ideas and their influence can only look back in amazement at the monumental folly that caused the intellectual leaders of the world, for more than a century, to buy into the 'fatal conceit' that socialism embodied – 'fatal conceit' being the wonderfully descriptive appellation recently introduced as the title of F.A. Hayek's last book

(1988). How did we, as members of the academies and intelligentsia, come to be trapped in the romantic myth that politically organized authority could direct our lives so as to satisfy our needs more adequately than we might satisfy them ourselves through voluntary agreement, association and exchange, one with another? I suspect that, literally, thousands of man-years will be spent in efforts fully to answer this question. I shall return to the question briefly later. But first I want to emphasize that the 'fatal conceit' was almost universal. Let us now beware of current attempts to limit acceptance of the socialist myth to those who were the explicit promulgators and defenders of the centrally planned authoritarian regimes of the USSR and its satellites. There were socialists among us everywhere, in all societies, at all levels of discourse, and, even in the face of the evidence that continues to accumulate, there are many who still cannot escape from the socialist mind-set. Even for those of us who have, somehow, shifted away from the mind-set of socialism, and who acknowledge, however begrudgingly, that the socialist god is dead, there may not have emerged any faith or belief in any nonsocialist alternative. We may accept socialism's failure; we may not accept the alternative represented by the free market or enterprise system, even as tempered by elements of the welfare or transfer state.

SOCIALISM AND INDIVIDUALISM

I shall, first, try to define socialism, lest we allow those who enjoy the exploitation of our language to shift the meaning of terms before we realize what is happening. Socialists everywhere, confronted with the evidence that economies organized, wholly or partially, on socialist principles cannot deliver the goods, are now making desperate efforts to redefine the term 'socialism' to mean something quite different from its received meaning, either in its historical development or in modern reality. To counter all such efforts at the outset, we can perhaps do no better than to consult the source books. The entry on socialism in *The New Palgrave: A Dictionary of Economics* is by Alec Nove, a distinguished British scholar, who is himself a socialist. Nove's definition is as follows:

> Let us provisionally accept the following as a definition of socialism; a society may be seen to be a socialist one if the major part of the means of production of goods and services are not in private hands, but are in some sense socially owned and operated, by state, socialised, or cooperative enterprises. (Alec Nove, 1987, p. 398).

As Nove emphasizes, the key elements in this definition are summarized in the shortened statement that 'the means of production . . . are not in private hands'.

Socialism, as a guiding principle for organization, is opposed directly to 'individualism', which could be summarized in the statement that 'the means of production are in private hands'. A more extended definition would include the corollary statement that the means of production, the resource capacities to produce that which is ultimately valued by persons, are *owned* by individuals (that is, *privately*) and that such ownership carries with it the liberty, and the responsibility, to make the relevant choices as to how, when, where and to what purpose these resource capacities will be put.

Only in an economy that emerges out of the complex exchange interrelationships among persons who privately own and control resource capacities can the incentives of resource suppliers be made compatible with the evaluations that persons as final demanders place on goods and services; only in such an economy can the resource suppliers, separately and independently, fully exploit the strictly localized information that emerges in the separate but interlinked markets; only in such an economy can the imaginative potential of individuals to create that which other persons may value be allowed to operate.

It is now almost universally acknowledged that such an economy 'works better' than a socialized economy in which decisions on resource use are made nonprivately, that is, by state or cooperative agencies. And the meaning of 'works better' is quite straightforward: the private-ownership, individualized economy produces a higher valued bundle of goods and services from the resource capacities available to the individuals in a politically organized community. The only proviso here is that the value scalar – the measure through which disparate goods and services are ultimately compared – must be that which emerges from the voluntary exchange process itself. If the value scalar is itself determined by the centralized socialist planners, there is, of course, no reason to think that the private ownership economy will 'work better' in generating more 'value' along this measure.

CLASSICAL POLITICAL ECONOMY

It is sometimes too easy to overlook the simple principles in our headlong rush to get into the complexities. Let me pause, therefore, to emphasize what I have already said here. The private-ownership, market economy 'works better' than the socialized economy; it produces more goods. But, and at the same time, it allows individuals more liberty to choose where, when and to what purpose they will put their capacities to produce values that they expect others to demand. Should we be surprised, therefore, when our history texts tell us about the genuine excitement that the discovery of the principles of classical political economy generated? Only with the philosophers of the eighteenth century did it come to be understood for the first time that the private-ownership economy could, indeed, make nations wealthy, but, at the same time, could ensure persons the liberty to make their own choices. These were heady ideas; it is little wonder that several generations of intellectual and political leaders were so aroused. Persons could be free from coercion by other persons and get rich at the same time, provided only that the state organized the legal-political framework for protection of private properties and for the enforcement of voluntary contracts. This discovery of the complementary values of freedom and well-being that the market order makes possible did indeed seem wonderful. And of course we know that this same complementarity is now being rediscovered all over again in so many lands.

Why, then, did the principles of classical political economy, which seemed so strongly to suggest the relative superiority of a market or free enterprise economy, lose their persuasive powers so quickly? Why did the intellectual leaders and social philosophers abandon *laissez-faire* from roughly the middle of the nineteenth century and throughout most of this century?

SOCIALISM TRIUMPHANT

We must, I think, appreciate the rhetorical genius of Marx in his ability to convert arguments advanced in support of market organization into what could be made to appear to be support for a particular distributional class, the capitalists. By clever substitution of emotion-laden terminology, the market system became 'capitalism', and the search of every person for his or her own advantage became the profit-seeking of the greedy capitalists. This rhetorical genius, coupled with totally erroneous economic analysis embedded into pseudo-scientific jargon about the laws of history, was highly successful in elevating the distributional issue to centre stage, to the relative neglect of the allocational and growth elements that were central in the classical teachings. And, further, the whole Marxian-socialist challenge was introduced into the political arena in the middle of the post-Hegelian epoch, during which the state was conceptualized only in a romantic vision completely divorced from the observable reality of politics.

(Let me pause to say here that I do not intend to present the socialist defence in caricature. I speak as one who shared fully in the socialist mind-set, from which, thanks to Frank Knight, I escaped relatively early in my career. But I appreciate the appeal of the Marxist-socialist ideas even if, now, I cannot explain it.)

There is no need to review in detail the history of the socialist century and a half. Governments everywhere resumed their natural proclivities to interfere with the liberties of persons to make exchanges and now supported by arguments that politicized control of economic decisions was necessary to correct for market failures. Lenin exploited the chaos of Russia to introduce the first fully socialist system of organization, the consequences of which we now know too well. But recall that during the early decades, the Soviet Union was held out as paradise by socialists in the West, both in Europe and America. After World War II, socialism reigned triumphant; Eastern Europe was absorbed into the Soviet political orbit; countries in Western Europe socialized their economies to greater or lesser degrees. Even where economies were largely allowed to remain free of politicized interferences, Keynesian-inspired macromanagement was supported by arguments about the tendency of capitalism to generate massive unemployment.

SOCIALISM IN RETREAT

The triumph of socialism, either in idea or reality, was never complete. There were isolated residues of understanding of classical political economy, and some markets were allowed to remain free from politicized direction, particularly in Western countries. Nonetheless, it remains accurate to describe the central and generalized thrust of politics as 'socialist' up to and including the decade of the 1950s and early 1960s.

Between the early 1960s and today, socialism became ill and died. What happened? There were two sides to the coin, which may be succinctly summarized as 'market success' and 'political failure'. The accumulation of empirical evidence must ultimately dispel romance. And the evidence did indeed accumulate over the three decades to demonstrate that free market economies performed much better than politically directed or planned economies. The German *Wirtschaftswunder* should not be overlooked in this potted history. The economic reforms that Erhard implemented were based on an avowed acceptance of the principles of a market economy, and the principles were demonstrated to work. Germany achieved economic recovery rapidly in the 1950s and 1960s. By contrast and comparison, the socialist experiments tried out in Britain in the late 1940s and early 1950s proved to be demonstrable failures. Nationalization did not produce the goods that had been promised. The Sputnik showpiece that seemed to suggest rapid Soviet development proved to be just that, a showpiece and nothing more. Honest evaluation suggested that the centralized economies of the Soviet Union, China and East European countries were not successful in producing goods and services. In the United States, the extended overreaching of the welfare state in the 1960s set off predictable citizen reaction.

Ideas also matter. And here the record of the academic economists remains, at best, a very mixed bag. The great debate about the possible efficiency of the centrally planned economy, the 1930s debate over socialist calculation between von Mises and Hayek on the one hand and Lange and Lerner on the other, was judged by economists to have been won by the socialist side.

Furthermore, the theoretical welfare economists of the early and middle decades of this century were primarily, indeed almost exclusively, concerned with demonstrating the failures of markets, with the purpose of providing a rationale for political interferences.

But the public-choice revolution in ideas about politics, and political failures, was also sparked primarily by academic economists. When the very elementary step is taken to extend the behavioural models of economics to apply to public choosers – to those who participate variously in political roles, as voters, politicians, bureaucrats, planners, party leaders and so on – the romantic vision that was essential to the whole socialist myth vanishes. If those who make decisions for others are finally seen as ordinary persons, how can the awesome delegation of authority that must characterize the centralized economy be justified? I do not suggest here, in any way, that public-choice theory set off the reaction against politicization, socialism and other variants of the controlled economy. The reaction, which has now extended over the whole world, was surely triggered directly by the many decades of the observed record of political failures. Public choice, as a set of ideas, was, I think, influential in providing an intellectual basis which allows observers to understand better what it is they can directly observe. Political failure was everywhere observed; public choice supplied the explanation as to why the observations were valid.

THE ABSENCE OF FAITH

I stated earlier that there were two sides to the coin; market success and political failure. Both the observations and the ideas that have been developed over the period of socialist retreat have concentrated on the second of these, that is, on political failure. There now exists widespread scepticism about the efficacy of politics and political solutions to achieve economic results. Bureaucracies are mistrusted; politicians are not the heroes of legend. The socialist principle of organization is not expected to work well. The faith in political and government nostrums has all but vanished, as a principle.

This loss of faith in politics, in socialism broadly defined, has not, however, been accompanied by any demonstrable renewal or reconversion to a faith in markets – the *laissez-faire* vision that was central to the teachings of the classical political economists. There remains a residual unwillingness to leave things alone, to allow the free market to organize itself (within a legal framework) in producing and evaluating that which persons value. We are left, therefore, with what is essentially an attitude of nihilism towards economic organization. Politics will not work, but there is no generalized willingness to leave things alone. There seems to be no widely shared organizing principle upon which persons can begin to think about the operations of a political economy.

THE NATURAL EMERGENCE OF LEVIATHAN

It is in this setting, which does seem to be descriptive of the era into which we are so rapidly moving, that the natural forces which generate the Leviathan state emerge and assume dominance. With no overriding principle that dictates how an economy is to be organized, the political structure is open to maximal exploitation by the pressures of well-organized interests which seek to exploit the powers of the state to secure differential profits. The special-interest, rent-seeking, churning state finds fertile ground for growth in this environment. And we observe quite arbitrary politicized interferences with markets, with the pattern of intervention being dependent strictly on the relative strengths of organized interests.

This setting, which I have referred to as Leviathan, has much in common with the mercantilist-protectionist politics that Adam Smith attacked so vehemently in his great book in 1776. Hence, in two centuries we seem to have come full circle. The selfsame barriers that Adam Smith sought to abolish are everywhere resurging, as if from the depths of history. And the selfsame arguments are heard in the land, both in support and in opposition. The arguments for Leviathan's extensions are not versions of the socialist's dream; they are, instead, simple efforts to claim a public interest in a single sector's private profit.

TOWARDS CONSTITUTIONAL LIMITS

There will be no escape from the protectionist-mercantilist regime that now threatens to be characteristic of the post-socialist politics in both Western and Eastern countries so long as we allow the ordinary or natural outcomes of majoritarian democratic processes to operate without adequate constitutional constraints. We have learned to understand interest-group politics; we no longer have a romantic vision as to how the state operates. If we have not rediscovered, and do not rediscover, and understand the precepts of *laissez-faire*, as organizing principles, it will be necessary to address that which we do know and have learned. If we know that politics fails and that its natural proclivity is to extend its reach beyond tolerable bounds, we may be led to incorporate constraints into a constitutional structure. Depoliticized economic order is within the realm of the politically-constitutionally possible, even if the accompanying faith in market organization is not fully regained. We can protect ourselves against the appetites of the monster that the Leviathan state threatens to become without really understanding and appreciating the efficiency-generating properties of the market.

A threshold was crossed in the eighteenth century when we learned how the rule of law, stability of private property and the withdrawal of political interference with private choices, could unleash the entrepreneurial energies that are latent within each of us. The modern age was born. Humankind seemed near to the ultimate realization of its socially organized potentiality only to have this future threatened and in part forestalled by the emergence of the socialist vision – a vision that has now been shown to be grounded in romance rather than in scientific understanding. The central flaw in the socialist vision was its failure to recognize the limits of politicized organization.

Recognizing the limits in order to avoid harm is as important as recognizing the potential that may be achieved within those limits. The organized polities of the nation-states, and the associations among those states, must be kept within constitutional boundaries. The death throes of socialism should not be allowed to distract attention from the continuing necessity to prevent the overreaching of the state-as-Leviathan, which becomes all the more dangerous because it does not depend on an ideology to give it focus. Ideas, and the institutions that emerge as these ideas are put into practice, can be killed off and replaced by other ideas and other institutions. The machinations of interest-driven politics are much more difficult to dislodge. Let us get on with the task.

NOTE

1. An earlier version of this chapter was delivered as the John Bonython Lecture in Sydney, Australia, in March 1990 (Buchanan, 1990a). *published*

11. Tacit presuppositions of political economy: implications for societies in transition

In this chapter, I shall discuss the limits on the transferability of the 'principles of political economy' to the understanding of those regimes which were, before 1989, classified as socialist. I suggest that we, as professional economists, understand capitalist or competitive regimes only within an intellectual construction that relies heavily on a conjectural history which, in itself, embodies a well-defined, even if subconscious, cultural perspective. From this proposition there follows the inference that, because we do not or may not have available a comparably useful conjectural history that can be applied to socialist regimes, those of us who classify ourselves as political economists may be limited in our understanding of those regimes. Our intellectual tools may not fit the task at hand.

The second section traces the several simple steps through which we construct our understanding of an economic order of markets. The third section extends the analysis to the generation of the exchange culture, which both informs the economists' enterprise and, through the effects of economists' understanding, influences the behavioural attitudes of participants in the market nexus. In the fourth section, I suggest the possible replacement of the basic exchange model, through which we understand market order, with a basic collective model, which may allow a better understanding of the collectivized command economy. The fifth section (comparably with the third section) extends the analysis to discuss features of the collective-command culture that are quite distinct from those that predominately exist in the exchange culture. The sixth section covers the necessary qualifications that must be placed on any reductionist enterprise and suggests that elements of both the exchange model and the collective model exist in any and all regimes. The seventh section briefly discusses the presumption about technological determination that informs the analysis. The final section suggests some implications concerning the advice that Western political economists may properly pass along to those involved at reform efforts in socialist countries.

My ultimate message is straightforward: only by understanding the limits of our enterprise can we exploit, both nontrivially and nonharmfully, the productivity of the intellectual capital stock that we inherit from our classical and neoclassical forbears.

FROM AUTARKY TO INTERDEPENDENCE: THE ROAD TO RICHES

How do we, as economists, *understand* the workings of the capitalist or market economies of the Western nation-states (including, of course, developed Asian countries) – economies that differ in themselves along many dimensions, and notably along that which measures the degree of politicization? Note that, prior to any effort at understanding, we must impose an order on that which we subject to direct or indirect observation. Empirical observation would, in itself, remain meaningless in the absence of a theoretical construction that allows us to relate the disparate elements, one to another and to the whole, in such fashion that produces coherence. As sophisticated scientists who command modern mathematical tools of analysis, we are able to work with, and to communicate in terms of, highly abstracted functional relationships among variables that may seem distant from any reality that may be sensorially perceived. I submit, however, that an understanding of 'the economy' cannot be achieved from a research programme that limits itself to a bare-bones idealization of skeletal structure. Economists may, of course, deceive themselves in thinking that they work with nothing beyond the abstracted functional relationships. But meaning attaches itself to abstractly defined relationships only through concrete, if idealized, exemplars.

'An economy containing N traders' – we think of persons, units of human consciousness, 'along with endowments of S goods' – we think of apples, oranges, deer and beaver. In other terms, we *populate* our abstracted universes of analysis with recognizable real things as a step towards achievement of ultimate understanding. This process of 'populating' our economists' analytical universe is itself complex and highly sophisticated. We think, initially and conjecturally, of a setting where two traders, A and B, possess beginning endowments of two well-defined 'goods' – a setting that opens up prospects for mutually advantageous exchange, provided that either initial endowments or relative evaluations should differ. From this beginning it becomes easy to increase the number of goods and the number of traders and to trace out the extended network of exchanges, always with central focus on the mutuality of advantage to all participants.

A somewhat more difficult extension, but one that remains easily manageable, involves the introduction of production in the place of the presumption of existing initial endowments. In this stage of conjectural idealization, persons possess no goods at the outset; instead, they possess capacities or talents to produce values, for themselves and for others, which may not take the form of physical goods. Again, however, to the extent that persons differ in tastes or talents, or that there exist advantages to specialization, production followed by exchange and consumption involves mutuality of advantages to all who participate.

The essential elements of the story are not modified as we take a further major extension from the imagined setting where individual producers-exchangers-consumers interact, one with another, in a whole network of pairwise trades, to a setting where individuals, as such, offer productive capacities (for example, labour) to 'firms', in exchange for units of generalized purchasing power (money) and, in turn, purchase from 'firms' desired end-items for consumption. We arrive, of course, at the familiar wheel of income that often introduces the student to economics – the wheel which basically depicts the simultaneous operation of the two conceptually distinct inclusive markets, one for productive services, the other for final goods.

My point of emphasis here is that this whole enterprise, which we may call the construction of our understanding of the economy, has as its central and pervasive theme the mutuality of advantage from exchange or trade, whether this be direct or indirect, simple or complex. The lesson that is derived from the simplest of models, that of two persons and two goods, remains embedded in our understanding of the operations of even the most complex institutional structures that describe the Western international economic order. The construction here is conjecturally historical in that we interpret the economy as having developed from autarky to increasing interdependence and, in the process of development, having increased the well-being of all persons who have participated.

THE CULTURE OF EXCHANGE

The understanding of the market or enterprise economic order that informs the thinking of Western political economists, and which does depend on the conjectural history sketched out above, has also sufficiently penetrated the cultural attitudes of persons who are not themselves economists, and who occupy varying roles as participants in economic process. The Western economic-political regimes are characterized by an exchange culture that incorporates, to some indeterminate but minimally required extent, the main lessons to be drawn from the understanding of their economists. I am not, of course, suggesting that noneconomists understand how a market economy works; if this were the case, what need would there be for those of us who call ourselves professionals?[1] Nonetheless, the ideas of the political economists have had consequences, and there is a modicum of generalized appreciation of the central theme from the economists' understanding.[2]

This appreciation shows up in at least two elements that describe the exchange culture. The first element may be called a 'toleration of trade and traders', again within minimally required limits. Persons who seek out and exploit trading opportunities (defined inclusively to cover entrepreneurial activity generally) have not been subjected to discriminatory treatment, scorn, derision and ridicule. And the personally accumulated gains from trading in the large have not been coveted, at least not directly, by those who stand willing to observe passively the productive and trading efforts of others. Emulation, rather than envy, has been the motivating force for many potential entrants.

I am not, of course, suggesting that the traditional hatred of trade, traders and, especially, trading profits, has ever been absent, even when the exchange culture has attained its widest domain. Punitive taxation of trading profits reflects the politicization of such motivation. And noneconomist intellectuals of all ages and places have remained critical of trade and exchange both as institutions and as praiseworthy occupational pursuits. Western regimes have, however, been successful in constraining the influence of the antiexchange mind-set. One source of such constraint has surely been the acceptance of the simple gains-from-trade theme.

A second element of the exchange culture is, however, even more significant than the first, and this element has to do with the general acceptance-acknowledgement of an *exchange role* by almost all members of Western regimes. Aside from those persons who may be classified as pure consumers, those who live off transfers from others, whether such transfers be organized privately or publicly, everyone in a Western economic order tends to perceive his or her own role as a simultaneous producer-*and*-consumer, that is to say, in terms of an exchange of values across markets. The person who supplies labour services does so in *exchange* for money wages, which are, as income, then *exchanged* for end-items of consumption value. The relationships are *reciprocal*, rather than unilateral. In this important sense, each producer-consumer considers himself or herself to be a trader and evaluates the trading relationship in positively valued terms.

To the extent that the market relationship between persons, or between persons and firms, is understood to be reciprocal, each party or agent to a transaction, in either productive services or final product markets, recognizes the connection between value offered and value received. The labourer who works harder expects to receive more pay, and the retailer who offers quality goods expects higher prices and more customers. Further, these direct exchanges of work for money and money for goods are themselves perceived as parts of the indirect exchange of work for goods.[3] As stated, these characteristics of a market order appear simplistically self-evident. The presence of a generalized culture of exchange has the effect of transmitting the sense of reciprocity, behaviourally, throughout the network of economic interdependence.

As with the toleration of trading and traders, qualifications must be introduced to the generalized presence of reciprocity in market relationships. The direct nexus between value offered and value received is often attenuated, and seriously, by institutionalized constraints that make the two sides of an apparent exchange seem independent to participants. Any departure from idealized piece-rate payment for productive services has the effect of attenuation, and, of course, such institutions as tenure and seniority in contracts tend to break the nexus. In either productive service or product markets, the observing economist has little difficulty in identifying literally hundreds of features that tend to move the relationships between buyers and sellers away from rather than towards the idealized reciprocity of the simple trade in apples and oranges between two traders. Nonetheless, I submit that the attitude of reciprocity in market relationships remains relatively pervasive in Western economies, even in those settings where, in some strict behavioural sense, there remains little or no rational foundations for such attitude. The salesclerk in the Sheraton Hotel in Houston, Texas, offers me a postcard *as if* she, personally, has an interest in my purchase, even when both of us know that her wage or position depends only in some extremely remote sense on her behaviour in our momentary relationship.

The exchange culture tends to foster the attitude of reciprocity, even in *as if* settings, and behaviour reflecting such an attitude tends in itself to promote a mutuality of expectations that becomes reinforcing. The economists' understanding of the elements of the idealized economy serves to influence the workings of the complex economy towards the idealized model from which it was conceptually derived. In this sense, even for economists, observing scientists have exerted an influence on that which is observed.

FROM COOPERATION TO CHAOS: THE ROAD TO RUIN

Western political economists find it difficult to observe economic interaction, whether conceptually or empirically, without reliance on the conjectural history outlined earlier and without interpretation from within the exchange culture. If we are to make progress in understanding non-Western economies as they operate, either before or after 1989, it may be necessary to start afresh and to think in terms of a different conjectural history. Western political economy describes the movement from autarky to interdependence as always generated by the individualized interests of those who participate in trades. This construction of our understanding may be vulnerable.

For a start, it may be necessary to exorcise the image of two isolated and independent traders, each of whom is presumed to be self-subsistent prior to trade, who meet, make trades and walk away with higher valued bundles of goods. To commence anew, we may replace this image by an idealized collective-cooperative-command setting in which, say, ten persons (families) confront a challenge that no one can handle alone – a challenge that, if not met, will ensure that no one will survive. Self-subsistence in a Hobbesian-like jungle is impossible; life is nonexistent rather than nasty, brutish and short. Cooperation among the several persons is necessary for simple survival, and to be effective, cooperation requires direction and command. A leader or coordinator must somehow emerge, or be chosen, who will take on the role of issuing orders to the separate members of the collective, assigning to each person some share in the work that is to be jointly done. From the work so organized, a result is accomplished, or, in economic parlance, some 'good' is produced. Postproduction, the leader or coordinator must also take on the role of assigning distributive shares.

In this most elementary model of the collective-command relationship, the position of the individual participant is profoundly different from that which is present in idealized exchange. In the idealized collective-command setting, there is, by construction, no threat potential available to the individual as determined by the threshold difference in utility between independent existence and participation in collective effort. *Exit is not an alternative.* The choices of the leader are, therefore, arbitrary, within wide limits, in the assignment both of relative shares in workload and reward. There is a necessary command or power relationship between the individual participant and the leader, over and beyond any such relationship that might, but need not, exist in an exchange setting.[4]

Even in a very small collective, there is little conscious linkage between the work that the individual supplies and the reward that is expected. Additional personal effort will not translate directly into expectation of additional personal reward, save as such linkage may emerge from the choices made by the commander – choices that necessarily involve wide ranges of discretion, which are recognized by all participants, including the commander.

In very small collectives, the individual may recognize that the success or failure of the whole combined endeavour depends critically on his or her own contribution, and conscious recognition of this interdependence may ensure general adherence to the orders issued by the coordinating authority. This sense of critical interdependence tends to be eroded, however, as the membership of the collective expands. Increasing interdependence along the size-of-membership dimension exerts effects that are directionally opposite to those that characterize increasing numbers in the exchange relationship. As noted, in the latter, increases in the numbers of traders tend to extend the mutuality of advantage.[5] By contrast, membership increases in collective relationships reduce the individual's conscious linkage between own-effort and collective result.[6] Differentially exerted individual self-interest, as potentially reflected in varying forms of free-ridership, diverges increasingly from uniform or general individual self-interest, as a member of the collective.

As the size and complexity of collective action increase, the set of rules, directives and orders issued to participants by the command-control authority must increase and, perhaps disproportionately, become increasingly constraining on behaviour. Beyond some limit, the constraints will be such as to prevent voluntaristic response, even in the direction of an extension of cooperative effort. The participant who may fully understand the ultimate linkage between own input and collective result and who may, because of this understanding combined with moral principle, seek to expand cooperative effort, may find such behavioural change impermissible under standing rules.

In its idealized limit, the large collective interaction operates effectively only when the command authority issues the proper set of rules and orders and when all participants fully obey these rules and orders as laid down. Idealized cooperative behaviour is defined in terms of following orders – of fulfilling the tasks assigned. Conversely, deviant or noncooperative behaviour is defined as any departure from the rules. And failure or success of the collective endeavour is measured by the degree of adherence to the rule-following norms, along with the control authority's correctness or incorrectness in the choice of norms.[7]

THE COMMAND CULTURE

In the discussion contained in the second section, I suggested that the conjectural history summarized under the phrase 'from autarky to interdependence' informs Western political economists' understanding of their own regimes, and, further, that principles derived from this understanding have, to some extent, been influential in fostering the development of an exchange culture in Western nations. In such culture, I suggested that there was a 'toleration for trade and traders', along with a sense of generalized participation in reciprocal market dealings, both of which elements have been important in facilitating economic development.

At the beginning of the fourth section, I suggested that, if we are to understand the economies of non-Western regimes, it may be necessary to jettison the conjectural history that is familiar to us and start anew with an alternative idealization – one that replaces the initial interaction of isolated traders with an initial communitarian-collective interaction from which the individual has no viable exit. This alternative starting place for conceptual analysis of behavioural interaction can be influential in the emergence and development of a culture that may remain characteristic of regimes that are defined by their participants in collective-communitarian terms.

By the very nature of the collective interaction that may be implicitly taken to be the most elemental feature of social grouping, cooperation requires that individual participants follow orders, that they do the tasks assigned to them and they accept the shares in goods that the command-control authority distributes to them. Failure to cooperate – to carry out the designated assignment, to fill the quota – must, again by the nature of the collective interaction, impose burdens on all other participants, who must either increase their own contributions to collective effort or suffer the consequences of a reduced joint product. (By contrast, in an idealized exchange setting, failure to cooperate on the part of an individual is signalled by an unwillingness to engage in trade, behaviour which, in the limiting case, imposes no burden on other potential traders.)

In the command culture derivative from the collective interaction model, neither of the two elements listed as characteristic of the exchange culture is present. There is likely to be little or no toleration for the person who deviates from the rules, whether for private or group advantage, and there will surely be a heightened sense of envy at the differential success of anyone who is seen to have secured such success by departing from known rules.

Consider the setting of an imaginary manorial village, where the shoemaker toils neither from benevolence nor self-interest, but because he is assigned to make shoes by the lord of the manor. Suppose that, one fine day, a little shoemaker discovers that his own talents are superior to shoemakers in neighbouring villages. And now, from self-interest, he 'markets' shoes to the mutual advantage of those who 'buy' and himself, as maker and seller. The conjectural history that produces the exchange culture stresses this mutuality of gain. But the shoemaker (the 'trader' in 'marketing' his shoes with foreigners, and thereby securing personal gain) imposes costs on those in his own village. Fewer or lower quality shoes are now available locally. The shoemaker's behaviour has disturbed the orderly routines by which goods, shoes and other things, are produced, distributed and consumed. The conjectural history that stresses the spillover damages imposed by the emergent trader's action produces the command culture in which the trader, and trade, always remain suspect.

Nor does the member-participant in the collective-command culture perceive himself or herself, as an individual, to be a part of, or as engaging in, a *reciprocal* exchange relationship with others, even at the most elemental level of consciousness concerning his or her own identified place in the social scheme of things. The shoemaker is supposed to act upon the orders of the collective authority, and he is not supposed to think in terms of voluntarily initiated action directed toward and tied to some reciprocal return of an enhanced distributive share. The Marxian norm – 'from each according to his ability, to each according to his need' – is more than an ideological slogan. It describes an idealization of collective reality, as this reality is interpreted by those who experience it. The exertion of effort creates no claim to share in product. Effort is directed toward *common* purposes, and linkage between effort and reward becomes the source of envy rather than emulation.

As indicated earlier, in very small collectives the sense of commonality, of cooperative sharing, both in supplying input and receiving output, may effectively supersede any strict sense of individualized reciprocity. Or, to put the point differently, in very small collectives cooperative sharing and reciprocity may be difficult to distinguish, one from another. But in large groups, with complex structures of authority and highly differentiated role assignments, the elementary nexus among sharers is almost necessarily attenuated. To the extent that a reciprocal relationship informs the individual's attitude towards the supply of effort, it is a relationship between the individual and the command-control authority that issues the instructions. The choice problem is akin to that posed by the highwayman, 'your money or your life', in this case becoming, 'your work or your punishment',[8] which is categorically different from 'your work or a cutback in your pay'.

In the earlier discussion of the exchange culture, I suggested that the theme of mutuality of gains from trade influences the observed behaviour of participants in the economy, even when the objectively described features of modern organizational reality may severely attenuate the relationship between an individual's supply offer and claims of distributive shares. In the hotel salesclerk example, I suggested that behaviour seems to be based on some as if norm of mutual advantage. In the alternative culture of collective-command discussed in this part of the chapter, there is no awareness, even at a subconscious level, of the generalized mutuality of advantage in exchange. The salesclerk in the Moscow hotel acts as if there is no connection whatsoever between the supply of effort and the individual's ultimate share in product. Behaviour in the two cultures is categorically different, even if the underlying organizational reality may be similar for the two settings.

CULTURAL INTERSECTION

I have contrasted two distinct understandings of the elemental economic relationships among persons, and I have suggested that these understandings produce distinct cultures that have observable behavioural consequences. I do not suggest that either of the two understandings and cultures is exclusive to the domain of either of the two associated organizational regimes. Capitalist economies, and especially as these operate within the constraints of democratic polities, contain within them features that are descriptive of collective-control cultures. And socialist economies, whether these be nominally democratic or authoritarian, contain features descriptive of exchange cultures. The intersections are perhaps worthy of brief discussion.

Any organized regime of social-political-economic order must, at some basic level, be considered as a scheme of cooperation. And, as such, the efficacy of the regime depends critically on the willingness of participants to abide by the rules, no matter what the source of these rules might be. This proposition applies to capitalist and socialist regimes alike, and it is a naive misconception to think of a capitalist regime as one that operates without constraints. But the rules of a capitalist order are minimal, and, ideally, these are summarized in the admonition 'obey the law', law that is general, impersonal and very limited in scope. There is a categorical difference between the constraint sets that confront the individual in a capitalist and a socialist order. Capitalism tends to minimize the political-bureaucratic direction of human behaviour and, at the same time, to allow for a wider range of individual initiative without invoking charges of noncooperation.[9]

Apart from the basic cooperation that is embodied in law-abiding behaviour, capitalist regimes, as they exist, contain sectors that necessarily violate the underlying 'exchange logic'. In the economies of Western nations, politicized or socialist sectors range in relative size from a quarter to more than one-half of total economic activity. For these very large public or governmental sectors, individual participation is not informed directly by precepts relevant to reciprocal exchange and is not reflective of behaviour in an exchange culture. Nor is the public sector of the modern nation-state modelled in exchange terms by more than a small minority of normative fiscal-political philosophers. The 'voluntary exchange theory of taxation' has surely not been dominant in the scientific discussion that has influenced Western political attitudes. Individuals make little or no connection between taxes paid (in response to the coercive impositions of governments) and the benefits (including transfers) received from government programmes. In application to the public sector, the dominant normative precept is that taxes should be based on 'ability to pay' and that benefits (including transfers) should be based on 'need' – precisely the precept that is contained in the Marxist slogan previously mentioned.

Individual behaviour in the public economy sectors of Western capitalist countries tends to be evaluated by collective-command norms rather than by those emergent from an exchange culture. The potential taxpayer who, while seeking his own differential advantage, discovers a means of avoiding an assigned liability is, indeed, imposing a cost on others in the fiscal nexus, prompting the charge that such behaviour is noncooperative. Individual initiative, reflective of a generalized trading instinct, in locating loopholes for the avoidance of tax liability or opportunities for claims to differential benefits and transfers, tends to be *destructive* of the achievement of the declared objectives of the welfare state.

These examples are sufficient to indicate that elements of the collective-command understanding of basic social relationships are pervasive in Western polities. But elements of the exchange conceptualization along with the consequent influence on individual behaviour also pervade socialist regimes. In the latter, there has always been a generalized recognition that persons respond to individually defined incentives – incentives that promise differential rewards for effort. Further, the highly centralized and collectivized structures of the Soviet Union always depended for their functioning on the activity of the defectors, of the 'traders', who work out mutually advantageous, if nominally illegal, deals among separate administrative-bureaucratic units in the system. But whereas the contribution of these genuine 'entrepreneurs' may have been acknowledged, their activities were, at the same time, treated as deviant or as outside ordinary and expected ways of doing things. And, of course, there were always sectors of socialist economies in which individuals engaged directly in reciprocal exchanges, fully cognizant of the relationship between effort and reward. But these genuinely private sectors were often very small relative to the size of the total economies.

TECHNOLOGICAL DETERMINACY?

My reductionist thesis is that the conjectural understanding of the economic process, and the influence of this understanding on behaviour, is an important source of difference between capitalist and socialist regimes, and that the exchange model and the collective-command model generate categorically different sets of behavioural attitudes. Economists will, of course, recognize that the distinction made here is identical to that emergent among persons who, in one setting, exchange private, or partitionable, goods and services and, in another setting, participate in arrangements for the provision of collective-consumption or public goods and services, defined technologically to be nonpartitionable and/or nonexcludable. The private goods – public goods distinction has been central in public economic analysis since Samuelson's (1954) seminal paper. For the most part, however, this whole analysis has incorporated the presumption that institutional organization is determined by the technological characteristics of the goods and services. By contrast, the presumption here is that the privateness–publicness distinction is applicable to the organizational structure of the regime rather than the underlying technology.[10]

The technology may, of course, affect the operation of any organizational structure. A fully partitionable good may be organizationally amenable to an exchange structure, and collectivization may invite noncooperative behaviour along several dimensions. On the other hand, a genuinely collective-consumption good may remain inadequately supplied in a simple exchange structure, although there is no assurance that collectivization, as it operates, will improve matters.

The 'organizational-behavioural technology' may be much more significant than the physical technology. As noted earlier, the collective-communitarian-command model of social interaction depends critically on individuals' sense of sharing in the joint or cooperative endeavour. This feature of the collective model is independent of the process through which decisions for the collective are made.[11] Other things equal, it seems clear that the sharing consciousness tends to be inversely related to the number of participants in the collective interaction. As collective groupings increase in membership size, free-ridership, generally defined, increases, and individual departures from assigned standards, norms or quotas become both more difficult to achieve and more vulnerable to peer criticism. Collective arrangements work best in small groups.

By contrast, the exchange model reduces interaction, arbitrarily, to two-person (one buyer-one seller) size and largely eliminates free-ridership while, at the same time, maximally encouraging individual initiative. And because each interaction is factored down to the two-person or two-unit exchange, there is no effective upper bound to the size of membership in the inclusive trading network. As its negative feature, however, the exchange model cannot readily be extended in logical structure to take directly into account the effects that simple exchanges exert on parties and groups that are not participants.[12]

CONCLUDING SPECULATIONS

My purpose in this chapter has been to examine the limits of the principles of Western political economy in application to the problems faced by failed socialist regimes as efforts are made to effect a transition to market economies under broadly democratic political constraints. First post-1989 impressions suggested to me that the Western political economists who proffered advice were not understood and, furthermore, that these economists themselves did not understand the nature of the problems that they were, presumably, trying to address. In an attempt to sort out what seemed to be intellectual confusion, I have suggested that there may exist differences in the basic conjectural histories through which our understanding of complex economic processes is constructed. To Western economists, the build-up from simple commodity exchange through complex institutional structures emphasizes the mutuality of trading gains, as these are variously motivated by the interest-seeking of traders (entrepreneurs). An exchange culture that finds its intellectual roots in the economists' construction extends to inform the attitudes of those who participate in the market nexus, as buyers-sellers of outputs, as agents for those organizations that buy and sell outputs, as buyers-sellers of inputs, as agents for those organizations that buy and sell inputs.

My central thesis is that we cannot understand the presuppositions upon which the whole socialist enterprise is based without shifting out of the mind-set described by the exchange model. I have offered an alternative conjectural history of social interaction, one in which persons are thought to be locked in a collective relationship from which exit is impossible. A collective-command structure is deemed to be necessary, regardless of how choices for the collective are made, and cooperative behaviour for an individual is defined to consist of behaviour in accordance with assigned rules and orders. Voluntary individual initiative tends to be destructive or noncooperative in this setting, and behaviour reflective of such initiative is adjudged to be noncooperative by participants.

What implications follow from acceptance of my thesis, even in the partial explanatory sense that I advance it? First of all, it seems evident that individual behaviour that is adjudged to be cooperative depends on the institutional setting within which such behaviour takes place. Adam Smith's butcher who acts in his own self-interest in selling meat does, indeed, benefit others and, in so doing, is behaving cooperatively in the positive-sum game of market exchange. But what about the Cuban butcher who has a bureaucratically-assigned monopoly on meat supply, and who acts self-interestedly when he delivers the whole week's quota to the hoarder who possesses the only freezer in town? The two traders gain, but others are damaged, and there may not exist alternative sellers from whom meat may be purchased. Until and unless the *institutions* of market exchange are in place in some proximate sense, as alternative to collectivized arrangements, Western political economists who simplistically suggest that black, underground or shadow markets should always be encouraged may exacerbate rather than smooth the transition process. (Would these same economists urge American policy steps designed to encourage rent-seeking efforts of interest groups aimed at securing differential gains through congressional politics? Charles Keating and the Senators expected to secure mutual gains from trade, but are we to ignore the spillover damages?)

An effectively working market economy requires both the institutional structure that facilitates the partitioning of parties to exchange and the presence of an exchange culture within which participants act as if they stand in a reciprocity relationship to those with whom transactions are made. Expansions and extensions in the small private sectors of the socialist regimes pass muster on these counts since these steps institutionalize the exchange culture. But 'privatization' of large-scale socialist enterprises, as such, may do little to implement the transition, even if the shares in ownership are widely dispersed. Radical decentralization and deconcentration, by contrast, may both exploit the residual collective sharing psychology and build a road toward reciprocity among separate small collectivities.

In Western regimes, markets work tolerably well, within the political-legal framework of widely dispersed property rights, when the workings of ordinary politics do not interfere excessively. They do so because they have evolved through a long history which has been interpreted and understood by experts in such fashion as to reinforce the behavioural attitudes necessary to make such institutions function. In failed socialist regimes, markets have neither the history nor the interpretation-understanding that informs behavioural attitudes. It seems naive in the extreme to assume that market order is 'natural' to the extent that it can emerge full blown without history, without institutional construction and, most importantly, without understanding.

A final caution. Lest Western political economists become too complacent about keeping their own place in the overall scheme of things, they should perhaps be reminded again that collective-communitarian-command models of interaction, with the accompanying mind-sets, continue to describe proportionately very large sectors of Western economies. Those who construct an understanding of the market order may, in fact, do their job best when they stay at home.

NOTES

1. Many noneconomists, and especially politicians and journalists, think that they do, in fact, understand the workings of economic process. The problems generated by 'everyman his own economist' have plagued political economy from its inception in the late eighteenth century.
2. I need not speculate on the relationship between the current teaching of economics and the carryover of some understanding into public attitudes. I can suggest, however, that the teaching of the classical political economists was influential in the formation of the institutions of Western social orders which, in turn, have tended to promote general public awareness of basic elements of the economists' understanding.
3. Alberto di Pierro has noted that the efficacy of the direct exchanges here depend critically on the translation of terms of trade into meaningful counters in the ultimate indirect exchange (di Pierro, 1990).
4. It is, of course, possible to model the operation of an economy made up of competitive collectives, with individual members exercizing free mobility among the several collective units. I submit, however, that in the absence of some conjectural sense of individual self-subsistence, such an economy could never emerge.
5. The categorical difference in the effects of numbers, as between private goods and public goods interactions, was noted early in Samuelson (1955).
6. For an early treatment of this point, see Buchanan (1954).
7. Note that the analysis here can remain noncommittal as to the sources for the objectives of the collective. An omniscient and benevolent authority could, by definition, match the collective's objectives ideally with individuals' evaluations. But even such an imagined ideal authority would achieve these objectives only if all individuals behave in accordance with the rules that the authority imposes on their behaviour.
8. For an extended discussion of the dual sense in which the citizen in a democratic polity 'exchanges' with government, see Chapter 17.
9. For an elaboration of the argument here, see Chapter 20.
10. See Buchanan (1968).
11. In collective interaction that may be described as 'democratic', the costs of reaching agreement will be related directly to the size of the decisive coalition. For an analysis, see Buchanan and

Tullock (1962). Such decision-making costs are, however, distinct from those that are emphasized in the analysis of this chapter. In the earlier analysis, we assumed, implicitly, that participants in the interaction would abide by collective decisions, once made. Or, in other terms, that all participants in the collective endeavour behave in ideally cooperative ways; there are no free riders.

12. The implication to be drawn would seem to be that market economies should be characterized by the presence of more severe negative externalities, in the form of environmental degradation, than socialist economies. The fact that, empirically, the results are precisely contrary to those that might be predicted analytically suggests that the objectives that guided the choices made by the decision makers for the collectivity in socialist economies were quite different from those that might have been derived from individual evaluations, as the latter might have been estimated by Western economists.

An additional explanatory element emerges when the sheer inefficiency of socialist economics is recognized. If total production is sufficiently low, there may be a much wider tolerance of environmental 'bads', even if the damages for all members of the inclusive collectivity are estimated and embodied in the decision calculus.

12. Asymmetrical reciprocity in market exchange: implications for economies in transition

Western visitors to those parts of the world that before 1991 were politically organized as the Soviet Union have been impressed by the attitudes of persons towards behaviour in ordinary exchanges – attitudes that seem to be so different from those in Western economies. The essential elements of an 'exchange culture' seem to be missing, and this absence, in itself, may be central to the effective functioning of market economies.[1] Individual participants in ordinary exchange relationships in Western economies act as if they understand the simplest of all economic principles, namely, that there are mutual gains from trade, that the benefits are reciprocal, that exchange is a positive-sum game. This as if understanding, which remains perhaps below our level of consciousness in the West, is largely missing from the public attitudes of citizens of the former Soviet Union, who behave as if the gains from trade do not exist, or at least are one-sided rather than mutual.

There is a familiar story that illustrates the thesis: in the Soviet Union, both parties to an exchange lose – one party loses the goods; the other party loses the money. This statement may offer a concise, if exaggerated, summary of the general attitude towards exchange that seems to describe the behaviour of many (of course, not all) persons in the republics that were formerly parts of the Soviet Union.

In this chapter, I propose to build upon, to extend and, in part, to modify these arguments. I propose to offer an *economic* explanation for some of the differences in behavioural attitudes that we observe, as between Western economies and those of the Eurasian republics. In the West, with developed market systems, economists concentrate initial attention on the mutuality of trading gains and on the *reciprocity* in any exchange relationship. And a recognition of this reciprocity seems to inform public participation in markets. What is often overlooked is the asymmetry in the reciprocal relationship between buyer and seller in developed money economies. The buyer of goods and/or services who offers, or 'sells', money in exchange possesses a bargaining advantage that is often overlooked. The central command economy reverses the direction of advantage, even when exchange dealings are permitted. The differences in the incentives that confront participants in the two organizational settings generate predictable differences in observed behaviour and in behavioural attitudes.

I should stress at the outset that my focus is exclusively on the economic, as opposed to the ideological, sources of explanation of observed behaviour in the exchange process. The ideological denigration of market exchange, as a general system of organizing economic relationships, may have exerted influences on individual behaviour over and beyond those analysed here. And, of course, at some higher system level where organizational-institutional decisions on structure were made, ideological motivation may explain why persons were confronted with the circumstances that contain divergent economic incentives.

In the second section, I shall introduce the formal analysis by reference to the workings of an idealized model of a barter economy in the absence of transactions costs. This model is introduced solely for the purpose of comparison with the workings of a money economy, still idealized, but as made minimally necessary by the presence of transactions costs. This second model is examined in the third section. In the fourth section, I shall identify the asymmetry in the reciprocal exchange relationship, even in the idealized money economy, and I indicate observable features of Western economies that do not falsify the hypothesis that such an asymmetry exists. The fifth section takes the obvious next step and extends the analysis to the command economy that does not allow full scope for the operation of the institutions of market exchange. The results suggest that the behavioural roles of participants in such economies may become quite different from those in market cultures. The final section discusses some of the implications of the analysis for problems of transition from a command to a market structure.

IDEALIZED EXCHANGE – A PURE BARTER ECONOMY

Consider a setting in which the exchange process operates ideally, in the analytical-conceptual sense and beyond any feasibility limits imposed by the limits to human capacities. Persons enter into exchange dealings, one with another, in the full knowledge of all potential trading opportunities. Further, the exchange network – the economy – is sufficiently large such that, for each and every buyer or seller in the market for each and every good or service, input or output, there exists large numbers of sellers or buyers, among whom any single buyer or seller may choose. Finally, there are no costs incurred by any buyer or seller in shifting custom from one alternative to another.

Note that, in such an idealized, zero transactions cost setting, no person, whether buyer or seller, in any exchange relationship secures any differential gain from exchanging with the single seller or buyer with whom a particular exchange is effectuated. Neither party's action, in making the particular cross-market transfer, generates benefits for the other, for the simple reason that alternative buyers or sellers to whom trade may be shifted are available at no cost. The gain emerges, of course, as between any person, whether buyer or seller, and 'the market', inclusively considered.

For my purpose, the noteworthy feature of this idealized model is the implied behavioural indifference that each participant in the exchange network will exhibit towards those with whom exchanges are made. In such a setting, nothing that might be called an 'exchange culture' would have meaning. Each participant may, if he or she chooses, behave as if he or she exists in total independence of others, despite the complete interdependence among all persons who participate in the inclusive network. No buyer need invest any effort in persuading, cajoling or convincing any seller to offer goods and services, and, similarly, no seller will find it rational to try to persuade any buyer to take his wares off the shelf. The reason is straightforward: there exists a sufficiently large number of alternative sellers or buyers to ensure that, if one person does not trade, a replacement immediately appears to whom trade can be shifted and at no differential cost.

IDEALIZED EXCHANGE WITH MONEY

I now propose to modify the idealized exchange model as previously described in only one respect. Assume, as before, that there are no costs of making exchanges, and that all participants have full knowledge about the qualities of goods. Further, assume, again as before, that the economy is large, and that there are many sellers and many buyers in the market for each good and service. Assume now, however, that there are limits to the knowledge that any participant has about the location of those persons in the economy who seek to purchase precisely the same good he or she seeks to sell, and vice versa. That is to say, direct barter is costly in the sense that each participant in a potential trade must undergo some search effort in locating the desired matching trading partner.

Recognition of the costs of search that make direct barter inefficient provides an economic explanation for the emergence of money, either in the form of some good that comes to be widely accepted as a medium of general exchange through some process of cultural evolution or in the form of some good or some symbolic representation, the value of which is guaranteed by the collective body that protects private property, that is, by the state. The existence of money allows sellers to eliminate costly searches for other persons who are themselves sellers of goods that are desired in exchange. Similarly, money allows buyers to purchase goods that they desire without the necessity of searching for persons who seek to buy precisely that which they offer in exchange as sellers. The familiar metaphor that refers to money as the lubricant of the exchange system is helpfully explanatory.

Under the severely restrictive conditions assumed to exist, however, the behaviourally relevant conclusions reached above with reference to the idealized exchange economy seem to continue to hold. Since there are many buyers and many sellers in the markets for any good or service, any input or output, the individual participant need not be at all concerned about the person with whom an exchange is effectuated. The seller of red shoes need not invest in efforts to convince potential buyers to purchase his stocks since, by definition, there exist alternative buyers who will purchase the stocks and with no cost to the seller. Similarly, the buyer of red apples need not invest in attempts to persuade any single apple seller to offer his wares, since, again by definition, there exist many alternative apple sellers to whom the apple buyer may turn and without cost. There is no economic basis for the emergence of any attitude other than behavioural indifference toward specifically identified cross-exchange partners.

ASYMMETRICAL RECIPROCITY

The summary analysis of the preceding paragraph is, I submit, incorrect at worst and misleading at best. The introduction of money, even under idealized settings for the operation of an exchange economy, modifies the presumed anonymity, and consequent symmetry, in the pairwise buyer–seller relationship; and this modification has important behavioural implications.

Consider, again, the working properties of an idealized money economy. Figure 12.1 reproduces the familiar 'wheel of income' diagram from introductory textbooks in economics. The individual at *A*, whom we may call *A*, who either possesses or produces a good or service (perhaps an input into some process) that is not desired for his or her own or internal use, enters one market as a seller of that good or service, which we may call *X*. If we ignore sequencing here, we can say that this individual simultaneously enters another market as a buyer of that good or service (or bundle of goods and services) that is desired for final end use; say this good or service is *Y*. The individual in question is a supplier of *X* and a demander of *Y*, in the two separated markets.

A person cannot, however, enter unilaterally in any market. The reciprocity relationship requires that each participant in an exchange enters simultaneously as buyer and seller. The individual identified above as the seller-supplier of *X* and the buyer-demander of *Y* enters the market for *X* and the market for *Y* in the necessary reciprocal positions as a buyer-demander of money (*M*) in the *X* market and a seller-supplier of money in the *Y* market. The generalized or fully fungible good, money, becomes the intermediate instrument of value that allows the individual entry into the two markets of his or her ultimate interest.

The asymmetry enters when we recognize that the money side of any exchange has an inherent 'transactions costs' advantage, which in turn improves

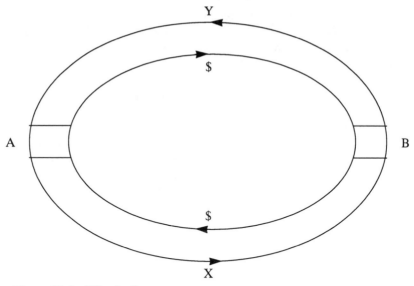

Figure 12.1   Wheel of income

the 'bargaining' power of the person who takes such a role. Consider, once again, a pure barter economy without money, but with some limits on knowledge. Clearly, the person who possesses or produces a good that is, relatively, more generally desired than others will find it less costly to effectuate exchanges for whatever good is ultimately desired. Money becomes the limiting case of a good that is generally desired by all participants in the exchange network, even if instrumentally rather than intrinsically. The trader who accepts money for units of any nonmoney good or service secures a nonspecific medium of value that facilitates reentry into any market. The ideal fungibility of money gives the supplier-seller of money an asymmetrical claim to the gains from exchange. By the very definition of what money is, the possessor, and hence potential supplier, of money faces lower transactions costs in completing any exchange than the possessor, and potential supplier, of any nonmoney good or service. The fungibility of money provides the possessor with enhanced power to 'walk away' from any exchange for goods and services – a power that the possessor of any nonmoney good or service simply does not have.

The basic asymmetry in the money–goods exchange is obscured by the proclivity of economic theorists to 'define away' the features of the exchange process that are sometimes of most interest. As noted, if transactions costs are, literally, defined away, there would be no need for money at all; the pure barter economy would operate with ideal efficiency. When the rigorous assumptions required for the working of a pure barter economy are modified, however, and money is recognized to be an efficiency-enhancing institution, attempts are made to idealize the operations of the money economy by postulating that each and every buyer and seller, whether of goods or money, faces a sufficiently large number of cross-exchange options to guarantee that no person has market or exchange power in the differential sense instanced above. Once transactions costs are introduced at all, however, there seems to be no plausibly acceptable logic for refusing to acknowledge differentials in 'bargaining' advantages as between those persons who enter markets as suppliers-sellers of money and those who enter as demanders-buyers. To put the same proposition conversely, it is the demanders-buyers of goods and services that have an asymmetrical advantage over the suppliers-sellers, and in all markets.

As we move away from the abstracted models for the working of a production-exchange economy and towards a more descriptively satisfying appreciation of the economy as it actually seems to function, the basic asymmetry identified here may become painfully obvious, and my whole discussion may be taken to represent trituration. I suggest, however, that the money–goods asymmetry assists in an understanding of much of the behaviour that we observe in developed economies, both historically and currently. The institutions of market exchange, as we know them, incorporate a recognition of this asymmetry, even to the extent that their familiarity breeds analytical oversight.

In markets as we know them, sellers of goods and services peddle their wares, advertise, create attractive displays, adopt attitudes of deferential demeanor toward potential buyers and behave, generally, as if their customers' interests are their own. 'We aim to please' – this slogan describes the attitudes of those traders on the goods and services side of the goods–money exchanges, rather than vice versa. And we should find ourselves surprised if this behaviour were absent. We do not observe buyers of goods and services setting up their own market stalls with signs that read 'we buy apples', except in unusual circumstances. In product markets, we see some, but not much, buyer advertising. Potential buyers of goods and services apparently feel under no compulsion to act as if the interests of a seller are of relevance. Such buyers remain behaviourally indifferent towards the interests of any identified seller.[2]

The distinction between the two sides of the money–goods exchange stressed here does not depend on the pricing institutions that are in place. In developed economies, sellers tend to offer their wares to potential buyers at quasi-fixed prices, and the latter remain free to purchase varying quantities. In many developing economies, by contrast, sellers do not fix prices in advance, save as some preliminary move in what becomes a complex bargaining game with buyers. In both sets of pricing arrangements, however, we observe sellers-suppliers in the active roles of seekers for potential buyers and investors in efforts at persuasion, rather than the opposite.

The asymmetry stressed here is, of course, implicitly recognized in the usage of the term *consumers' sovereignty* to describe the exchange economy. This term, which might be better replaced by *buyers' sovereignty*, suggests that sellers of goods and services, or suppliers, are, and must be, responsive to the interests of buyers, and, hence, that the latter are the ultimate sources of evaluation. Conventional discussion of the consumers' sovereignty feature of market economies does not, however, take much note of the relevant behavioural implications.

An alternative way of discussing the asymmetry in the money–goods exchange relationship is to introduce the differential specificity of valued assets, as held by each party prior to exchange. Whether we analyse a pure exchange economy, in which persons commence with determinate endowments of goods, or a production-exchange economy, in which persons commence with endowments of talents that may be organized to produce goods, the potential supplier in any exchange for money is, by definition, locked in, relatively, by the specificity of the valued asset in possession, pre-exchange, and, for this reason, is more vulnerable to terms of trade manipulation than the potential cross-exchange demander, whose pre-exchange valued asset takes the form of money.[3]

ASYMMETRY INVERSION IN COMMAND ECONOMIES

How would it be possible to remove or even to reverse the asymmetry in the basic exchange relationship in an economy? Reversion to a system of barter through some prohibition of a generalized money medium could remove the asymmetry here, but only at the expense of gross inefficiencies occasioned by the costs of search. In such an economy – one without money but with transactions costs – each market participant is both a buyer and a seller of goods (services), and there is no generalized advantage to either side of an exchange. As noted earlier, there would be particularized advantage to either the buyer or seller of the goods that are in relatively wider usage in the economy.

Let us consider, now, an economy in which money has been introduced, but where money is not, in itself, a sufficient medium to ensure the effectuation of an exchange. Such an economy would be described by money prices for goods, but accompanied by some set of complementary nonmonetary 'prices', or arrangements, that would be required to complete a transaction. The nominal money prices for goods and services would be politically established – and at a level below those prices that would clear markets, that would equate demand and supply. Straightforward public-choice analysis of the incentives of persons in bureaucratic authority to set money prices suggests that such prices will remain always below market-clearing levels.[4] Bureaucrats lose any rationing authority if prices are set at market-clearing levels, and such authority is desired both for its own sake and as a source for the extraction of favours (rents). There will tend to exist excess demands for the supplies of goods brought forth in all markets. Each seller will tend to face more demanders for his or her product than can possibly be satisfied.

In such a setting, any reason that a seller-supplier might have for acting as if he or she is motivated by the interests of buyers is absent. Sellers will be behaviourally indifferent towards each and all potential buyers; they will have no incentive to please particular buyers, not even to the extent of providing quality merchandise, since there will always be buyers ready and willing to purchase whatever is made available to them.

Consider, by contrast, the behavioural stance of the participant who enters the exchange relationship as a potential buyer, who possesses a stock of money in the hope of securing goods and services. Each person in such a role will face the frustration experienced in an inability to get the goods in the quantities desired and of the quality standards wanted. Buyers, with money, become the residual claimants to the gains from exchange, a role that is directly contrary to that which buyers occupy in the well-functioning money economy, as analysed earlier. 'Buyers' sovereignty', which was mentioned earlier as a shorthand description of the central feature of the exchange economy, is replaced by 'sellers' sovereignty', provided we are careful to include within the 'sellers' category those persons who hold bureaucratic authority to establish arrangements for nonprice rationing among demanders of goods and services.

In the command economy as sketched out in capsule here, buyers of goods and services become the supplicants, who must curry favour with the sellers and their agents, who must, somehow 'aim to please' over and beyond some mere offer of generalized purchasing power in the form of money. Sellers remain indifferent to the pleas of buyers, and not only because of the excess number of demanders. Sellers also realize that if they exchange goods for money, they, too, must return to other markets, as buyers, who must, in turn, expect to encounter the frustrations of buyers throughout the system.

The chronic 'shortage' of goods that describe the workings of the command economy stems directly from the imposed politicization of money prices, as does the generalized supplication of buyers toward sellers-suppliers, including the relevant members of the bureaucratic apparatus. The institution of money, as such, is not allowed to serve its standard efficiency-enhancing function. The nonprice rationing arrangements, which emerge as supplementary to money prices, become analogous, in their economic effects, to the search costs that barter involves in the absence of money.

The command economy, with politicized money prices, along with supplementary rationing arrangements, will be characterized by a 'money overhang' – a supply of money that is in excess of that which is needed in exchange transactions, at the politically set money prices. Indeed, without such money overhang the authority that is exercised by the whole price-control regime loses its 'bite'. Unless potential consumers-buyers are provided with more money (through wage payments) than they can spend on products, at the controlled prices, the authority of bureaucrats to ration scarce supplies becomes unnecessary. This excess money supply, in its turn, sets up additional incentives for the emergence of exchange transactions that are outside the boundaries of legitimacy in some formal sense. Black, shadow or underground markets will emerge more readily when persons are unable to satisfy their demands for goods through standard exchange channels and when they have available, at the same time, unused and unusable stocks of money. As this shadow sector increases in size over time, as measured either by the volume of transactions or by the number of participants, the behavioural norms that describe the operation of the whole legal order must be undermined.

The fact that money is not allowed fully to perform its efficiency-enhancing role in the economy must also set in motion evolutionary pressures toward the emergence of some good that will secure general acceptability as 'real money', quite distinct from the money issued by the state monopoly. In Russia, and in other former socialist economies, the currency of developed nations (dollars, marks, Swiss francs) has emerged to fill this role, at least in part. And, in the shadow exchanges between these monies and goods, the asymmetry observed in Western economies is partially restored. Sellers of goods do, indeed, seek out and court potential buyers who are thought to possess hard currencies.

This transitional stage aside, however, the point to be emphasized is that, in the command economy, as it traditionally functions, the whole economic culture is dramatically different from that which we observe in Western market economies. The near total absence of seller-supplier efforts to attract custom and to please potential buyers shocked Western observers who visited the territories of the former Soviet Union. The paucity of billboards in the Moscow of 1990 was not primarily attributable to regulatory prohibition. This result emerged directly from the fact that no seller-supplier of any good or service felt any economic pressure to respond to customer interests or to expand the demands for product. The sales clerk at the kiosk, as a selling agent, behaved very differently from her Western counterpart, but not because of ethnic origins; she behaved differently because in the Russian mind-set that permeated the citizenry generally, the seller-purveyor of goods was not concerned about customers.

The pre-1990 Russian visitor to the United States was equally surprised when the behaviour of sellers-suppliers was observed, both directly and indirectly. Such a visitor was overwhelmed by the neon blazes, by multicoloured billboards, slick magazine pages and the television commercials, as well as behaviourally by the stance of those persons who acted as agents for suppliers of almost all goods and services. Coming out of an economic culture where buyers were the universal supplicants, the Russian visitor stood aghast at the supplication of sellers and their agents. Neither this Russian visitor nor his American counterpart in Moscow understood that the dramatic differences in the two cultures can be explained, at least in large part, by variations in the incentive structures. The American setting allows the asymmetry in the money–goods exchange relationship to be played out fully in the development and operation of its market institutions. The Soviet Union, by contrast, attempted, throughout its existence, to counter this asymmetry by the politicization of money prices, with an acknowledged major increase in the costs of making transactions, but also with the unrecognized impetus given to the emergence and operation of an economic culture that must be subversive in any effort to move toward the market structure.

IMPLICATIONS FOR THE TRANSITION FROM A COMMAND TO A MARKET ECONOMY

This chapter is not presented as a contribution to the explanation of the operation of either an exchange (market) economy or a command (socialized) economy. My emphasis is on and my interest is in the behavioural differences that the separate systems tend to motivate and to accentuate – differences that are readily observable – and on the implications of these differences for the problems of transition from a command to a market economy – the transition that the countries of Central and Eastern Europe now face.

In Chapter 11, I concentrated on the apparent failure of participants in the socialist economy to recognize the reciprocal nature of the exchange relationship and the presence of mutuality of gain to all parties. I did not, of course, suggest that participants in the developed market economies of the West explicitly understand even this most elementary principle of economics, and that a comparable understanding was missing in the command economies. I did suggest, however, that the basic principle of reciprocal exchange had come to inform the consciousness of many persons in Western economies, even if there seems to be little or no articulation of such a principle within the range of ordinary competence.

In that chapter, which was advanced only in an exploratory fashion (as is this one), I attributed the absence of such an 'exchange mentality' or mind-set to the conjectural history that persons accept as descriptive of their social development. I suggested that in Western societies, and especially in the United States, the central notion of gains-from-trade emerges naturally from a historical imagination that traces economic and social development from family independence and self-sufficiency (the frontier homestead) through stages of increasing interdependence as specialization proceeds, always accompanied by increasing standards of living. In this imagined history, however, the exit option, the potential for withdrawal into independence, remains at the back edge of understanding and interpretation, thereby ensuring that the expansion of trade and exchange must enhance well-being for all members of the society.

I suggested that participants in the former Soviet economy carried with them no such historical imagination of economic development, and that there was no comparable conjectural history of self-sufficient independence from which the economy emerged. Instead, cooperation was always imagined, not as achievement of mutual gains through exchange, but as taking place within a collective-community enterprise. Individual cooperative behaviour, even as idealized, was modelled exclusively as the fulfilling of tasks assigned in a collective endeavour, assigned by some command authority. When I sketched the elements of my analysis to a Russian intellectual, he aptly described, and accepted, the thesis as, 'the Russians are natural slaves; the Yankees are natural traders'.

I see no reason to back off from or to withdraw the arguments made in Chapter 11; I remain convinced that the analysis contributes to an understanding of some of the difficulties in making the transition from a command to a market economy. I think, however, that the arguments advanced in the present chapter supplement and extend those of Chapter 11 usefully and allow me to offer an economic explanation of some of the apparent differences in mind-sets that need not be so critically dependent on a presumed divergence in historical imaginations. The importance of historical imagination may have been exerted at a more fundamental level than that discussed earlier. An imagination that is grounded on the liberty and independence of individual families might have proved a formidable barrier against collectivization of the economy. A 'socialized United States' may never have been within the realm of the possible. History, and the historical imagination that it shapes, matters. And different national experiences may affect the feasibility of adaptation to different organizational structures. In the view of many observers, Poland's role in the revolution against the Communist regime was due, in part, to the historical position of the Catholic Church.

The possible oversight of the earlier treatment lay in my failure to appreciate that the 'exchange mentality' that I took to be descriptive of Western attitudes towards markets generally, is manifested largely, even if not exclusively, in the observed activities of those who find themselves in roles as sellers-suppliers (or their agents) of goods and services, and that their behaviour finds its origins, at least in part, in the asymmetry of the goods–money exchange. Conversely, I generalized the behavioural indifference of sellers or selling agents in the former Soviet Union to the whole culture, without noting that the structure within which exchanges takes place removes incentives for sellers to behave in ways comparable to their Western counterparts.

Entrepreneurial or leadership roles in implementing exchanges-transfers of valued goods among persons and units in the command-control economies have been taken by those persons who possess differential access to nonmoney means of influencing choices, through personalized relationships, through extra-market barter arrangements, through sublegal bribes, payoffs, kickbacks. In other words, the entrepreneurial talents that have been rewarded in the command economy, as it operated, were those of the 'fixers' rather than those which might have represented some differential ability to recognize latent demand in nonexisting goods and to design and organize the production of such goods in response to such demand. In other words, there was little or no supply-side entrepreneurship, as such, in dramatic contrast with Western-style capitalist economies, where, at least in principle, such entrepreneurship should remain a dominant feature.

The entrepreneurship manifested in the activities of the fixers is not, of course, absent from Western economies, especially as these economies have developed to include large and rapidly growing socialized or public sectors. As governments have grown, in all dimensions, over the course of the century, there has been the developing recognition that private profits may be located in the exploitation of public as well as private opportunities.[5] Entrepreneurs who seek to capture the rents created by the artificially contrived scarcities stemming from politicized economic regulation, sometimes called 'rent-seekers', are behaviourally similar to those that emerge in the more pervasive regulatory structure of command economies. We need only point to the thousands of lawyer-lobbyists whose activity consists exclusively in exploiting loopholes in the complexities of tax law and in seeking the creation of still further loopholes through new legislative changes.

The unanswered empirical question is whether or not the scarce set of entrepreneurial talents are generalizable over the two quite distinct roles. And the answer here will be critical for the problems of transition. Is a successful rent-seeker, who has demonstrated an adeptness at implementing value transfers in a regulated-politicized setting, likely to be equally successful when, as and if the incentive structure shifts and success requires that attention be paid to organizing production to meet demands of consumers? Or do the distinct entrepreneurial roles require quite divergent talents? These questions stand as a challenge to my economist peers who place their primary reliance on direct empirical results.

My own intuition and interpretation suggest that the experience of the command economy, in which there has been little or no differential reward offered for supply-side creativity, will exert relatively long-lasting effects, and that the transition to a market economy will be made more difficult because of this absence of an entrepreneurial tradition. Those persons who have been skillful in responding to the disequilibria of the command structure may find the switch to the new role beyond their limits.

Entrepreneurs are, of course, emerging in the transition economies. Both those who were and might have been the fixers and those who held positions of bureaucratic authority are moving to take advantage of the opportunities opened up by institutional changes. The question is not so much whether entrepreneurship will emerge as whether that which does emerge will prove sufficiently creative to stimulate the impoverished and sluggish economies in ways that may prove necessary to ensure that the revolution's ultimate result will be positive.

A useful distinction may be made at this point between the Kirznerian and the Schumpeterian definitions of entrepreneurship – a distinction that has been the source of longstanding debates within the subdiscipline of Austrian economics. Israel Kirzner, who has long stressed the importance of the entrepreneurial function in an economy, models the entrepreneur as responding to disequilibria, essentially as an arbitrageur, who locates and exploits disparities in potential exchange values as among separate locations, persons and production opportunities.[6] In this conceptualization of the entrepreneurial role, there should be relatively little difficulty encountered in transforming the fixer of the command economy into the equilibrating supply-side organizer of production and distribution in the operative market economy. By contrast, Joseph Schumpeter models the entrepreneur as a disequilibrating force, as a creator of destruction to established ways of doing things, as a disrupter of existing and predicted channels of exchange.[7] In this conceptualization, the supply-side entrepreneur acts quite differently from the arbitrageur, even if the latter is defined in the broadest possible terms. The entrepreneur creates that which does not exist independently of his or her action. To the extent that the ongoing market or capitalist economy is understood to be progressively created by Schumpeterian entrepreneurs, there can be no easy transition from the command system, quite independently from the institutional reforms that may be put in place.

Both types of entrepreneur can coexist as highly productive contributors to the successful transition toward market economies and to the growth of such economies, once established. In my own view, the supply-side or Schumpeterian entrepreneur is unlikely to become dominant in the economies that are now in transition. And, indeed, such entrepreneurs may have almost disappeared in Western economies. In this perspective, while successful transition to a market economy is possible for the former command systems, there will be no *Wirtschaftswunder* (economic miracle) in the near term, East or West.

NOTES

1. See Chapter 11.
2. Labour markets may seem to offer an exception to the generalizations suggested here. The absence of homogeneity among separate units demanded may offset, or even reverse, the direction of effect emphasized here generally.

3. The relationship between differential asset specificity, as between parties to contract and the vulnerability to opportunistic behaviour, has been discussed by Armen Alchian and Susan Woodward (1987).

   More generally, economists have analysed the effects of asymmetric information in the operation of exchange. The pioneer in these efforts was George Akerlof (1970).
4. See Levy (1990).
5. For a generalized discussion, see Buchanan, Tollison and Tullock (1980).
6. Israel Kirzner (1973).
7. Joseph A. Schumpeter (1934).

13. Consumption without production: the impossible idyll of socialism[1]

The element of the socialist construction that is most important in explaining its failure is the rupture of the nexus between production and consumption – a rupture that would have guaranteed socialism's failure even in some imaginary world where knowledge might have been perfect. The incentive to produce value is missing in the idealized socialist construction, and thereby poverty is ensured.

In one sense, the argument is embarrassingly simple, so much so that I apologize in advance for the apparent insult to the intelligence of my audience. But, in some defence here, let me suggest that often the elementary verities are indeed overlooked precisely because they are so self-evident. And recall the fable where only the small boy really did see that the king had no clothes.

I shall proceed as follows. In the second section, I shall offer a summary sketch of the whole argument. The third section presents an economic parable that is an alternative to that which informs the analysis of modern economists. The simplified and abstracted model of 'an economy' requires no allocation, as such, and there is no evaluation, by anyone, as among separate goods and services in the ordinary sense. The model is designed, in part, to eliminate the market's role or function both in setting a value scale and in allocating resources. The fourth section modifies the model to allow for the introduction, first, of collectivism, second, of authoritarian control and finally, third, of rent extraction by those who control. Only in the fifth and sixth sections do I shift discussion and analysis to more 'realistic' models of economic interaction, in which evaluative, allocational, organizational and distributional functions of regimes, whether market or hierarchy, must be compared and contrasted. The seventh section briefly discusses some of the possible reasons why economists have neglected the emphasized elementary principle. The final section examines some of the implications of the analysis for an understanding of both the 'post-socialist' and the 'nonsocialist' regimes emergent in the 1990s.

CONSUMPTION AND PRODUCTION

In Munich's Alte Pinakothek, there is a Breughel painting, *Schlaraffenland*, that depicts the eternal idyll of men who can think of worlds other than their own.

122

Fat peasants lounge about and find their open mouths filled immediately with morsels of the finest foods. Consumption by everyone without production by anyone – this state of existence describes that which can be imagined but never realized. The myth of the fall jolts the dreamer into sobering reality; in order for anyone to consume, someone must produce. Only by the sweat of some brow does the food for Breughel's peasants come into being. The myth of Eden before the apple was eaten – the myth of nature's abundance – must be entirely exorcised from scientific thought if we are to understand man's many failures, as well as his successes, in attempts to better his own condition.

The source of socialism's failure is located precisely in the scientific error that allowed a divorce between production and consumption – a scientific error that is ultimately derivative from the flawed analytical parables of both classical and neoclassical economics. Both parables embody the presupposed reality of scarcity, of land in the strict classical setting, of resources more generally defined in the more sophisticated neoclassical alternative. And, as all economists are wont to remind us, scarcity makes choice necessary. Hence, some allocation of that which is scarce must be chosen, by someone, somehow or by some process. And, as David Hume suggested, scarcity also opens up avenues for considerations of justice.

I submit that these familiar parables of scarcity have prompted scientific error because they allow analysts to forget the necessary linkage between production and consumption – a linkage that a more appropriate parable might have placed in full light. In some ultimate sense, we live in a world that is accurately described by neither 'abundance' nor 'scarcity'. These two imagined states do not exhaust potential reality. We need go no further than Biblical mythology. Abundance in the garden is not simply replaced by scarcity beyond the boundaries. Post-Eden man must produce that which he desires to consume, even to survive at all. A 'choice' to produce is a 'choice' to consume; and production does involve the allocation of 'something' to 'something' rather than to 'something else'. But the ordinary calculus of allocative choice that is familiar from the economists' models does not capture the elemental behavioural enterprise at all and, indeed, distracts attention from common sense understanding. *Ab initio*, there is no glob of value to be allocated, no manna from heaven, nature or anywhere else. Value must first be produced in order to exist, and the production of value of one sort does not imply the sacrifice of produced value of yet another sort, at least not in the standard meaning of these terms. As Jeremy Bentham implied, the calculus is one of pain *and* pleasure, and the pleasure of anticipated consumption is achieved only by the incurrence of pain. That which is avoided by not producing is the pain or disutility of effort rather than the sacrifice of some produced alternative that might have been consumed. Opportunity cost must be related to choice, and the cost of the choice to incur pain to produce value is measured by the pain itself, by the disutility of effort. This cost is captured only in some reckoning of the pleasure of pain avoidance.

Production takes place in real time, of course, and time itself does seem to have an objective limit. But time, as such, need not be the operative constraint on productive activity. Production of that which has value requires adjustment among many margins simultaneously, only one of which involves the time dimension that is objectively measurable. Physical exertion, time rates of action, carefulness in observation, alertness to environmental change, applied cause–effect reasoning, behavioural attitudes towards risk, personally expressed rates of discount – these seem to be only a few of the many possible attributes that enter into productive effort that cannot be reduced to the unidimensional measure of real time. Shifts along any of these, and other, behavioural margins will affect the measured value that emerges from productive effort.

As a producer-consumer, the individual may be modelled as maximizing utility by adjusting along the several margins, but such an exercise is little more than a forced translation into economists' jargon. It may be nonetheless helpful to think of the individual-as-consumer motivating the individual-as-producer and to define a personalized equilibrium, of sorts, where the promised utility of that which is produced-to-be-consumed matches the promised disutility or pain of the production effort required to produce it, always at the appropriate margins.

This simple exercise in personal economics may be contrasted with a model in which the linkage between production and consumption does not exist. Consider a setting in which persons are expected to produce without consuming that which they produce, currently or in future time periods, either directly or indirectly. In the total absence of such linkage, why should any person produce value at all?

This sketch is perhaps sufficient to indicate the thrust of my simplistic argument. But I shall try to make the structure of analysis more interesting to sceptics by outlining some details of an alternative parable to either the classical or neoclassical economic world-as-modelled.

THE PARABLE OF THE BUFFALO

In early America, the Plains Indians produced and consumed a single good: buffalo, which met all of their basic needs – food, clothing, shelter. (Reminder: This is a parable, not a history.) Neither buffalo nor land was scarce. But the buffalo did not convert themselves into directly consumable articles of food, clothing and housing. These articles came into being only through a process of production that required effort embodying time, imagination, dexterity, strength, speed and many other attributes. The final products, meat, hides and fur, were 'scarce' in the sense that no one attained satiety. Any person would have preferred more product, provided that he or she was not required to produce it.

The family was the economic unit in this society, and we assume that the advantages of specialization were internal to the family producing and consuming unit. We assume, further, that each family, along with all of its members, respected the 'rights' of other families to the product values, in varying form, that had been produced but not yet consumed. In this imagined economy, each family would extend its productive effort, as described in the several dimensions of adjustment noted earlier, to the point at which the expected positive value in consumption equals the expected negative value involved in further production. In the language of economists, we can say that each family attained a position that could be classified to be 'efficient'. But note that there is no meaning of the term *efficiency* as applied to any unit larger than the single family. There is no interdependence; each family produces that which it consumes. And there is no aggregative or overall 'resource' capacity that is 'allocated'. Similarly, there is no interfamily set of 'prices', even shadow prices, that may be compared, one with another.

In this imagined world, families would, of course, be predicted to differ both in their relative preferences for produced goods and effort avoidance and in their relative capacities to convert effort into produced goods. The 'society' including many families would not be characterized by equality either in observed outlay of effort (including time) or in production-consumption of buffalo in its finally used form.

COLLECTIVE PRODUCTION, COMMUNAL CONSUMPTION AND AUTHORITARIAN ALLOCATION

Remain within the basic parable of the buffalo and suppose that members of the inclusive buffalo producing-consuming society observe the inequalities among the constituent families. Suppose, further, that all of the many families agree to collectivize production by placing all that is produced in a single common depot, from which each family is to get back an equal share (per person). Each family is now expected to exert effort to produce buffalo, as before, but that which is produced is now for common rather than own consumption. Production and consumption are now separate rather than simultaneous choices.

The predicted results are familiar. A family will attain personal equilibrium in its productive activity when the disutility associated with extended effort matches the value that it places on its proportionate share in the consumption of that which is produced plus whatever value might be placed on the consumption of others in the inclusive society. If there are N families in the society, the producing family's own share in that which it produces is only $1/N$. Unless the family values the consumption of others equally with its own, it will attain production equilibrium at some lesser input of effort along all of the dimensions of input adjustment. Each family will produce a lower value of product than it produced in the autarkic setting before the production and consumption decisions were divorced.

In its consumption choices, each family will move quickly to the limit allowed by the equal-sharing rule, and, at this level of consumption, each family will seek, if at all possible, to extend its own consumption, at the expense of other families if possible. A lower value of product will be produced and consumed in the inclusive society, and the product that is produced will be of a quality that is inferior to that previously generated. Further, each family will find itself dissatisfied with its share of that which is produced.

Note that this result will tend to emerge even in the setting where all families, initially, might have agreed upon the collectivization of production and the equal sharing of that which is produced. The basic organizational change will have succeeded in its presumed objective of equalizing consumption of produced goods as among the separate families in the society. But the overall quantity and quality of production and consumption will be lower, perhaps substantially lower, than in the private property regime. Productive effort will not, however, be equalized after the regime change examined here, and the disparities in effort as among the separate families may be increased rather than decreased by the collectivization of production. Those families that are more productive in converting effort into output and those that suffer less disutility from any outlay of effort will find that they place higher values of product into the common depot than they are allowed to take out. And those families that are less productive and those that are less willing to endure the disutility of effort will find that they take out more than they contribute to the common pool. The first group, which we may call the *net producers*, will consider themselves to be exploited by the second group, which we can call the *net consumers*. And the sense of unfairness generated among members of the first group will tend to alter the equilibrium adjustment toward lowered rates of production and lowered quality standards.

The failures of 'pure' socialism, in the form described, will seem evident to everyone, and the next stage of 'reform' must involve the assignment of authority to some agent who will be empowered to set production quotas and modify consumption shares. In some idealized omniscience, the agent might assign to each family in its capacity as a producing unit a quota that is the same as that which might have been observed under the autarkic equilibrium adjustment. In this idealized setting, full equalization in consumption might be achieved without sacrifice of production; the producing units would be coerced into supplying effort over and beyond that which they would voluntarily choose to supply.

In practice, however, there is no way that even the most benevolent agent might find out just what the personalized equilibria of producing units might have been under the earlier regime. At best, productive effort can be monitored only along the objectively measurable dimensions of adjustment. As noted, hours or days spent in supplying work seem to be objective units, but these involve only one of the many dimensions of productive effort. The agent can assign working times to persons and families, but there seems to be no way that adjustments along the other dimensions can be brought under the agent's control. Forced out of the preferred level of effort, the producer surely will pay less attention to quality. At best, the authority who is empowered to assign production quotas can increase output in the society somewhat above that level attained under 'pure' socialism. But total product will remain well below that observed in the autarkic private property model, and the quality of produced goods will be inferior.

The next stage in 'reform' will involve some relaxation of the equal-sharing rule for consumption. Even the most benevolent agent will recognize that total production in the society can be increased if the net producers are given shares in consumption in some positive relationship to shares in production. Such reform may take shape by allowing all producing units to retain, for their own usage, some specified share of the value that is produced. Each producing unit may, for illustration, be allowed to retain one-half of the value its effort generates, with only the remaining one-half allocated to the common depot for subsequent sharing along all units in the society.

Such a modification in the incentive structure will restore, to the extent measured by the relevant share, the nexus between production and consumption, and the change can be predicted to increase, perhaps dramatically, the size of the total value of product along with the quality of output. Such a partial restoration of the nexus cannot, however, be predicted to return production to that level that would have been attained under autarkic production-consumption in this parable. The partial socialization of the economic process will have directionally predictable results. And, of course, the effects on total product value will be directly related to the size of the socialization-privatization ratio. A society that socializes one-half of its value produced will produce less than a society that socializes one-quarter.[2]

The collectivization-socialization process, whether this be total or partial, requires the establishment and continuing operation of an authority that is empowered to act to set production targets and/or quotas, if desired, and to police whatever consumption-sharing arrangements are chosen. Only in the setting where production and consumption are strictly tied together, as in the autarkic model of this parable, is the authority strictly limited to a protective role. To this point, I have assumed that the allocative-distributive authority is benevolent in the sense that it acts exclusively as an agent for the members of the society and behaves in such fashion as to exhibit no interests of its own. Even in this limit, of course, persons who act in such positions must themselves receive consumption shares, thereby inserting a bureaucratic wedge of sorts between total value generated and value returned to ordinary persons in the society.

The assumption of benevolence on the part of those in positions of authority cannot be sustained. These persons will have their own economic interests, and their positions will be such as to allow these interests to be furthered without directly related checks. It becomes relatively easy for persons charged with allocative and distributive authority, even in the confines of the simple buffalo parable here, to exact rents from the economy – rents over and beyond those consumption shares that would measure their alternative contributions to production. The bureaucratic rents will ensure that the rupture between production and consumption is larger than that indicated directly by the share in product devoted to communal purposes. As a partial offset to this effect, the control authority will have an all-encompassing interest in promoting the highest possible production, because such authority becomes a residual claimant of sorts.[3]

I have gone to some length to show why and how socialism, whether total or partial, would fail in the overly simplified economy modelled in the parable of the buffalo. I have extended the discussion for the purpose of suggesting that, even in the absence of allocative and evaluation problems of the standard sort, any attempted separation of the production and consumption choices creates value shortfalls by comparison with the setting in which these choices merge into one.

FROM THE SIMPLE TO THE COMPLEX ECONOMY: PRODUCTION AND CONSUMPTION IN MARKET EXCHANGE

It is a relatively straightforward procedure to shift from the simple parable of the one-good buffalo economy under autarkic organization towards a complex exchange economy characterized by input specialization, many final goods and an operative market structure in which exchanges are facilitated by a set of prices defined in terms of a numeraire. For my purpose, the important point of note is that this conjectural shift from a simple to a complex economy may be effected without any rupture in the production-consumption nexus. The individual production of one good followed by exchange for a numeraire good that is, in turn, exchanged for units of some finally desired good becomes a process through which the individual indirectly produces the final items of consumption. Nor is the nexus broken when a person or family sells its productive input services for money wages which are utilized in turn to purchase final end items in other markets. Despite the apparent circuitousness of the process, participating individuals fully understand that, in making choices to offer inputs to the market, they are indirectly producing the consumption services that they desire. Adam Smith's butcher produces the meat that we desire out of his own interest, as an ultimate consumer of other goods.

The science of economics, commencing with Adam Smith, is that body of analysis that provides the understanding of how the complex network of market interdependence operates so as to maintain the production-consumption linkage while at the same time achieving the coordination among the separated individual choices that is required to generate the maximum value of total product, as determined by the preferences of those who participate in the process. How does 'the market', which necessarily places separate producing-consuming units in positions of mutual dependence, achieve a result that is analogous to that achieved only in fully autarkic independence in the simple buffalo economy sketched out earlier? As economists (and perhaps only economists) know, these results emerge without the operation of any consciously registered allocative or evaluative choices on the part of anyone. 'The market', as an organizational structure, exploits the separated, and independent, choices made by individuals and groups, in many input and output exchange processes, in such a way that an allocation of productive effort among many possible uses is made, and that a value scale, represented by a set of input and output prices, is established – a scale that, in turn, allows disparate bundles of goods to be compared, one with another.

As in the one-good economy, individuals attain their own equilibria when the disutility of production effort at the margin matches the promised utility of that which such effort produces, and these equilibria can be labelled to be 'efficient' in some meaningful sense. Because of the interdependence of separate individuals through the network of markets here, however, the term 'efficiency' can also be applied to the whole structure of results, provided care is taken to avoid the confusion generated by some presupposition that there exists some 'scarce' resource to be allocated independently of individuals' actions in production. To the extent that there may exist gains from further exchanges, some persons have not attained their own personalized equilibria, and, as a consequence, the overall results may properly be labelled to be 'inefficient'.

In the idealized workings of the complex exchange economy, with many goods produced by highly specialized inputs, individuals and families would be predicted to differ both as to preferences between productive effort and value produced and as to rates at which valued output can be generated from productive inputs. The interdependent market economy will be characterized by observed inequalities both in effort supplied and in rates of consumption of final goods.

COLLECTIVE PRODUCTION, COMMUNAL
CONSUMPTION AND AUTHORITARIAN ALLOCATION
IN A COMPLEX ECONOMY

Let us now suppose that the observed inequalities prompt a revolution in the economic regime and that the complex market economy is replaced by a full-fledged socialist order. (The presence or absence of a consensus in support of such a revolutionary change is not relevant to the analysis here.) Production is collectivized in the sense that all of the value generated is collected into a common depot from which equal consumption shares are assigned to all participants in the society. As was the case in the one-good economy examined earlier, individuals (families) as producers will no longer have an incentive to supply effort, whereas individuals as consumers will seek to increase their aliquot share beyond the limits assigned. An authority empowered to assign production quotas and to enforce consumption share limits will be necessary. But whereas the task of such an authority may have seemed large even in the simple one-good setting, here the task is enormously increased by comparison. Producing units must not only be assigned rates of input supply, they must also be assigned to this or that productive process or 'industry'. Persons must be directed to work in the brewery, on the wheat farm or in the steel factory. And the making of any such assignment among the many possible uses of productive effort, even as monitored, requires the presence of some value scale that will allow trade-offs to be made as among the different end-items. Is the additional wheat that might be produced by a shift of inputs from steel production 'worth' the loss of steel production involved in the shift?

The early critics of socialist central planning, notably von Mises and Hayek, were clearly on target in their emphasis on the magnitude of the task that any putative planning authority must face in any economy that involves many goods. And the stress on the informational-knowledge requirements necessary to accomplish any results, even to a tolerable degree of 'efficiency', was well placed. Further, the dramatic contrast drawn between the market's unique ability to exploit information through the voluntary choices of individuals in an interlinked network of exchanges and any bureaucratic authority's effort to achieve comparable results should have been (but was not) convincing to everyone. In the absence of a value scale emergent from the choices of individuals as producers-consumers in a market order, the allocative choices made by any authority must be, to some degree, arbitrary. As a result, the bundle of goods finally produced fails to correspond with that bundle that persons might have preferred. That value which is produced in such an economy and becomes finally available for consumption is not directly related to that which might have been desired by those who actually do the producing, under the coercion of the authority. The allocative 'distortion' acts to drive a further wedge between production and consumption, over and beyond that which is represented by the mere separation of production and consumption choices, along with the extraction of bureaucratic rents.

The task that faces the authoritarian agent in a complex economy is incomparably more difficult than that which might be faced in a simple economy, and, indeed, so difficult that it may be considered to be impossible. For this very reason, however, once the socialist order is politically emplaced, the potential for the extraction of bureaucratic rents is enhanced. Because it is called upon to do so much more, the bureaucracy must be larger, and must claim a larger share of rent, even if it remains totally benevolent. And the enormous expansion in the dimensions of allocative control creates like expansion in the opportunities for rent extraction by those agents who use office to further their own economic interests. In sum, we can say that the distributive, allocative and bureaucratic sources of the separation between production and consumption become increasingly constraining as the economy grows more complex.

SOURCES OF SCIENTIFIC DISTRACTION

My purpose in an earlier section was not to show how a complex economy functions under a set of market arrangements, and my purpose in the previous section was not to show why any attempted socialist organization of such an economy must fail. My purpose was, instead, to suggest that concentration both on the positive analysis of the workings of a complex market economy, with normative overtones, and on the potential disastrous consequences of any attempted collectivization of such economies may have acted to distract attention from the most basic element in the whole socialist experiment – the attempt to divorce the production from the consumption of economic value. The ultimate sources of this relative oversight may be located in the parables of resource scarcity that are foundational in both classical and neoclassical economic theory.

My point here can be demonstrated by accepting, for purposes of argument, and working within, one simplified version of the scarcity parable. Suppose that there does, indeed, exist a scarce resource, in the usual sense, a glob of potential 'capacity', from which may be generated a whole set of desired end items of consumption goods and services, but a set that is not sufficient to satiate persons in the relevant group. This resource exists as potential capacity; it does not require production. The 'function' of the economic process or economic order is to allocate this scarce resource among alternative end uses. We are squarely inside the classic Robbins' definition of what 'the economic problem' is (1932).

Relevant and useful economic analysis can be brought to bear which will suggest that the assignment to many persons of separate ownership shares in the scarce resource, along with the liberty to organize processes that convert the resource into end-items of consumption, and the liberty of entering into voluntary exchanges will generate allocative results that maximize the value of the scarce resource in terms of the preferences of the economy's participants. This sentence summarizes the neoclassical paradigm, which I presume is cleansed of all its peripherally discovered 'failures' (which are, in any case, unrelated to my discussion).

Assume now that a socialist transformation is implemented. The scarce resource is placed under collective ownership and control, and a planning authority is assigned the task of allocating the resource among uses and of organizing the conversion processes. I submit here that it was within this paradigm that von Mises and Hayek mounted their criticism of socialism – a criticism that did, indeed, demonstrate the infeasibility of the socialist effort, and which based such a demonstration on the relative superiority of market arrangements in utilizing information available to individuals throughout the economy. That is to say, von Mises and Hayek argued that, even if no production of the source of economic value is required, socialism fails as an allocative mechanism relative to the market, provided only that the ultimate objective is the satisfaction of the preferences of members of the economy.

Within its limits, this argument is now acknowledged to have been successful, despite its failure to gain early acceptance. What was overlooked, however, was the central socialist element, the separation of the production of value from its consumption. We must ask, and try to answer, the question: why did economists fail to understand that value must first be produced before it can be allocated?

I suggest that one answer may be identified in economists' failure fully to escape from the classical notion that value is embodied in objectively observable 'things' and conceptually separate from the evaluation process that takes place within the consciousness of persons. In other words, the dimensionality of economic value is considered to be objective rather than subjective. Persons exchange 'commodities for commodities', as embodiments of objectified value, rather than anticipated utilities. In part, economists' reluctance to incorporate the utility dimension fully in their formal structure of analysis stems from their desire to apply the readily available mathematical logic of the calculus. A scarce resource, objectively measured, can be 'allocated', and the simple principle of maximization can be used readily. But do we not also observe this principle being extended to utility, with much of formal theory couched in terms of utility maximization? As economists all recognize, however, utility as employed in such exercises has no independent objectifiable existence; it is merely a term meaning *that which is maximized* and with no operational content. The 'utility' of theory comes into being with choices among alternatives; it does not exist as a potential value subject to allocation, as such. A shift from the basic scarcity parable, in which objectively measurable resources are available to be allocated, to a parable in which utility gains emerge only when, as and if some evaluation process prompts productive effort, the disutility of which is overmatched by the utility value of that which such effort brings forth, would require a reformulation of the foundations of economic theory. The idealized market order would maximize value, as determined by the preferences of participants, and as constrained by the capacities of participants to produce values, but, even conceptually, there could be no 'calculus of maximization' independently of the voluntary choices made by participants themselves. The intellectual exercise that socialism embodies could never have been undertaken.

In the introduction, I apologized for the elementary nature of the whole argument. Hence, I should not be interpreted at this point to suggest that the basic flaw in the socialist experiment, the attempted divorce of production from consumption, has been totally neglected. The thrust of the argument is as old as Aristotle's defence of private property, and incentive compatibility is an important research programme in modern economics. I do suggest, however, that those who have made early contributions to analysis here have not directly extended the argument's logic to the socialist enterprise. The incompatibility of the incentive structure was not a central feature of the socialist calculation debates of the 1930s.

Incentive structures entered modern economics by way of the theories of property rights, bureaucracy and entrepreneurship. In each case, however, the analysis was largely, if not wholly, limited to institutional comparison within the partially politicized Western-style economies. Armen Alchian's early work on the economics of property rights led him to advance predictions about observable differences between proprietary and nonproprietary institutions, but he did not, to my knowledge, extend discussion to socialist economies, as inclusive organizational structures (Alchian, 1977). Gordon Tullock's (1965) pioneering effort to use incentive structures to analyse modern bureaucracies was limited in application to Western countries. Israel Kirzner's emphasis on the entrepreneurial component in all economic behaviour can be interpreted to embody a recognition of the necessary production-consumption nexus; however, his criticism was directed at the economists who sought to understand market structures (Kirzner, 1973). My own early work was motivated by a concern to clarify the notion of opportunity cost, and although I did include a section on socialist choice that may now be interpreted as precursory to my argument in this chapter, I did not sense the extended relevance and applicability of my own analysis (Buchanan, 1969). To my knowledge, only in a short paper by Alberto di Pierro (1990) has the argument been applied directly to the collapse of socialism.[4]

IMPLICATIONS AND PROSPECTS

In my interpretation, the presumed motive force for socialist transformation is distributional. Production is separated from consumption in order to achieve distributional objectives. By contrast, in an idealized market structure, persons, if they so choose, may consume that share in economic value that they produce. Any increase in a consumption share beyond that which is produced must, *pari passu*, imply that someone else in the economy produces more value than he or she retains for consumption.

This interpretation suggests that there is a spectrum along which the socialization of an economy may be conceptually measured. At the one extreme, there is the pure market economy with no separation between production and potential consumption. At the opposing limit, there is pure or total socialization, where all value that is produced is placed in a pool for common sharing among all persons in the collectivity. Real world economies are located variously along this spectrum. The modern welfare states, which coercively transfer large shares of produced value to persons who produce little or nothing, are not different, in kind, from socialist states that offer enhanced consumption shares as incentives to producers. In both cases, a wedge is driven between production and consumption, with predictable shortfalls in value generation.

In the highly simplified buffalo economy described earlier, the welfare-transfer state and the socialist state are essentially similar in all respects, since all that matters for productive incentives are the shares of value that producers are allowed to retain. In a complex economy with many end-uses of value, there may be major differences between the operation of the welfare-transfer state and the socialist state. These differences stem, of course, from the fact that, in a complex economy, there does exist an allocation problem that is not present in the simple one-good model. The welfare-transfer state may be organized so as to allow market organization to direct production without political or bureaucratic intervention in the process. By contrast, the socialist state may be characterized by bureaucratic barriers to market forces. As a consequence, in any comparative evaluation, the welfare-transfer state can be predicted to secure a somewhat higher value of economic product, for any given size wedge between production and consumption, than the state that retains the apparatus of socialist organization. But the basic feature that separates production from consumption remains common to the two organizational structures.

The political economies of Western countries have been transformed gradually over the course of this century toward the socialist pole. The share of total value taken in taxation, largely if not wholly for distributional purpose, has increased dramatically. The separation between production and potential consumption has been less than total but, nonetheless, has been extended beyond any limits of earlier predictions. For the most part and with some exceptions, these political economies have retained market structures for the organization of production; collectivist-socialist organization, as such, has been avoided in most settings, and, even where experiments in nationalization have been carried out, there has been a movement toward denationalization (privatization) in the most recent decade. For these Western economies, there seems little prospect for movement towards socialist organization, but, at the same time, there seems almost no prospect for any dramatic reduction in the size of the transfer sector.

Political and economic revolution has occurred in those countries that carried out the grand socialist experiments early in the century. This revolution was sparked in large part by the demonstrable failure of socialist organization to produce economic value – a failure that seems attributable, first, to the effort to separate production from consumption and, second, to the infeasibility of authoritarian allocation. These countries are now in periods of transition, with unpredictable prospects. For some of these economies, however, there surely exists the unparalleled opportunity to locate closer to the pole of market organization than those positions that describe Western welfare states. The 'baggage' of the welfare state, reflected through the complex interplay of client and bureaucratic pressure groups on the political process, need not emerge to prominence immediately in the post-socialist settings. If, and to the extent that, post-socialist countries can 'seize the day', we can predict that their prospects for development are relatively unlimited.

In conclusion, I return to the central, and very elementary, point of this chapter. If individuals are allowed the liberty to produce value in the expectation that they are, themselves, to be allowed to consume that which they produce, they can surely be predicted to produce a higher value of whatever it is that they may want than in any other setting.

My whole discussion has been restricted to the simple economics of the matter. I have deliberately left aside any treatment of ethical considerations. What ethical claims do those who produce no value have on those who do produce such value? The economics seems clear enough, the ethics remain, for me, shrouded in mist.

NOTES

1. This chapter was initially presented as the 1992 Hayek Lecture, University of Freiburg, Germany.
2. Some economists may suggest that a larger product may be forthcoming when producers are allowed to retain less than the total value produced because of the possible presence of a strong income effect that may offset a substitution effect. This logic is, however, inapplicable here because, for the society as a whole, the income effects are cancelling. The return of the socialized share of value, in any sharing arrangement, ensures that, in net, only a substitution effect remains.
3. On this point see Mancur Olson (1991).
4. The inverse form of the argument was presented by Joseph H. Carens (1981). That is, the critical importance of moral incentives for the efficacy of socialist organization was recognized, but still within the context of potential, even if idealized realization.

14. Structure-induced behaviour in markets and in politics

Perhaps the most salient difference between political and market institutions is measured by distance along an exit dimension. In an idealized competitive setting, in each market, each participant as buyer (seller) confronts another as seller (buyer), and either party can exit from the interaction at zero cost. By contrast, in the stylized case of an inclusive democratic polity, each participant confronts all others in every collective interaction, from which no participant can exit. The presence or absence of the exit option, or, more generally, the costs of exercising such an option, should affect the behaviour of persons who engage in continuing sequences of interaction, whether in markets or in politics. Effects should be expected to emerge from the intertemporal feedbacks that serve to constrain behaviour differently in the two institutional settings. 'That which is rational' in sequential market interactions may seem to embody a different 'morality' than 'that which is rational' in sequential political interactions.[1]

Critics of rational choice models of behaviour, as such models are conventionally interpreted, may acknowledge that institutional structure can influence criteria for rational choice. Such critics may, however, fail to appreciate that departures from the dictates of rationality, as may be motivated by presumed ethical-moral norms, may be quite differently 'penalized' in separate institutional settings. That is to say, the opportunity costs of 'other-regardingness' may vary as between market and political structures, in which case, the survivability or sustainability of character traits summarized under 'morality' may be critically linked to descriptive features of the interaction process itself.

My aim in this chapter is to analyse the differential influences of market and political structures on the sustainability of behavioural patterns. I shall argue that, because of the presence of an operative exit option, individual behaviour in market relationships is more constrained, externally, than in political interaction. At the same time (and interestingly), the individual may act in furtherance of moral rules that violate canons of rationality with lower opportunity costs in market than in political relationships. Individuals who exhibit 'other-regardingness' survive relatively better in the selective, evolution-like process of continuing market exchange than in the comparable sequence described in the operation of unconstrained majoritarian democracy. The participant in such politics is more or less forced, by elementary criteria of survivability, to choose and to act in furtherance of narrow or differential interest, at least to an extent that need not be paralleled in markets.

This comparative result may, in part, be mitigated by explicit constitutional constraints on the operations of politics. Such constraints can take three forms. First, politics can be modified to allow for and to incorporate some of the market's exit features. The constitutional establishment and enforcement of a federal structure of governance allows individuals, within limits, access to potential exit, thereby indirectly limiting resort to exploitative efforts to further special interests. Second, majoritarian democracy may be replaced, at least in part, by consensual democracy that requires general agreement on political actions. Third, the range for politicization may at least conceivably be constitutionally restricted to actions that are generalizable in effects over the inclusive membership of the polity, in which case differential interests, as such, are nonexistent. Discussion here is concentrated on the third type of constitutional constraints.

The organization of the chapter is as follows. The second section presents a model of stylized market choice to demonstrate that, when embedded in a temporal sequence, participants are severely restricted in their opportunistic departures from the behaviour that exhibits the standard 'morality of the marketplace'. Such behaviour does not, in commonplace discourse, depart from self-interest, institutionally defined, but the analysis does suggest that participants who do, indeed, choose to behave in accordance with norms for 'other-regardingness' may sustain such behaviour within plausibly broad limits. The third section presents models of stylized political choice in a constitutional setting of unlimited majoritarian democracy. As again embedded in a temporal sequence, the analysis is designed to demonstrate that the participant, first, faces no direct constraint against possibly opportunistic behaviour and, second, is required to act in terms of differential self-interest in order to survive at all in the evolution-like processes of political selection. Finally, and as a part of the same analysis, any attempt by an individual to adhere to an other-regardingness motivation can be shown to be short-lived, at least relative to its market analogue. The fourth section modifies the analysis to consider models of constitutionally constrained political interactions. I do not, explicitly, discuss either the introduction of operative exit options through schemes of federalism, subsidiarity and the like or the replacement of majority rule by a rule of unanimity. I concentrate attention on the effects of constitutional restrictions on the range of political action. The fifth section contains a discussion of applications and implications, and the final section concludes the chapter.

MODELS OF MARKETS

In the highly abstracted and limiting model of competitive market exchange, no participant possesses power over another, in any sense of being able to affect another's well-being, either positively or negatively. An exchange or trade between two parties is instantaneous, and each party is able to observe accurately the descriptive qualities of the goods entered into trade – goods that are presumed to be physically homogeneous over varying quantities. Further, each party confronts a sufficiently large number of alternative traders from whom the same goods may be purchased (to whom the same goods may be sold) on identical terms. And there is no cost involved in switching custom as among alternative traders.

Consideration of the properties of the exchange or market relationship in this highly abstracted setting for generalized competitive equilibrium led David Gauthier to characterize the market as a 'morally free zone' (Gauthier, 1985). Any attempt on the part of any participant in exchange to secure opportunistic advantage must, in the model, close off any prospect for trade. No potential trading partner would enter into an exchange relationship with anyone who seeks to take undue advantage. And the generalized failure to enter exchange is, of course, equivalent to a generalized exit from exchange.

Gauthier was criticized for his 'morals free' characterization of the market (Buchanan, 1991c) on the grounds that his treatment seems to transform properties of an idealized model into the descriptive reality of institutional operation. In any real exchange each trader can, through his or her own behaviour, exert at least some effect on the well-being of the person on the other side of the prospective bargain. Few exchanges are instantaneous; goods are not homogeneous; quality is not readily observable. Fraud, deceit and default are always possible. Further, there are costs involved both in securing information about alternative sellers and buyers and in switching custom from one to another (Mueller, 1989).

Recognition of any or all of these departures from the model's idealization requires an acknowledgement that opportunistic behaviour can occur in the market relationship, that any trader may attempt to take advantage of a trading partner without immediate rejection from consummation of an exchange transaction. To the extent that opportunities for 'cheating' are present, the market exchange relationship is 'morally laden' rather than 'morally free'. And the efficacy of the relationship depends critically on the generalized adherence of participants to what may be called the 'morality of the market', that is, to behavioural standards that do not extend to include generalized opportunistic exploitation of particular trading situations. Adam Smith's butcher offers meat for sale in furtherance of his own self-interest; such behaviour lies within the morality of the marketplace. But it is also in the butcher's self-interest, strictly measured at the day of sale, to put his hand heavily on the scales – a behavioural pattern that would be adjudged to violate the market's implied morality.

Economists have tended to neglect the morality of market behaviour because the presence of the exit option acts to place external limits on the extent to which opportunistic exploitation can take place in operating market structures. Even when we recognize that information concerning market alternatives is costly to obtain, and, further, that any shift of custom creates transactions costs, the potential exercise of exit (and entry) places severe limits on departures from ordinary and accepted standards for market conduct. And this aspect or feature of market relationships, generally, can best be appreciated if a temporal dimension is introduced so that any particular act of exchange may be treated as one in a possible continuing sequence over several periods. An individual who, by contrast, enters a one-time trading relationship may expect to be subjected to opportunistic exploitation, since, by definition, there is little or no expectation that the particular pairing will recur. Examples are familiar: the tout at the travelling show, the taxi driver in a large city and especially as first encountered at an airport by foreign visitors. But if and to the extent that repeated or continuing custom in an ongoing relationship is a part of the overall exchange process, the potential for exit will surely constrain resort to opportunistic behaviour. A trader who is exploited may shift custom to another, and new trading partners may enter to offer trade on nonexploitative terms. Adam Smith's butcher who does, indeed, defraud by weight faces little or no return custom. The 'discipline of continuous dealings' moves the exchange process much further towards the abstracted idealization used by Gauthier than straightforward examination of isolated trades might suggest or that many economists themselves appreciate.

My purpose here is neither to array differing market-like institutions in terms of their tendencies to promote nonopportunistic behaviour nor to evaluate the relative importance of an operative exit option in ensuring that the market order, generally, works reasonably well. My point is simply that the prospect for exit from particular exchange pairings over a temporal sequence restricts the pursuit of opportunistic self-interest by traders, whether or not such traders may ultimately be guided by a generalized inner morality that would exclude such opportunism.[2] That is to say, traders are forced, by the success-survival criteria of the institutional process, to behave as if they seek to further their own interest in a nonexploitative fashion, to behave in accordance with what we may call the 'morality of the market', quite independently of inner motivation.

To this point, I have allowed participants in exchange processes to have available only two behavioural alternatives, both of which may be grounded in the axioms of rational choice. I have presumed, implicitly, that traders are motivated by measured economic interest, which may or may not be constrained by the exit option as it operates in a temporal sequence of interactions. For my general aim in this chapter, I do not want to limit analysis and discussion to rational choice models of the standard sort. I want to examine prospects for individual market behaviour that is motivated by genuine 'other-regardingness'. Consider, then, a trader who enters into an exchange with the interests of others elevated to a status equal to his or her own. Are there elements in market relationships, as constrained by pressures of an exit option, that prevent departure from market morality in this direction akin to those elements that limit exploitative behaviour in the other direction?

Somewhat interestingly perhaps, the exit option itself provides an insurance policy, of sorts, that allows other-regarding behaviour to survive, within limits. Consider a person who has in hand a stock of goods, the potential market value for which is in excess of the anticipated cost of reproduction, but who has no desire or interest to return more than such cost from sale. The goods may be offered to buyers who will be able to realize net rental values. Such buyers will not, of course, choose to exit from such favourable terms of exchange. But the seller, also, retains an exit option, and he or she will not market goods below those values that ensure his or her survival as a participant in the process. In this setting, the seller may remain a viable economic unit despite the exhibition of altruism in his or her trading stance. (If we look at market relationships in this way, it is not surprising that the behaviour described as 'pricing at cost' should have been singled out for attention by those medieval scholastics who did concern themselves directly with the morality of exchange.)

My emphasis here is upon the behavioural traits that tend to be encouraged in the evolution of market exchange relationships over extended temporal sequences. As noted, opportunistic attempts to exploit differential advantages may take place. But such behaviour reduces the prospect that practitioners will survive over the long run. The potential for exit by those who are subjected to the exploitation offers the societal feedback mechanism that ensures the ultimate demise of the trader or trading firm that deceives, defrauds, defaults or otherwise seeks to gain differentially advantageous terms of trade. To the extent that 'codes of conduct' come to be established in some process of cultural evolution, as stressed by Hayek (1979), we should not expect such codes to incorporate opportunistic advantage-seeking through trade. And while the selection process that takes place within markets does not actively encourage the evolution of behaviour that reflects norms of 'other-regardingness', there is no feedback generated from potential exit that will discourage the evolution of such behaviour so long as the tripwire exit at cost-price terms remains available. The market will, of course, operate to ensure that persons who extend altruism to the extreme limit of disregard for their own survival will not, in fact, survive. St Francis has nothing to offer after the one-time dissipation of goods.

MODELS OF POLITICS

In the earlier discussion of exit as a feature of market interaction, attention was concentrated on the ability of any trader (buyer or seller) to withdraw from a specific exchange relationship and to shift to a comparable relationship with another trading partner. A more fundamental possibility for market exit tends to be overlooked in this preliminary overview. An individual may, presumably, withdraw altogether from the market or exchange nexus even if the costs of so doing are high. That is to say, entry into any market network is itself voluntary. The individual retains the option of withdrawing from the market 'game' itself.

Politics is different at this basic level of comparison. An individual is a member of a politically-organized community; he or she does not voluntarily choose to enter the political relationship, at least in the stylized model that excludes prospects for in or out migration. Even within a political relationship, however, there is no exit option potentially to be exercized as among alternative trading sets. Persons cannot choose among collectivities, except in federal-like structures that may allow for Tiebout-type adjustments. Individuals are 'locked in' to the political nexus, independently of their own active participation or the absence thereof.

The political relationship is 'morally laden', even in the most stylized of models. Regardless of what person or group may be assigned the authority to make choices for the polity, the nonexcludability from effects ensures that the well-being of others than the chooser(s) may be modified, positively or negatively, by any choice that is made.

Political interaction is inherently more complex than market interaction, and any effort to model politics abstractly seems to involve dramatic departures from any semblance of observable reality. In its most general sense, politics is a process of complex exchange among all members of a polity – an exchange in which each participant gives up value through taxes and secures a reciprocal return of value through programme benefits. The 'exchange' terms stipulate the shares in taxes and benefits assigned to each party to the inclusive transaction.

This basic political exchange among citizens tends to be obscured in much analysis because of the intrusion of a second, and quite distinct, 'exchange' between each person and 'government' or 'the state' in which taxes are paid to such an entity in apparent 'exchange' for programme benefits. The introduction of this second exchange between the individual and the government prompts inquiry into processes through which agents of governance are selected and monitored. I do not propose to examine the set of problems raised by this second exchange here.[3] I shall restrict analysis to a stylized model of the complex exchange among all members of a polity, thereby abstracting from all questions that involve the institutionalization of government as a means of effectuating the ultimate exchange among citizens. I want to model politics 'as if' collective decisions emerge from an inclusive town meeting in which all members of the polity participate.

Even in this highly abstract model, it is necessary to specify the rules under which political-collective decisions are made. I shall limit analysis to simple models of majority voting. Agreement among a number of voters sufficient to make up a majority is required to implement collective action, regardless of the attitudes or positions of members of a minority.

In the stylized model to be considered first, there are no constitutional limits on the range and scope for political-collective action. A majority coalition may impose taxes differentially on members of a minority with revenues then used either to finance public goods that yield generalized benefits to all citizens or to finance transfers differentially paid out to members of the majority coalition. In this setting, the dominant majority strategy will tend to be that which involves taxes on persons in a minority and transfers to persons in a majority (Flowers and Danzon, 1984). In a large electorate, the minimal winning coalition will find it advantageous to implement such a straightforward differential tax-differential transfer regime unless the prospective aggregate benefits of a public good, assumed to be uniformly distributed, are at least double the aggregate tax costs.

Consider an expectational setting in which each member of a polity considers membership in a minimally winning majority coalition to be equally likely with membership in a losing minority coalition. The winning coalition is empowered to implement collective action without constraints as to either the type of action or the distribution of costs and benefits. The only constitutional guarantee is that no majority can set collective action for more than the current period. A new electoral process, with possibly a new majority, takes place in each period.

In this abstracted setting, with some heroic simplifications, we are able to model the politics of any period as a simple two-person matrix relationship between the individual who is a member of the majority and the individual who is a member of the minority. Collective action in providing a public good is available that will yield a net surplus over costs. The ordinal payoff structure is that depicted in Figure 14.1. Note that the effective majority, whether this be the As or Bs, can choose among three separate solutions or outcomes, each one of which specifies the projected payoffs to each player. The fourth solution, Cell IV, is not possible by the logic of the structure, as described.

If an individual becomes a member of the As, and these persons make up the minimally winning coalition, the solution will be that shown in Cell III; in which members of the coalition of As exploit members of the minority, the Bs. The majority will not choose the Cell I outcome that involves the sharing of tax costs for the purchase of the public good. The situation is, of course, reversed if the Bs make up the winning coalition, in which case the solution is in Cell II, with the As being subjected to collective exploitation.

		B	
		Pays net tax	Pays no tax and receives transfer
A	Pays net tax	I $^1/_2, ^1/_2$	II −1, 2
	Pays no tax and receives transfer	III 2, −1	IV (0, 0)

Figure 14.1

Consider what might happen if and when a majority of voters, say the *A*s, attempts to act in 'the public interest'. Rather than impose taxes on the members of the *B* coalition, with transfers to the *A*s, the fiscal scheme chosen involves generalized tax financing of a public good that benefits all persons. This behaviour becomes fully analogous to the honest trader in the market who does not cheat on terms. The majority achieves the preferred Cell I solution in the period considered. But note that this majority remains highly vulnerable to defection by some of its members to a different, and less 'honest', majority that might be formed during the next period. The salutary effects of the behaviour during the first period may be dissipated quickly by the formation of the new, and exploiting, majority. There is no way that members of the majority who choose to 'play fair', to behave nonopportunistically, can exit from their political relationship with all other members of the inclusive polity. In recognition of this structure of interaction, participants in the political game, as modelled here, must play the exploiting strategy if they are to survive. They cannot avoid being played for a sucker, and repeatedly, unless they, too, seek to place others in the role of suckers when the opportunity warrants.

The absence of exit guarantees that the individual remains vulnerable to the 'mining' of whatever value he or she may possess or produce. In the market, at each and every level of interaction, 'voluntariness' remains a characteristic feature because the individual may walk away from the game, no matter how inclusively it may be defined. In majoritarian politics, by dramatic contrast, the individual can, at best, try to get 'his or her share', not in the net surplus that collective action makes possible, but in the aggregate total of value possessed or produced by all members of the polity.

TOWARDS CONSTITUTIONAL REFORM

The model of unconstrained majoritarian politics sketched out in the previous section is extreme, but it does, nonetheless, draw attention directly to the structural features that generate the undesirable results, measured both in the failures to achieve the potential cooperative surpluses from collective action and in the failures of the incentive system to facilitate the survival of nonopportunistic individual behaviour. Unconstrained majoritarian politics produces the 'churning state', to employ Anthony de Jasay's accurately descriptive term (de Jasay, 1985).

The simplified analytical construction in the previous section is helpful because it points to the two separate, but indirectly related, avenues for constitutional or structural reform within a single polity, either one of which might mitigate, even if not eliminate, failures along both of the dimensions noted. Clearly, the nonsymmetrical or off-diagonal majoritarian solutions, as shown in Cells II and III in Figure 14.1, are achievable only through the coerced imposition of the effective majority on the minority. As Wicksell recognized, the replacement of majority rule by an effective rule of unanimity would guarantee that such off-diagonal results could never be attained (Wicksell, 1896). Persons engaged in collective choice processes would, in this case, be forced to consider only those schemes that exclude exploitation, that is, those schemes that involve some sharing of cooperative surplus over and beyond that *status quo* position. I shall not discuss the Wicksellian thrust for constitutional reform here, in part because I have analysed it at some length in earlier works (see in particular, Buchanan and Tullock, 1962). I shall, instead, concentrate on a second, and different, direction for constitutional reform, which builds upon a provisional acceptance of majority rule as a central feature of democratic politics.

The matrix illustration in Figure 14.1 suggests immediately that direct conflicts between sets of participants, in this case between members of majority and minority coalitions, arise only because there exist potential solutions or outcomes that can only be attained without the agreement or acquiescence of one or more of the parties to the interaction. To generate any of the nonvoluntary outcomes, the separate players or participants must be placed in nonsymmetrical roles or positions, defined either in terms of actions taken or effects externally imposed. That is to say, *differences* between the participants must be introduced, whether these differences take the form of action or the effects of action. And these differences produce differentials in payoffs, allowing for a classification of participants as between winners and losers, between positive and negative payoffs, in absolute as well as relative terms, by comparison with some conceptualized exit benchmark.

The prospect of 'winning' by imposing net costs upon 'losers' becomes the attractor for the choice of participants, and it is this prospect that distracts-diverts attention from the potential opportunities for mutuality of gain through symmetrical sharing for common purpose. Constitutional reform may eliminate the *off-diagonal* solutions that embody differences between participants in action or effect that lie beyond the limits of possible voluntariness. If those outcomes (Cells II and III) that emerge only because the participants are made to be different by the coerciveness of the decision rule are placed constitutionally beyond the limits of politics, the decision rule itself may be retained.

In the highly simplified construction of Figure 14.1, it is evident that if the off-diagonal solutions are prohibited, then *any* decision rule will produce the Pareto-preferred outcome of Cell I. In this setting, whether the As or the Bs make up a majority, or whether some effective unanimity rule requires agreement among all the As and Bs, this result is invariant. In such a rarified setting, there is no basis for discussion about possible definitions of what is 'in the public interest', and no difference between self-regarding and other-regarding action, at least as observable in choice behaviour.

Any move toward descriptive reality must allow for the existence of a multiplicity of potential political outcomes, all within the Pareto-preferred set and Pareto superior to the conceptualized exit outcome in Cell IV of Figure 14.1. That is to say, there may be many nonexploitative political alternatives, each one of which involves collective action aimed at generating some mutually advantageous sharing of a potential surplus, but which differ, among themselves, in the distributional consequences. Consider the set of payoff alternatives: $(.9, .1), (.8, .2), (.7, .3), (.1, .9)$. Each one of these sets of payoffs dominates the $(0, 0)$ result, but neither of them imposes coerced loss on either party. Distributional results may motivate choice, and a majority made up of As may select the $(.9, .1)$ outcome whereas a majority made up of the Bs may select the $(.2, .9)$ alternative. But the generalized political 'discussion' here seems logically equivalent to that present in exchange when traders bicker over terms, with full recognition of the omnipresent exit option. In one sense, the game remains one of distributional politics, but it is distributional politics constrained by constitutional limits on the off-diagonals.

The participant in such constrained politics, whether in a role as a voter in a potential majority coalition, or as an elected agent for others, may behave in furtherance of a personalized definition of 'the public interest' without expecting to suffer the penalty of subsequent exploitation. The 'sucker's payoff' is excluded from the set of allowable results and with feedbacks on political behaviour generally. The political rhetoric of 'public interest' takes on some meaning in such constrained majoritarian politics, as contrasted with the absurdities in the pronouncements that often accompany the discussion of pork-barrel politics.

Analytic construction tends to objectify the subjective reality of social interaction, and the exercise in this paper is no exception. Implicitly, the model of the majoritarian political game incorporates the assumption that participants can identify political actions that are exploitative and distinguish these actions from those that embody a mutually advantageous sharing of potential collective surplus. This assumption, as stated, can be accepted to be psychologically descriptive, but its acceptance does not allow the inference that such subjective evaluations by the affected parties need correspond with any attempted objectification by the analyst. In this context, it would perhaps have been more accurate to have left off any labels for the rows and columns of Figure 14.1 and to use the matrix of interaction only to indicate the presence of the payoff alternatives, as subjectively perceived by the participants, however these might be identified and classified. Note particularly that, in such a reconstruction, the payoff alternatives may not be classified similarly by the separate participants. Action considered to be exploitative by members of a coerced minority may not be considered as such by members of the majority.

Problems raised by the inherent subjectivity of the evaluation of political alternatives may be illustrated by the fact that, clearly, some tax financing of net transfers to some members of the polity is considered to be generative of a collective surplus beneficial to those who are the net taxpayers, even by the latter. In this instance, the analytical construction of the model raises questions as to the extent and the limit of such net transfers – questions that will be partially addressed in the following section.

APPLICATIONS, EXTENSIONS, IMPLICATIONS

The whole discussion in the two previous sections may be criticized for its implied presumption that majoritarian politics, as it has historically evolved and as it operates, contains within its existing rules or constitutional structure none of the constraints that the analysis suggested to be necessary to ensure against the mutual exploitation suffered by rotating minorities. Such criticism, as might be advanced by a staunch defender of majoritarian politics, could point to the formal constitutional prohibitions against discriminatory treatment among members of the polity – prohibitions that find their traditional origins in the rule of law, in the precept that all persons be subjected to equal treatment under the law.

To an extent, the existence of such precepts in application to the operation of majoritarian politics must be acknowledged, *and appreciated*. There are constitutional limits that prevent majorities from denying the voting franchise to particular persons; there are limits placed on the deliberately discriminatory treatment of persons or groups in respect to some forms of political regulation; there are limits beyond which politically-driven discrimination in taxation might not go. And, indeed, it is the existence of such constitutional limits, and the traditional understanding of these limits in constitutional law, that have prevented the most overt forms of exploitation by politics from taking place. The purpose of my discussion becomes, in this sense, both precautionary and definitional. The importance of generality in the applicability of law, as interpreted by judges, has been extended to wide areas of human interaction. But the equal importance of such generality in the applicability to politically-driven action has not been adequately recognized, and notably in this century's transformation of majoritarian politics into the regulatory and transfer state.

Any effort on the part of a legislative majority to tax, subsidize or regulate differentially a group of persons classified by personal characteristics, such as gender, race, ethnicity, religion or geography would be judged unconstitutional. By dramatic contrast, almost any action by a legislative majority to tax, subsidize or regulate differentially a group of persons classified by economic characteristics, such as amount and type of wealth and income, occupational status, profession, industry, product category, form of organization and size of association, would be left constitutionally unchallenged.

With reference to the simplified construction in the two previous sections, application to the politics of the United States in the 1990s suggests that some off-diagonals are beyond recognized constitutional boundaries. But it is also emphatically clear that many possible off-diagonal solutions are both constitutionally permissible and become increasingly characteristic of modern democratic politics.

Consider restrictive trade policy, whether in the form of tariffs or quotas on imports, negotiated agreements, internal subsidies, 'dumping' legislation or 'fairness' requirements. Representatives of a sufficiently inclusive coalition of industries may succeed in securing legislative enactment of a set of such policies to be applied *differentially* only to the industries so designated (Buchanan and Lee, 1991). Such legislative action would take place with little or no argument to the effect that, if protection is extended to one industry or product category, the precept of equal treatment or generality would suggest extension of like or similar protection to all industries. And, indeed, as either elementary economics or our simple matrix illustration makes clear, if such a straightforward extension of constitutional law should be made, if the off-diagonal solutions that necessarily incorporate differential treatment should be eliminated, any and all support for politically enforced restrictions on trade would vanish.

It is instructive to think of the position of the legislative agent, perhaps an economist by training, who participates in trade policy debates, out of which a majority coalition is formed and a policy stance emerges. The agent may understand and appreciate that a regime of universalizable free trade is genuinely 'in the public interest' and should be preferred to a regime of trade restriction, either partial or total. Such an agent cannot, however, act in furtherance of the general 'good' and hope to survive electorally. The agent will be forced, by the structure of the political game, to seek differential protection for the industry concentrated in his or her constituency, to seek membership in the successful majority coalition, even at the recognized expense of both those outside the coalition and the inclusive 'public', as measured in some aggregate welfare index. By comparison, think of this same agent involved in a discussion of the alternatives: universalizable free trade and universalizable restriction. In this setting, both alternatives lie along the diagonal, and the agent who understands simple economics can, indeed, mount an argument and act in furtherance of 'the public interest'. There is no structurally-induced pressure on the agent to depart from the moral precept of generality.

Constitutional reform aimed at eliminating differential treatment – at removing the off-diagonals – seems relatively straightforward, at least at the level of discussion here, in application to politically-imposed economic regulation, as in the trade policy illustration. Comparable reform is much more difficult to discuss in application to transfer politics, in which majority coalitions include persons who, quite explicitly, seek monetary payoffs at the expense of those outside the coalition.

On one interpretation of the argument that I have advanced, full application of the precept for generality of treatment would require that all persons be subjected to equal-per-head taxes and be eligible for equal-per-head transfers. Such a regime would, of course, eliminate off-diagonal solutions, but, at the same time, it would not allow any net fiscal transfers to be implemented. And, as noted earlier, some redistributional role for the fisc seems to be broadly acceptable, even among those persons who must be placed in positions of net taxpayers rather than potential recipients of transfers. There is a categorical difference, however, between the collective 'purchase' of distributional adjustments that might conceptually be utility enhancing for all parties and majoritarian imposition of taxes to finance transfers beyond such limits. Even if explicit generality, defined as measurable equality, becomes contradictory in any scheme of collective transfers, steps in the direction of greater generality can do much to reduce the felt sense of fiscal exploitation.

A first and obvious step is that which would make all taxation general through the elimination of special tax treatment of identified sources. The argument for generality here lends support to schemes like the flat tax, with the same rate being applied to all income and over all persons. Such a scheme, if coupled with equal-per-head transfers, or demogrants, to all persons, would go far towards extending generality norms to fiscal action even in the operation of the transfer state. Differing persons would, of course, be differentially affected, but in their roles both as taxpayers and recipients, there is a sense in which all would seem to be treated equally. In terms of the metaphorical PD construction earlier, the flat tax-demogrant scheme might be considered to be quasi-diagonal.

An important by-product effect of any move towards generality in political treatment has not been mentioned. The promised opportunity to secure differentially favoured treatment, through shared membership in a successful majority coalition, provides incentives for rent-seeking investment that wastes economic value over and beyond any direct transfer between winner and loser in the political game. A special tax exemption will, indeed, allow those exempted to secure pecuniary gain at the expense of those who are provided no such treatment. But this gain–loss calculus may be matched or even exceeded by investment in efforts at persuading political agents to provide such discriminatory treatment in the first place. To the extent that constitutional rules prohibit discriminatory treatment through the political process, the incentives for rent-seeking are correspondingly reduced.

CONCLUSION

The discussion in the two previous sections may have seemed to depart from the main argument, as summarized in the title 'Structure-induced behaviour in markets and in politics'. The implications of the absence of the exit option in political interaction for the behaviour of participants seem clear enough. There is no feedback loop that works to impose penalties on those who behave opportunistically in majoritarian politics, and the rewards promised from such behaviour are such as to ensure its survival in the ongoing evolutionary process. Participants must play distributional politics if such play is allowed by the rules. The discussion in the two previous sections was aimed to demonstrate how the rules might be changed so as to restrict alternatives within the political choice set to those that might be chosen by a majority but yet remain meaningfully classifiable as 'within the public interest'.

The analysis suggests that much of the familiar criticism of market organization that is based on its underlying morality of 'greed' or 'unconstrained pursuit of self-interest' is wrongly conceived and applied. The standard question: 'relative to what?' must be raised. To the extent that the exit option eliminates or reduces opportunistic behaviour (the off-diagonals), the structure of markets induces behaviour that exhibits a morality of fairness, quite independently of an underlying motivation. If 'greed' is defined as the seeking of gain at the expense of trading partners, this behaviour is precisely that sort which will not survive as a personal characteristic in an ongoing market order. On the other hand, and by contrast, this pattern of behaviour will find its reward in the play of distributional politics.

The widespread dissatisfaction with modern majoritarian politics stems from a hazy recognition that the 'politics of greed' guarantees a mutuality of opportunity loss for all citizens. Escape from the genuine dilemma requires that some constitutional means be found that will effectively change the constraints within which political behaviour takes place. Politics must be restricted to the discussion and implementation of actions that are properly classified as alternative 'public goods' that promise benefits to all members of the polity.

NOTES

1. The specific origins of this paper, along with the central argument, owes much to the important analysis developed by Roger Congleton and Viktor Vanberg (1992). For earlier analyses that are precursory, see Buchanan (1954); Downs (1957); Tullock (1967b); Hirschman (1970). For preliminary statements of some of the argument, see Buchanan (1992a).
2. Congleton and Vanberg work within the repeated PD game paradigm to demonstrate that an 'exit if other defects' strategy tends to be successful, even against the tit-for-tat strategy.
3. See Chapter 17 for a discussion and comparison of the two exchanges.

15. The epistemological feasibility of free markets[1]

One of F.A. Hayek's most important achievements is his contribution to an understanding of how markets utilize knowledge. However, Hayek himself did not specifically examine the epistemological underpinnings of market institutions or rules that must, themselves, emerge from some process of 'choice'. Presumably, he did not make such an extension of inquiry because of his concentration on the evolutionary origins of institutions, with the consequent implication that no choice, as such, need inform the historical record.

It is first necessary to clear up a possible ambiguity that may arise from a failure to distinguish between the claim for evaluative or normative superiority of evolutionary *laissez-faire* and the much more sweeping claim that the course of evolutionary development cannot be modified by human action. In his persuasive criticism of what he called 'rational constructivism' (or 'constructive rationalism'), Hayek can be interpreted as making the first of these two claims. Although he may not himself have been clear here, Hayek should not be interpreted as making the second claim that efforts at institutional reconstruction, no matter how bungled and misguided, and no matter how inefficacious in results, do not, and cannot, exert effects at all. After all, 'socialism happened', a fact of history that Hayek surely did not choose to ignore.

Over the course of two centuries, efforts have been made to reconstruct the order of societies, and institutional structures have been changed because of these efforts. Hayek is convincing when he suggests that the development of these societies would have been 'better', by several agreed upon standards, had the efforts at reconstruction not been made at all. But, to my knowledge, Hayek did not directly recognize that, once any effort at social reconstruction was made and was observed to have effects, explicit 'social choice' became a necessary element in the human condition.

We start from the social order that exists and as shaped in part by past efforts at reconstruction. The institutions of order have been chosen in some process, and this fact of choice is understood to have occurred. Any direction for change, for future development, is also recognized as something to be chosen, quite independently of the causal nexus between choice and consequences. Even to allow the process of cultural evolution to work, to leave institutional change alone, requires choice. 'To leave alone' is, itself, a choice alternative.

Once this elementary point is recognized, it becomes appropriate to examine the epistemological environment within which choice takes place. If to leave alone is one choice alternative among many, what sort of generalized public understanding is required for this alternative to emerge? The classical liberal, in the role of social engineer, may, of course, recommend institutional *laissez-faire* as a preferred policy stance. But why, and under what conditions, should members of the citizenry, or of some ultimate political decision authority, accept this advice more readily than that proffered by any other social engineer?

PRELIMINARY STIPULATIONS

For purposes of clarifying the discussion here, let me stipulate that if there should be adequate understanding of the working properties of market institutions, then these institutions would be chosen as the basic framework within which persons carry out their economic activities. My concern in this stipulation is to set aside all argument about the efficiency enhancing attributes of markets. I simply postulate that market organization does, indeed, generate a higher-valued bundle of goods and services than alternative forms of organization, with evaluations based on the preferences of those persons who are participants. In this stipulation that the market organization of the economy produces more value than alternative institutional arrangements, I am quite deliberately bypassing the whole set of issues concerning the scientific content of 'economics' as a discipline. The stipulation implies that the required understanding of the working properties of markets is achieved through scientific inquiry, in all respects analogous to other fields of knowledge. The initial stipulation also implies that efficiency in the standard sense is the agreed-on objective for economic organization. Neither distributional considerations nor extramarket environmental concerns are relevant for the choice calculus of the political decision maker.

I want also to emphasize that my subject of inquiry is *epistemological* rather than *political* feasibility. There may exist many types of constitutional-political decision structures that fail to generate organizational choices for the polity that correspond to results that would emerge from considerations of the generalized interest of participants. Decision structures may be such that special or differential interests may dominate any selection of alternatives that would further the general or all-encompassing interest. I can circumvent this difficulty either by postulating that the constitutional rules are so stylized as to prevent any subversion of the general interest or by assuming that political choosers are classical utilitarians.

Given such preliminaries, the problem to be addressed can be simply stated: do persons, as political choosers in their roles as participants in political processes, possess the capacities to make informed selections among the relevant organizational alternatives, which, in this case, would be the selection of the market? And, if they do not possess such capacities, can they be expected to defer to the experts, in this case, the economists, who are presumably competent to make accurate institutional comparisons?

We must, of course, recognize that only on a few occasions in history are persons faced with choices among inclusive and comprehensive institutional-constitutional alternatives. The effective choices are rarely in such stark form as that between 'socialism' and 'the market', even in those societies that have gone through genuine revolutionary upheavals. The choices actually faced by participants in the politically-organized communities are likely to be incremental or piecemeal, with particular reference to identified subsectors of the economy. The choices are likely to take such forms as: should the existing politicized and bureaucratized production and/or distribution of, say, bread be abandoned, wholly or partially? Or, vice versa, should the existing decentralized and nonpoliticized market for bread, both in its production and distribution, be replaced by a collectivized alternative, again in whole or in part? Or, even less comprehensively, should the market price for bread be collectively controlled, either directly or indirectly through taxes or subsidies?

Consider, then, the position of the potential political chooser, whether citizen, elected politician, party leader or bureaucrat, who is confronted with such institutional choice. (Recall that I have explicitly ruled out motivations based on narrowly identified interests; the chooser is presumed to act on estimates of the general interest.) Clearly, some understanding of how the institutional alternatives work must inform the choice calculus. It is this understanding and its relationship to the market in particular that I want to examine in some detail.[2]

Before proceeding, however, institutional history must be acknowledged to be relevant for any such choice. As noted earlier, no choices are made *carte blanche*. An institutional structure always exists, and this structure has worked, after some fashion, whether efficaciously or not, and persons have observed its working properties. Effectively, institutional choice is always between some institutional-organizational *status quo* and some proposed alternatives, the working properties of which cannot be observed directly, except possibly in foreign settings. Institutional choice is not analogous to the choice among items in a Greek restaurant kitchen, each one of which is observed to be available. Institutional choice is between that which is and that which might be but is not. This fact alone suggests that the temperament of the chooser may become relevant. The conservative's choice may be biased towards that which is; the radical's choice may be biased towards that which is not but might be.

Again, however, the presence or absence of such a temperamental bias or its direction is not my primary concern in this chapter. My concern is exclusively with the understanding or knowledge of the institutional alternatives that is present in the mind of the potential chooser, whichever alternative may describe the *status quo*.

MINIMAL ECONOMIC UNDERSTANDING

I suggest that there is a minimal level or degree of elementary economic understanding required in order that the potential chooser be led to select the market alternative, under the conditions stipulated, through the process of an internal rational calculus, whether the dimension for choice involves small or incremental adjustment towards or away from an operative market system or comprehensive change in overall economic organization. Absent such minimal understanding, the collectivized alternative tends to be chosen over the market because it tends to be more in accord with the 'natural' mind-set of the person who remains nonsophisticated in economics.

This vulgar mind-set has been reinforced rather than offset by the allocation-maximization paradigm of the economic theory of this century – the paradigm that provided the central logic upon which the idealized models of collectivization were constructed. To the extent that the market is conceptualized as a 'device' or a 'mechanism', or even is discussed in terms of its 'functions', it is necessarily seen to be more complex in its operation than the more directly focused, and centralized, control process of the collectivized alternative. Adequately, even if minimally understood, the market is not to be conceived analogously to a mechanism, but, instead, as a process within which separate persons interact in furtherance of their own purposes and, in so doing, generate an order. This order of the market may, of course, be described in terms of its results by a vector of valued inputs and outputs, but this vector itself emerges from the process and does not, and cannot, exist independently of the process through which it is generated.[3]

It is an elementary or minimal understanding of this *order* of the market that must inform the choices that are to be made among institutional alternatives, in the small or in the large. Absent this, the collectivization alternative will tend to trump the market in the chooser's rational, even if ignorant, calculus. The collectivist alternative is clearly sensed to have an order, no matter how badly it may be predicted to work, and it stands opposed to what must seem to be a chaotic pattern of results with no internal logic. Order takes precedence over disorder. Quite literally, the market is, indeed, 'out of control' by any person or any authority, and this absence of control is taken to imply the absence of any order in the pattern of results. 'The blind forces of the market' – this derogation reflects the unknowledge of those market critics who mouth it.

It is as if those who do not possess the minimal understanding here think of demand and supply relationships in total independence of any incentive response behaviour on the part of persons who participate in economic activities. It is as if both input and output prices (terms of trade) are arbitrarily settled through some complex bargaining among groups that possess varying degrees of effective economic power, with all participants in the economy being recipients of pure rents (producers' and consumers'). And, of course, in such a setting, resource allocation among end-uses is also quite arbitrary, within broad limits. In such an imagined model of economic reality, the results would, indeed, be chaotic, with no discernible order, and no predictability, either to an observer or to an internal participant.

As this somewhat forced and artificial image might suggest, however, the understanding required to make more informed choice may be quite minimal. As between the market and the collectivist institutional alternatives, under the conditions stipulated, the person who chooses need only to know that demand for any good or service is inversely related to price and that, conversely, the supply of any good or service is directly related to price, that markets clear and that resources move to the most valued uses. (That is to say, demand curves slope downward, supply curves slope upward, prices are set at the intersections, resource returns are equalized among uses.)

ECONOMIC LEARNING AND FEEDBACKS FROM REALITY

The minimal understanding of economic *science* sketched out here is not a part of our intuitive perception of social reality. Such an understanding must be learned, either through some intellectual exposure to the elementary principles or some directly sensed feedback from personal experience. And it is in this latter feature that economic science differs dramatically from natural science. If I choose to deny the existence of gravity and jump off a building, the harsh realities of physics catch up very quickly to bring me into recognition and acceptance, if, indeed, I survive at all. If, however, I should, analogously, deny the existence of the laws of demand and supply and proceed to join with others politically in efforts to impose some preferred allocative and distributive result, the feedback from reality is likely to be much more complex and to require a longer time for general recognition. This century witnessed the grandest social science experiment in all of history. The whole socialist scheme was based on a denial of the elementary laws of economics. And, as we know, seven decades were necessary before the efforts at centralized collective control failed sufficiently to force acceptance of basic institutional-organizational change.

At a less comprehensive level of institutional choice, the feedbacks from reality are likely to prove even less effective in modifying the natural mind-set of the economically nonsophisticated. Throughout history, political communities, with the acquiescence of citizens, have destroyed potential economic value by the deliberate restriction and control of markets, based in part on a simple failure to understand the most elementary principles of economic science. It is important in this context to recognize that piecemeal politicization of markets destroys value that *might have been* generated but that was never brought into existence. That is to say, the choice-influenced opportunity costs of market restriction are never observed directly by those who bear them (Buchanan, 1969). There is nothing here that is akin to the hard surface of the ground for forcing immediate recognition of error as in the gravity analogue.

The low-skilled person who might have been employed in the absence of the politically-imposed minimum wage restriction will never, personally, experience the loss of value from that which exists. And the utilitarian participant in the collective-political choice that considers imposing the minimum wage restriction will not experience the feedback relationship from reality that might substitute for an absence of elementary economic understanding. Modern empirical economists might raise objection at this point and suggest that persons who do not really understand the principles can be convinced as to the truths of basic propositions by confrontation with empirical evidence. But the relationship between empirical evidence and the structure of belief remains mysterious, and in economics particularly the difficulties and lags in experimentation make it unlikely that the marshalling of evidence will genuinely convince those who remain ignorant of the causal sources in behaviour.

The institutional-organizational failure of 'socialism in the large' seems to have done nothing towards generating an understanding of the elementary logic of markets. The grand experiment served to refute the hypothesis that centralized control of a national economy can produce goods and services of comparable value with those produced through the workings of a market order, along with the complementary hypothesis that the rate of growth in value under collectivized control is comparable. But the linkage between the observed failure of socialism in the large and the value-reducing effects of piecemeal efforts towards 'socialism in the small' can be appreciated only by those who do possess the required minimal knowledge of economic science. Until and unless it is recognized that the failures of the grand experiments were rooted in the denial of the behavioural laws that elementary economics teaches, there can be no carryover from the evidence of the failure of these experiments to the assessment of the potential success or failure of piecemeal market intervention which are informed by similar denials of the basic economic regularities.

A 1993 EXAMPLE

In his press conference on 23 March 1993, President Clinton made the following statement:

> I was astonished that the Bush administration overruled its own customs office and gave a $300 million-a-year freebie to the Japanese for no reason (referring to estimates of minivan tariffs) and we got nothing, and I emphasize nothing, in return (*Wall Street Journal*, 24 March 1993).

This statement can be interpreted, I submit, only on the supposition that Clinton does not understand elementary economics. The statement makes sense only on some presumption that the supply of Japanese minivans exported to the United States is totally invariant with the net return to supplying firms, in which case the exclusive beneficiary is the US Treasury, while the Japanese firms bear the full cost. (The supply curve of Japanese minivans is vertical.)

The Clinton statement is particularly disturbing since it was made by someone who is clearly in a position of decision-making authority and also by someone who has demonstrated a high level of general intelligence. As we shift attention to the degree of possible economic sophistication attained by the citizenry, generally, those to whom ordinary politicians seek to respond, the prospects become discouraging indeed. How can free markets survive at all in the face of generalized economic ignorance?

DEFERENCE TO EXPERTS

One way out of the morass created by widespread economic unknowledge might seem to be that offered by some enhancement of the authority of the experts, in this case, the professional economists, to whom citizens and politicians might defer in some acknowledgement of their own scientific limitations. Professionals in this discipline, however, have never come close to commanding such intellectual authority, and economics has been plagued from its disciplinary establishment by the proclivity of everyone to act as his or her own economist. This phenomenon is due in part, but only in part, to the ambiguity in feedback between error and reality noted earlier. It is also due in part to the failure of economists themselves to stick to their knitting, to keep attention focused on the elementary verities (Hutt, 1936). Further, the public's disrespect for economists as intellectual gurus stems from the economists' own misunderstanding of what the basic principles of their science tell them. Economists, too, were victims of the 'fatal conceit' that allowed socialism to happen.

Above all these, however, there remains still another important reason why the scientists and the science of economics fail to command the intellectual respect that seems to describe public and political attitudes toward natural scientists and science – a reason that was noted by Thomas Hobbes more than three centuries ago. The laws of natural science, of physics and chemistry, do not seem to bear directly on the interests of persons and groups, because these laws are not considered to be amenable to human choices, whether private or public. The laws of natural science are, indeed, 'natural'.[4]

By contrast, the laws of economics seem to be artificial because both the objects of inquiry, the choices of animate human beings and the outcome of such choices, describe a social reality that is, itself, clearly not invariant. There is a general failure to make the distinction between choices made within the institutional parameters that contain incentives for personal behaviour – choices that can be scientifically analysed and tested – and choices of the parameters themselves – choices that cannot, at least not directly, be scientifically predictable. Because institutional structures are themselves subject to choice, and can be modified deliberately, it becomes relatively easy for misunderstanding to arise concerning the ultimate malleability of economic actors. From such a misunderstanding the idea emerges that there are no laws of economics comparable to those of the hard or natural sciences, and that the so-called 'science' is without content, leaving institutions vulnerable to shaping by the pressures of particular interests, with little or no feedback from reality.[5] These considerations are independently important and warrant extended treatment. However, they are not my central concern here. I have stipulated that there is, indeed, scientific content in economics. The discussion here is intended only to suggest that dispute over this scientific content, if present, makes it more difficult for the professional scientists to command respect.

ARE FREE MARKETS EPISTEMOLOGICALLY FEASIBLE?

Public choice economists perhaps have rushed too hurriedly towards the discovery of interest-based explanations for collectivized restrictions on market activity, although the major contribution of public choice in dispelling the romantic myth of the benevolent state should be acknowledged. But, relatively, there has been a neglect of explanations for market restrictions based on economic ignorance and/or illiteracy. Political choosers, whether these be voters, elected politicians, bureaucrats or judges, may lack an understanding of even the most elementary principles of economic science, in which case the choices made among institutional alternatives may reflect honest error rather than any direct promotion of narrowly defined and special interest.

The capacity to understand elementary economics may be less general among even the most informed elements of the citizenry than we may have implicitly assumed. Free markets may be vulnerable to politicization that is motivated neither by differential interest nor by some rejection of the efficiency norm but, instead, by simple misunderstanding of how markets work. Frank Knight once remarked that he could not distinguish between those critics of the market who based their criticism on the market's failure to work as it was supposed to work and those critics who based their criticism on the results that emerge because the market worked as economists described. My thesis is that there is an important third source of criticism; persons seek to subvert the market order because they do not understand how it does work.

The implication for pedagogy is clear. Economists have failed to promulgate the elementary principles of their science so as to secure the generalized understanding for informed political-constitutional choice. Think of the enormous value of the marginal product of some economist who might have taught President Clinton the elementary principles that would have caused him to think differently about Japanese minivans.

Somewhat more specifically to the point of this chapter, the implication is that we should pay more attention to the human capacity to understand social processes as a basis for making informed choices among institutional-organizational alternatives. Such choices will be made, willy-nilly, and the limits of understanding may be a more serious impediment to the exploitation of maximal value potential than any limits imposed by physically measured resources. The capacity to understand, to know, is also a valuable resource, and this capacity must surely extend to economic interaction. Economists, back to our blackboards!

NOTES

1. Material in this chapter was presented at a Hayek Conference, Bleibach, Germany, in June 1993.
2. In an earlier paper, Viktor Vanberg and I made a distinction between 'interests' and 'theories' in constitutional choice (Vanberg and Buchanan, 1989). In this terminology, my concern in this paper is exclusively with 'theories'.
3. See Buchanan (1982) for an elaboration of this point.
4. Some qualification should be introduced here with reference to modern developments in science that do suggest prospects for interfering with 'laws of nature'. But note also that precisely as these potential interferences have seemed to become possible, controversy has emerged on the scientific level that did not describe behaviour in earlier periods.
5. In his provocative book, *The End of History and the Last Man* (1992), Francis Fukuyama suggests that, after the great revolutions of 1989–91, political communities everywhere will organize economic activities through markets. He argues that this result represents an acceptance of the central hypotheses of economic science. From my perspective, Fukuyama ignores the required linkage between the public-political understanding of these hypotheses and the constitutional choice for market institutions. For further discussion, see Chapter 25.

16. Who cares whether the commons are privatized?

Neoclassical welfare economics contains precise definitions of the necessary conditions that must be satisfied in order to meet the criteria of efficiency or optimality in the allocation and use of scarce resources. Failure to satisfy any of these conditions implies a shortfall in economic value below that which might be produced, with value being measured by the ultimate evaluations of the individual participants in the whole economic nexus. From this elementary base, economists, generally, have inferred that overall value maximization, that is, efficiency or optimality, is an appropriate welfare objective, in the sense that it allows for appropriately qualified normative judgements in the comparisons among alternative institutional structures. The Pareto construction, and perhaps especially as this is amended to incorporate Wicksellian agreement as the necessary epistemological test, allows economists to translate the whole neoclassical exercise into meaningful hypotheses about individual expressions of support for institutional changes.[1]

Individuals in their roles as generalized consumers are presumed to be interested in the satisfaction of the efficiency norm, since this result ensures that the most highly valued bundle of end-items for final use is made available from any given expenditure of resources. From this interest, it is presumed that individuals, as consumers, will positively support reforms that aim at maximizing total product value in some aggregative sense. Some neoclassical economists have elevated the presumed welfare of the nonspecialized consumer to independent criterial significance in the evaluation of policy proposals.[2]

Especially since the development of public-choice theory, economists have recognized that individuals' interests as consumers need not track their interests as producers, and that, due to the presumed greater specialization among persons in their producer roles, generalized support for efficiency in resource use may not find expression in politicized decision structures. That is to say, politically expressed preferences may not suggest to legislators that economic efficiency, as such, finds much constituency support.

In this chapter, I shall challenge a basic presupposition in this familiar chain of neoclassical and public-choice, welfare logic – a challenge which, if accepted, will weaken still further the presumption that aggregative efficiency in resource use is a politically viable objective alternative to the more obvious separated interests of producer groups. I shall suggest here that, within the neoclassical analytical framework, such aggregative efficiency is not necessarily an economic interest to individuals, *even in their roles as generalized consumers-producers*, quite apart from differential interests in market restrictions. That is to say, even if we could supervene or otherwise neglect the revealed preferences of persons who act in furtherance of their specialized roles as producers, there may remain situations which observing economists classify to be demonstrably inefficient but which do not, in any sense, provoke the reform interests of persons as generalized consumers-producers. The second section presents these results through the use of a familiar and highly simplified set of examples of commons overusage.

If the results can be generalized to apply to relevant barriers to allocative efficiency over and beyond those that are normally discussed under the 'tragedy of the commons' rubric, the analysis would seem to suggest that generalized individual interest in, and support for, efficiency-enhancing schemes for reform may require the satisfaction of specific distributional criteria. The third section examines these issues. The central proposition that efficiency, as a normative objective for reform, will not secure widespread support in the absence of these distributional requirements, depends critically, however, on acceptance of the analytical framework of neoclassical economic theory. The fourth section relates the whole exercise to the relevant underlying presuppositions of neoclassical theory and demonstrates that a particular change in these presuppositions may restore the efficiency support inferences that economists tend to draw from their constructions.

BACK TO BASICS: SOME DEER–BEAVER ANALYTICS

We can scarcely do better than return to Adam Smith (1776) and to examine his model of the deer–beaver economy with the purpose of assessing support for efficiency as a policy norm. Let us suppose that the long-run equilibrium or natural price ratio is two deer for one beaver, which reflects relative input costs: one day's labour to kill a deer, two day's labour to kill a beaver. Persons are homogeneous, both in endowments and in preferences, and labour is the only factor. The input–output relationships are assumed to be invariant over the relevant margins of production. They do not rule out, however, the presence of commons phenomena over certain areas of the forest. Assume that persons (who are equally adept as deer or beaver hunters, although there is clear advantage to specialization) are allowed to choose freely between the two productive activities. And further assume that the whole forest remains open to all hunters, whether of deer or beaver. There is no ownership of the forest, or any part thereof.

But suppose now that there exists a relatively small glen, within the larger forest, where deer abound, and that hunting deer in this part of the forest is much more productive, over some initial ranges of use, than elsewhere. Deer hunters will rationally exploit the opportunities of the glen so long as the net returns from their outlay exceeds that attainable from other parts of the forest. In familiar terms, the productive glen is a scarce resource, and if it is treated as if it is not, usage will be extended to the point at which its total value is dissipated. We have here a classic example of the tragedy of the commons imbedded inframarginally within Smith's classic illustration.

Aggregate value in this simple economy can be increased by privatizing the ownership of the glen. Suppose, now, that some person, anyone, claims an ownership right, encloses the glen and charges fees for hunting deer. Overall efficiency in the economy increases; a resource that was valueless as used earlier now produces value.[3]

But who gains from the enhanced efficiency with which resources are now utilized? Note particularly that consumers, as such, do not gain, since the price vector does not change. One beaver still exchanges for two deer; both absolute and relative prices are unchanged by the efficiency-enhancing privatization. Individuals, in their roles as producers, neither gain nor lose. In the commons equilibrium, the overexploitation of the glen was such that the returns were equalized on the more productive and the less productive parts of the forest. The gains from privatization accrue solely and exclusively to the person or persons who are successful in seizing, or otherwise securing, the ownership rights. The owner or owners secure the full value produced by the efficient usage of the scarce resource. No other persons in the economy, regardless of their roles as consumers and/or producers, gain. But it is important to recognize also that, if we neglect short-run adjustments, no one loses either. Consumers or producers neither lose nor gain from the privatization. Basically, the stance of persons who fully understand, articulate and express their economic interest, strictly speaking, should be one of indifference towards proposals to privatize the commons.

Even within the confines of this extremely simplified model, the analysis suggests that support for institutional change that takes the form of privatization of resources previously used in common may be very narrowly limited, although opposition to such change may also not be widespread. If, however, persons are less than fully informed about the workings of the economy, if personal envy affects individual attitudes or if there should exist elements of human capital specialized to the use of the commons, we should expect that these modifications in the model would find expression in opposition to rather than support for privatization.

Widespread or general support in favour of privatization as an institutional reform would seem to be forthcoming only if large numbers of persons could somehow be brought within the group that shares the benefits of ownership, as these might be capitalized upon the act of establishing such ownership. I shall return to this point later.

Economists will perhaps criticize the restrictiveness of the elementary Smithean model. The privatization of marginally irrelevant commons may be acknowledged to generate little if any generalized interests on the part of consumers and/or producers, despite the efficiency-enhancing results of such privatization. But, say the economists, values are set at the margins, and the whole analysis may be inapplicable to privatization in settings where margins are affected.

We may readily modify the Smithean setting to examine the efficacy of this possible criticism. Under the same general assumptions, let us now suppose that, as before, a beaver can be produced upon the outlay of two days' labour, and that this input–output relationship remains constant over all possible ranges of supply. Suppose, however, that a comparable production relationship does not characterize deer production. From the outset of production, assume that deer are produced under increasing costs. As more units are produced, the outlay per unit, measured in labour time, increases.

In this case, the whole forest becomes the overly exploited commons for the hunting of deer while it remains without value for the hunting of beaver. If there is no ownership, deer hunters will enter into production so long as the net return per day's labour exceeds or equals that in the production of beaver. A day's labour in deer must, therefore, yield the value equivalent of one-half a beaver in equilibrium. In orthodox efficiency terms, in the commons solution there will be too many persons hunting deer relative to beaver. Upon privatization of the forest for deer production, the rational owner (owners) will commence to charge fees for deer-hunting permits. Fewer persons will produce deer; the quantity of deer produced may decrease, stay the same or increase, depending on the location of the pre- and post-privatization equilibria on the production frontier. In the post-privatization equilibrium, the relative price of deer may increase, stay the same or decrease.[4]

In this model, the determinacy of the equilibrium price ratio is, of course, no longer present. We cannot predict how many deer will exchange for one beaver either before or after ownership is established; the price ratio, in either case, will depend on both the relative demands and the relative costs of the two goods. Privatization, of course, will increase aggregative value; the previously nonvalued resource will be optimally combined with complementary inputs in production; the newly established owner (owners) of the scarce resource will secure the full value of its addition to the economy's total product.

But what can we say about support for efficiency-enhancing privatization in this setting? It is no longer so easy to separate consumer and producer roles, especially when we recognize that there is a second productive resource – land for deer production – that affects valuation at the relevant margins of adjustment.

The presence of constant input costs in production of one of the goods provides a base that anchors the productivity of this input, labour. Under the assumptions of the model, a day's labour can never be valued (in equilibrium) more highly than one-half a beaver, whether employed in deer or beaver production, so long as both goods are demanded in the final equilibrium. But privatization will reduce inputs into deer production and may increase, leave unchanged or even decrease the relative price of deer. At issue is whether the deer-beaver bundle that is purchased by the worker-consumer, who is not an owner, will be valued at a higher or lower total than the bundle purchased before privatization.

We know, of course, that the economy, considered as a whole, is more efficient after privatization, and that a larger value of goods is produced. Ratios between marginal rates of substitution in production are brought into equality with ratios between marginal rates of substitution in consumption, and the production possibility frontier for the whole economy is shifted outward by the change. But the economy cannot be considered as a unit for purposes of my exercise in this chapter. Disaggregation is necessary, and particularly as between the owner (owners) of the valuable resource (land in deer production) that is privatized and others who remain strictly as workers-consumers.

I suggest that the results attained from analysis of the first model carry over to this model, although formal proof might be difficult to present. In any case, I leave such proof (or disproof) to others. The intuitively convincing logic is, however, straightforward. Workers-consumers who do not share in the newly created value of ownership are faced with an incentive structure, which takes the form of rental prices for use of the land for deer production, that guarantees efficient allocation of labour as between the two goods. The rental value of the land in deer production will be equal to its marginal product, evaluated in the post-privatization equilibrium price ratio. Workers, in either deer or beaver production, will earn their marginal product, and payment of land rentals and wages will exhaust total value produced in the economy. The latter result holds so long as we maintain the neoclassical postulate of constant returns to scale. And there is nothing within the example here to suggest departure from this postulate.[5]

But will the worker-consumer who does not share in the newly created ownership value be better or worse off than before privatization? The marginal value product of a day's labour will, of course, be higher. But the relevant comparison is that between marginal value product, evaluated at the post-privatization equilibrium ratio of prices, and the *average value product*, evaluated at the pre-privatization equilibrium ratio. And there seems no way, *a priori*, to make this comparison, since, as noted earlier, the price ratio may move in either direction or remain unchanged.

The possible effects on the economic position of the worker-consumer, who does not share in the value of land ownership, would seem, in any case, to be of the second order of smalls and would not be sufficiently important to motivate expressions of support or opposition. Nonowners, therefore, will tend to be relatively indifferent as to privatization when proposed as an institutional reform, although, as noted with reference to the first model, they will perhaps tilt towards opposition as we depart from presumptions of full information, no specificity and complete rationality.[6]

DISTRIBUTIONAL CONSTRAINTS IN EFFICIENCY GAINS

The criteria for allocative efficiency are not affected, of course, by the simple point that the examples are designed to demonstrate. Since aggregate economic value is increased by any removal of barriers to efficient resource use, there must exist some structure of institutional reform that will increase the well-being of some members of the relevant community while damaging no one. The efficiency-enhancing privatization of the commons may not benefit nonowners, generally, but neither does it cause them harm. The net beneficiaries are those who secure the ownership rights, regardless of how these rights are assigned. And, in the examples, there is a once-and-for-all increase in present value attributable to the attainment of ownership of the value-producing resource, which carries the authority to control usage.

Those persons who apply their resources to the use of the commons before privatization may neither gain nor lose from the shift to private ownership (save in the short run), despite the fact that, post-ownership, they face rental fees for usage. By construction, in equilibrium these users earn competitive rates of returns on their outlay either before or after the establishment of private ownership. In one sense, no one in the community bears or suffers the incidence of the inefficiency that the absence of private ownership creates. The loss is to be reckoned here only in terms of foregone opportunities rather than consciously sensed damages or harms. On the other hand, the restriction of the usage of a facility, through pricing or otherwise, that was previously available on some unrestricted basis, may be opposed, in part, irrationally, especially if users consider that the rights have been arbitrarily assigned. In this setting, in particular, envy may emerge to tilt the balance towards maintenance of the *status quo* tragedy of the commons. Such a prospect, which may well loom large in real situations, suggests that some Wicksellian test should be incorporated into early considerations of institutional change, and that users of the relevant resource to be privatized be assigned at least some share in the value created by privatization.

The analysis prompts an interesting question: who 'owns' the commons? Who has an ethical claim to the value that the scarce resource could produce but which is not being produced? All members of the community, as politically organized?

The state, as such? All who participate in the production-exchange-consumption nexus? Users of the commons? Consumers of the goods produced on the commons? A more relevant question might be: how can privatization of the commons take place at all? The ownership rights have value, and anyone who has the authority to assign these rights has the means to capture this value.[7] And will not the prospect of securing such authority itself set off rent-seeking investment that may, in some limiting cases, dissipate in advance the net efficiency gains from the establishment of ownership rights?

The whole analysis suggests that the standard economists' concentration on the efficiency-enhancing properties of privatization is not sufficient independently to carry much weight in discussions of institutional reform. The distribution of the value of the ownership rights to be created becomes important in generating the required political support for any efficiency-enhancing proposal. Efficiency *per se* must be replaced by efficiency 'for whom'. Some of the implications are clear. Proposals to privatize scarce facilities through auction, with funds collected from successful bidders to be used either to reduce taxes or to expand public programme benefits, tend to ensure wide sharing in the value created by the reform. Proposals to assign ownership rights directly to users may or may not succeed in stimulating sufficiently broad support for effective privatization. Proposals to assign newly created ownership rights to the 'managers', to that small set of persons who have acted in supervisory roles in the collective enterprise that has been described to contain elements of the commons tragedy, will almost surely fail to find support beyond a very narrow constituency, despite the promised efficiency gains. Distribution as well as allocation matters.

RESTORING EFFICIENCY AS A SUPPORTABLE POLICY NORM

If we restrict analyses of economies to the limits imposed by the presuppositions of neoclassical theory, efficiency, as such, seems to have quite limited authority, on its own and independently of distributional considerations. But it is important to recognize that we need not be bound by the conventional limits of neoclassical theory, and that efficiency may emerge as a broadly supportable policy norm, quite independently of distributional constraints, under some modifications in the presuppositions of this theory. In particular, I refer to the constant returns postulate that is required to prove the allocative efficiency of competitive equilibrium. If we substitute the postulate of economy-wide and generalized increasing returns for that of constant returns, we can derive a logic of generalized support for the efficiency gains that privatization of the commons creates, quite apart from distributional limits, even if, at the same time, we must perforce abandon the central theorems of neoclassical welfare economics, as these are normally discussed.

The establishment of ownership rights adds to value in the economy and, in the orthodox logic, the increment to value accrues primarily, if not solely, to those who secure these rights. But suppose we depart from the constant-returns postulate and consider a many-good economy that is described by economy-wide and generalized increasing returns; a larger production-exchange nexus ensures that the value of output produced per unit of input increases as the economy expands. In this case, all persons in the economy, and not only newly established owners of valued resources previously used as commons, will secure some indirect gain consequent on the expansion in the size of the economy that the value of the resource represents. Even if they secure no direct share in the ownership, and hence in the imputed value therefrom, persons will find that, in the larger economy that emerges as resources are more effectively utilized, input–output ratios move in their favour. There will exist a generalized interest in economic efficiency in the large – an interest which should translate ultimately into politically expressed support.

The whole exercise suggests that orthodox treatment of the whole set of related issues that can be brought under the tragedy of the commons dilemma, along with the efficiency gains promised by privatization, may have been flawed by an unquestioned adherence to the postulates of neoclassical economic theory. In this, as in other areas of current relevance and importance, modern economists need to examine some of the implications of these neoclassical postulates.[8] When and if they do so, they may find it necessary to rethink, and possibly to reconstruct, some of the foundations of their discipline.

NOTES

1. See Buchanan (1959) and (1962) for elaboration of the arguments.
2. See Hutt (1936).
3. See Knight (1924) for the classic analysis.
4. The indeterminacy here stems from the shift in the production frontier that privatization, and subsequent optimal usage of the now valued resource, represents. For a general discussion, even if on a somewhat different point, see Goetz and Buchanan (1971).
5. In this setting, the constant-returns postulate would seem to be 'innocuous' in the sense noted in Prescott and Mehra (1980, p. 1367).
6. Implicitly, I have assumed that a resource-using public sector does not exist. If public goods are collectively supplied and collectively financed, or if collective transfers are present, the results will be modified.
7. See Buchanan (1973) for an elaboration of this argument.
8. In my own case, it was my stubborn refusal to accept the neoclassical implications that the quantity of effort supplied by others exert no effect on my own welfare that eventually led me into the necessary abandonment of the constant-returns postulate. See Buchanan and Yoon (1995) which contains substantially all of the important contributions in the increasing-returns tradition, from Adam Smith through to modern theories of endogenous growth.

PART III

Constitutional Understanding

17.   The individual as participant in political exchange

An important element in James S. Coleman's scientific enterprise has been the derivation of collective organization and collective action from the rational-choice behaviour of individual decision makers. It is not therefore surprising that he was a contributor to *Public Choice* (Coleman, 1968) and an active participant in the Public Choice Society, when both the journal and the Society were in their infancy. In a very real sense, Coleman's was always a 'public choice' perspective, as this somewhat misnamed, and widely misunderstood, subdiscipline emerged into viability as a research programme.

On several occasions, I have suggested that a necessary component in the public choice perspective is a conception of politics as a complex exchange process in which individuals participate in some sense analogous to their participation in markets (Buchanan, 1983). I have compared and contrasted this exchange model of politics with (1) the pure conflict model and (2) the truth-judgement model. My concern has been to demonstrate the relative superiority of the exchange model, both for descriptive analyses of observed political reality and for any normative justification of government as political agency. I have not directed sufficient attention to explication of the several variants of the exchange model itself, which becomes the self-assigned objective for this chapter.

In the second section, I set out the two distinct 'exchanges' in which the individual may be presumed to participate in the role as a member of an organized polity. The third section describes in some detail the idealized operation of the voluntaristic exchange model and extends its potential applicability by shifting attention to the constitutional stage of interaction. The fourth section examines the second model – that of coerced or unequal Hobbesian 'exchange' between the monolithic sovereign and the individual citizen. The fifth section discusses the institutional marriage of the two exchange models in political regimes.

EXCHANGE *AMONG* INDIVIDUALS AND EXCHANGE *BETWEEN* THE INDIVIDUAL AND THE COLLECTIVITY

In its most abstracted formulation, political exchange takes place among all members of the set of individuals who share a common objective and who can secure this objective more effectively through joint rather than separate action. This setting describes the familiar public-goods model of interaction; individuals are conceived to be exchanging, one with another, shares in the costs of the joint undertaking. Note that, in this formulation, there is no 'state' or 'government', as such. Politics is limited to the cooperative activity that is involved in the joint *demand* for the commonly desired 'good', which is, presumably, 'purchased' directly from ordinary suppliers on a market.

The exchange involved here is complex because of the necessary inclusion of all participants who share in the demand enterprise. There is no possible factoring down of the exchange into a single-buyer/single-seller relationship. And, because of the nonexcludability characteristics of the 'good', all participants must be brought simultaneously into the contract. Bargaining among participants takes place along two dimensions – that which measures the relative shares in the costs of the good that is to be purchased and that which measures the quantity to be purchased.

In its idealized limits, this is a model of purely voluntary exchange – analogous in important respects to exchange in private goods markets, with the significant exception being the extension in the number of participants. The relevant exchange takes place among demanders; the derivative exchange between demanders (as a collective group or as a corporate actor) and some single supplying agent is treated as an ordinary market relationship, with the good that is purchased being supplied at a competitive price.

As some public-choice critics noted early, the political exchange model in orthodox public-goods analysis is exclusively limited to the demand side of the fiscal process and leaves out of account any organization of public-goods supply. In real-world politics, governments do, indeed, exist, and they can scarcely be modelled as passive transmitters of the preferences of citizens, who have presumably completed the trade-offs among themselves so as to arrive at some collective determination of cost shares and public goods quantity. As they are observed to function, governments *extract* tax payments from and *supply* goods and services to citizens; the transaction between each citizen, as taxpayer-beneficiary, and government would seem amenable to analysis in terms of 'political exchange' between government-as-supplier and the individual-as-demander, much as with the case of an ordinary exchange between the seller and the buyer in the market-place.

Such an 'exchange' is, however, quite different from either a market transaction in private goods or the idealized contractual agreement on cost shares in the pure public goods setting. A central characteristic of exchange is absent; the individual does not *voluntarily* participate in the fiscal exchange with government, at least in a sense that is analogous to ordinary market behaviour. The individual does not retain the relatively low-cost *exit* option that remains ever present in the market, nor does the individual retain the effective veto power that is present in the idealized Wicksellian contract for the demand of collectively purchased goods. In direct fiscal exchange, the government confronts the individual, as taxpayer, with a bill that he or she is required to pay, upon pain of penalty for failure. At the same time, the government supplies to the individual some flow of goods and services from which some benefits are enjoyed. But there is no individual behavioural adjustment available at relatively low cost – adjustment that can ensure that, at least at the margin, benefits are subjectively measured to be equal to costs. If such adjustment to the 'exchange' offered by the fisc were possible, the individual would, of course, accept the flow of services offered while at the same time withholding all payments. Voluntariness, in this sense, is clearly impossible in this transaction between the government and the individual.

The presence or absence of this central feature of exchange does not modify the formal definition of the conditions that must be met to ensure that the *results* of the overall or inclusive relationship between the individual and others in the political unit, including those who act in roles as governmental agents, are analogous to those that emerge in market exchange. And it may be useful here to specify precisely the idealized fiscal process in its entirety, if for no other reason than to suggest the incentive incompatibilities that must arise at some critical spots where persons confront choice alternatives.

Consider, then, a setting, where all members of a political community enter initially into a discussion-dialogue on the prospect for collective action directed towards the purchase of a good that is to be made available for consumption-usage by all persons simultaneously. An agreement is signified when and as each person, voluntarily, accepts an obligation to contribute a specified sum towards the joint costs in exchange with matching contributions specified for all other members of the group. The complex agreement describes the allocation of cost shares (tax prices) among persons as well as the quantity of the good that is to be purchased and subsequently made available.

Government then enters the calculus solely as an *agent* directed to implement the agreement that has been reached through the voluntary exchange among members. Acting as agent, for the collectivity of persons, government then confronts each citizen with a tax charge – the one that the member in question has agreed to pay – and then uses funds so collected to finance and to supply the collective-consumption good in precisely the quantity that had been earlier agreed to by all members.

Each individual attains an 'equilibrium' at which the assigned tax price per unit of good is equal to his or her relative marginal evaluation of the good, defined in some numeraire. In this sense, each person is in a position that is allocatively analogous to that attained by his or her own individualized behavioural adjustment in the market for a partitionable private good. But despite this formal equivalence in positions, note that the individual in the exchange with government-as-agent here is not faced with an incentive compatible structure, one that will be voluntarily sustained. The individual will find it rational to defect on the prior agreement; the individual will seek to become a free rider; the benefits of the nonexcludable public good will be available independently of the individual's own behaviour. Hence, the government-as-agent must be assigned powers of coercion; persons must be forced to contribute shares in the financing of the collectively consumed good, even if they have agreed to the terms of the more inclusive 'exchange'.

If, however, the government-as-agent is assigned powers of coercion over citizens in order to overcome the incentive incompatibility in citizens' behaviour, another potential incentive incompatibility emerges as government is allowed to depart from its role as idealized agent. It will be useful to specify precisely the form that the coercive charges levied by government must take, if government should strictly remain in the role of idealized agent. The government could not, in this role, be empowered to *tax* in any orthodox meaning of the term; it could not impose a coercive charge against any measurable base such as income, expenditure or use of particular goods. Each individual must be confronted with the tax price per unit of public good that he has agreed to pay in the inclusive contractual process. But since, by the nature of this charge, the individual cannot behaviourally adjust so as to modify his or her liability (per unit of public good), there is no direct negative feedback exerted on government when it departs from its idealized role, either by levying higher than agreed taxes or utilizing some share of funds collected to finance goods for agents' rather than citizens' benefits. Just as individual citizens have incentives to free ride in the absence of governmental coercion, government itself, through its agents, has incentives to depart from the terms of its own mandate by exploiting its coercive powers.

CONSTITUTIONAL EXTENSION OF THE MODEL OF EXCHANGE AMONG INDIVIDUALS

The procedural requirements that any pure model of voluntary fiscal exchange must meet in order to accomplish the defined purpose are indeed extreme. Unanimous agreement among all members of the polity must be reached on each and every component item in the budget. Each outlay must be treated separately in the collective decision calculus. Further, government must be established and assigned powers of coercion to enforce the agreed upon contractual terms, but means must be found to restrict government to these limits. Recognizing the immense practical difficulties of approximating such requirements, it is all too easy to reject the voluntary-exchange model out of hand, even as an ideal conceptualization of the relationship between the individual and the collectivity in which membership is claimed.

If, however, the exchange model is modified by shifting attention to the level of *constitutional* choice, essential elements may be retained, while moving some considerable distance towards plausibly recognizable institutional features of real-world politics. Suppose that the separate individual members of the political community acknowledge that the costs of attempting to reach agreement on each and every item of proposed collective outlay will be prohibitive. But suppose, further, that they also recognize that any assignment of coercive powers to government must be accompanied by restrictions or limits on the arbitrary usage of such powers. In this setting, agreement may be reached on a structure of collective decision making that will facilitate collective action while at the same time keeping the exercise of coercion in check (Buchanan and Tullock, 1962). In place of idealized agreement on each and every proposal to inaugurate joint action, a legislative body, periodically elected by voting, may be empowered to use majority voting rules to make spending and taxing decisions, provided that the degree of arbitrary discrimination in these decisions is limited by some appropriate criteria of generality. That is to say, legislative majorities may be authorized to impose taxes on all citizens, but only so long as taxes are levied on acceptable, and well-defined, criteria of generality. Supporters of legislative minorities cannot be singled out for discriminatory tax treatment, nor can supporters of majorities be discriminatorily favoured. Analogous constitutional criteria of generality may be applied to the distribution of benefits from goods and services that government is authorized to finance with tax funds, although this fully symmetrical application is much less familiar in observed fiscal systems.

The provisions that establish the whole structure, involving the voting franchise, the periodicity of elections, the voting rule among the electorate, the size of the legislative body, the bases of representation, the voting rule within the legislature itself, the veto powers of the executive, the range and scope of legislative powers, fiscal and nonfiscal and so on – these may be set out in a political constitution for the community. And *agreement*, or potential agreement, on the provisions in the constitution provides the ultimate legitimation for action taken within the terms of the structure that is described.

Note that this shift of idealized agreement to the constitutional level allows for very substantial departures from the procedural conditions described earlier as those necessary to bring any fiscal exchange into close analogy to market exchange. The process through which constitutional agreement is reached, conceptually, remains contractual, and remains in this sense 'political exchange', in which each individual trades off or exchanges his or her own interests with others. Each person or group accepts the potential constraints defined by the constitution in exchange for the like acceptance of comparable constraints by others in the community. But, acting strictly within the constitutional limits that may have been accepted, a legislative majority may impose tax charges upon an individual as means of financing outlay that the individual values much less than the private goods that might be purchased by the tax funds extracted. There need be little, if any, relationship here between the tax charges that are imposed coercively on an individual and the value that is placed by that individual on the flow of goods and services made available by the government. Almost every person in the polity will prefer a budgetary mix different from that which is provided, and, universally, each person will prefer a tax structure that involves lower charges against his or her own account. Further, there may exist substantial numbers of citizens who consider themselves to be net losers in the complex fiscal exchange process which includes the whole taxing-spending package; they may value the total flow of benefits from public goods and services lower than the value of taxes extracted.

The limits on such fiscal exploitation rest in the constitutionally dictated electoral processes. A government, acting through the constitutionally authorized legislative majority, is subject to electoral replacement in whole or in part if its combined package of outlays and taxes gets too far beyond the limits dictated by the ultimate preferences of a majority of citizens in the polity. But such limits are broad indeed, so much so that the conceptualization of the fiscal process in the exchange metaphor may be called into question.

There are two difficulties with the exchange or contractual model of politics that must be acknowledged, even at the level of abstract analytical discourse. The first invokes the familiar and long-standing criticism of any contract theory of the state. Individuals find themselves born into membership in an ongoing political structure, with a well-defined set of constitutional rules. They have never participated in any process from which general agreement on the set of constitutional rules in existence might have emerged. In this situation, which is acknowledged to be descriptive of empirical reality, how can the individual's acquiescence in the constraints of politics be meaningfully discussed as an element of an 'exchange' with others?

At this point, those who defend contractual or exchange models find it useful to introduce conceptual as opposed to actual agreement as a device for retaining some explanatory value. The exercise becomes one of potential legitimation of existing constitutional structures rather than one of the historical explanation. Could the existing rules that define the overall operations of the polity have been agreed upon by all citizens if, indeed, there could have been some imagined initial dialogue? At this point, the potential conflict among the separate interests of persons and groups is mitigated by resort to constructions that introduce a veil of ignorance or uncertainty.

Even if this major criticism of the exchange or contract model of politics is somehow countered, there remains a second difficulty, related to the incentive incompatibility previously noted. In a large-number polity, individuals will have little or no incentive to become informed about relevant choice alternatives or even to participate actively in any discussion leading to ultimate agreement upon the general constitutional rules that define the constraints upon their actions, either privately or publicly. That is to say, it remains fully rational and in their own interest for persons to remain disinterested in such processes, and this disinterestedness, in turn, offers the opportunity for exploitation by potential political entrepreneurs who seek to exploit emotion-based prejudices, as opposed to reasoned expressions of interests (Brennan and Buchanan, 1984; Buchanan and Vanberg, 1989).

'EXCHANGE' BETWEEN THE INDIVIDUAL AND THE SOVEREIGN

Recognition of the attenuated nature of any exchange model derived directly from the democratic-contractual setting, even as extended to the constitutional as opposed to the within constitutional level of political action, prompts attention to the alternative conceptualization noted earlier; that in which the basic model becomes one in which there is a two-party relationship between the citizen and the government (state or sovereign). This model can also be interpreted in exchange terms, although in a sense that sharply contrasts to that examined in the democratic setting previously discussed.

The setting for the second model presumes some prior existence, or the initial emergence of, a putative sovereign entity which confronts the individual (any individual, every individual) with the ultimate 'choice': pay tribute in 'exchange' for the protection and security of person and property offered, along with whatever other goods and services the sovereign chooses to make available. This fundamental Hobbesian challenge is nonvoluntary, in any other than a purely semantic sense, and it is equivalent to the highwayman's offer: 'your money or your life'. And, of course, this sort of exchange takes familiar nonpolitical form in the various mafia-like protective rackets operated by organized criminal syndicates.

Historically, this model for political 'exchange' may well be more descriptive than any version of the democratic, contractual model, which involves the agreement of citizens on the rules under which they will live politically. Most states, or governments, emerge from conquest and coercion; rarely have constitutions emerged from general contractual process. But note that, in the noncontractual model for governance, for the individual's relation to the state, the source of the legitimacy of coercion becomes quite different from that which characterizes the voluntary-exchange, and participatory, model earlier described. In the basic Hobbesian contract between the individual and the sovereign, the exercise of coercion by the latter is legitimate only to the extent that the value of the security (and other services) thereby guaranteed exceeds the value of the resources extracted from the individual. The government, as the sovereign agency, is armed with the exclusive monopoly of coercive force, and it makes no pretence of offering to the individual that bundle of goods and services that most closely correspond to the latter's preferences, analogously to the response of producers-suppliers of goods in the market place.

The 'political exchange' involved here is unequal in two separate respects, making it categorically different from exchange among persons in competitively organized markets for private partitionable goods. The sovereign is a monopolist and possesses, thereby, power to set 'price' on its own terms. Secondly, the sovereign also exercises monopoly control over the good, or bundle of goods, that the individual 'purchases'. The government can supply the bundle of goods and services along with the prices charged for this bundle in accordance with its own objectives, which may or may not include explicit concern for the satisfaction of individuals' preferences for public goods. To the extent that the government seeks to enhance the value base upon which it can levy claims, that is, so long as the sovereign acts as a residual claimant of economic value in the system, it will be motivated to tax and to spend in such fashion as to ensure that measured economic growth will take place. An 'efficient' sovereign, in this sense, may place a greater emphasis on growth enhancing public goods and on growth promoting taxation than the preferences of citizens would dictate.

Whether or not the sovereign will act in this way will depend, in part, upon the effective time-horizon that guides its action. Because of its monopoly position, the sovereign has available for exploitation the whole resource base of the political economy. But uncertainty about the length of its own tenure, as sovereign, may provide the motivation for an inefficient drawdown, or mining, of the value potential in the economy.

INSTITUTIONAL MARRIAGE: THE SOVEREIGN WITHIN ELECTORAL AND CONSTITUTIONAL CONSTRAINTS

The two models of 'political exchange' that have been discussed embody categorically different relationships between the individual citizen and political authority. In its idealized limiting case, there is no independently motivated sovereign in the first model. Such authority exists exclusively for the purpose of carrying out the expressed objectives of citizens, particularly the joint consumption of public goods. In the second model, by dramatic contrast, the political authority, as an independently existent 'person', or association, finds its own expected utility enhanced by specializing in the supply of services which it 'sells', monopolistically, to the citizens as demanders-users.

Analytical models are, of course, constructed with the aim of imposing some sort of intellectual order on complex reality, and widely different models carry with them differing perspectives on the reality subject to observation. It is not at all surprising, therefore, that any empirical description of political institutions would, in most cases, identify features of each model. In a sense, it is necessary that individuals in most political settings must live with the continuing tensions created by the conflicts imposed by the two 'exchange' relationships. This result applies to individuals in their roles as citizens who, on the one hand, participate in electoral processes and in constitutional dialogue and, on the other hand, face the monolithic and coercive agency of government. But, the result also applies to those persons who find themselves in roles of political agent, who are constrained, through electoral feedback mechanisms, to satisfy the preferences of citizens, but who, at the same time, face opportunities to further their own agendas.

Differing political structures reflect differing weightings of the two models, as reflective of the relationships sensed by individuals. Concentrated authoritarian regimes may be almost totally described by the second model, in which the individual, as citizen, faces unequal exchange with the monopolistic sovereign which, itself, remains unconstrained by either electoral or constitutional feedbacks. Romania before 1989 offers the polar case. Regimes described as parliamentary and majoritarian move considerably along the spectrum towards the participatory-voluntaristic pole. But the individual-as-citizen remains subject to the dictates of the parliamentary majority in office, subject only to the prospect of removal through electoral processes. The market analogue to parliamentary majoritarianism is that of the monopolist franchisee, who holds a franchise (for example, cable television) subject to periodic renewal. The constitutional democracy, along the lines of the US structure, shifts the weights somewhat further toward the voluntaristic model of political exchange, while remaining some distance from the ideal. Legislative majorities are constrained both by electoral feedbacks and by explicitly constitutional restrictions, and majorities reflect some bargained vector of interests which may shift as among separate policy issues. Majorities do not 'govern' in the parliamentary sense, and, because they do not, there is a somewhat greater sense of direct participation by citizens in political process. At the same time, there is a loss of the possible consistency in ordering that comes with the replacement of the monolithic, if constrained, Hobbesian sovereign.

It is not within my purview to join the debates among political scientists concerning the relative strengths and weaknesses of parliamentary and nonparliamentary political regimes. But the thrust of my argument is clear. In any and all political regimes there is a sense in which the individual citizen, *qua* individual, feels locked into the unequal and bilateral 'exchange' with the monopolistic sovereign, essentially the second of the models discussed above. To the extent that institutional-constitutional structures shift the weighting so that the individual senses governmental responsiveness to his or her expressed preferences, there must exist a greater acceptance of shared responsibility for political outcomes, no matter how such outcomes may be assessed externally.[1]

Hence, the 'political exchange' that matters, in any normatively meaningful sense remains the first model discussed, even if the location of consent of agreement must be shifted almost exclusively to the constitutional level, and even if the individual fully acknowledges the strict irrationality of rational inquiry and discourse. In realpolitik, the Hobbesian sovereign always exists, but we tolerate its incursions if we know that we share in the construction of the constraints that limits its behaviour.

CONCLUSION

By necessity, the individual in a democracy participates simultaneously in the two political exchanges isolated for discussion in this chapter. On the one hand, there is the idealized exchange among equals derivative from the universality of the electoral franchise, which may find expression in consensual support for the constitutional structure that constrains the activity of agents who act on behalf of the collective unit. On the other hand, and in contrast, there is the exchange between unequals, which materializes in the continuing and unavoidable confrontation between the individual and the collective unit. Note that the first of these 'exchange' relationships may remain below the individual's level of conscious evaluation; the second 'exchange' is, by comparison, brought into the individual's explicit attention span by the simple necessity to pay taxes. The selfsame person who 'agrees', implicitly or explicitly, with fellow citizens in consensual support for the basic rules of political order may, in accordance with the dictates of rational interest, seek to subvert these rules as a player in the two-party game with the sovereign collective. The tensions created by the requirement that the individual act in these two roles provide the source of the fundamental political dilemma.

A final note: I have limited discussion in this chapter to the two relationships of exchange in politics. It is obvious that the same duality exists in the structure of any large organization. The individual, as a participant in the collective, trades off interests with others in the attempted achievement of jointly shared objectives. At the same time, the individual, as subject to the constraints internal to the collective, bargains with the collective, as a unit, in attempts to further his or her particularized interests.

NOTE

1. Robert Nozick's clever 'Tale of the Slave' obscures the relevant distinction here. The individual who participates, as one voter in a large-number electoral process, may be subject to the external dictates of the collective unit, and, objectively, his position need be no different from the slave subject to the dictates of the master. But the two situations may be dramatically different to the individual, and this difference may exert behavioural effects. See Robert Nozick (1974).

18. Democracy within constitutional limits

It is not easy for Western political economists either to understand post-revolutionary developments in the former socialist countries or to proffer meaningful normative advice. The histories of these societies must evolve spontaneously, even if necessity dictates a dramatic compression of the time-scale, at least in any comparative sense. At best, political economists who are external to the process can isolate and identify features of Western institutions that may be worth noting, and especially in a precautionary fashion, by those who may find themselves in positions to make critical choices during the institution-building phases of transition.

In this chapter, I shall draw largely upon my own country, the United States, as a source for identifying elements of current political structure that reflects departures from the normative standards that were both expressed in our founding documents and embodied in our political history for a significantly long period. It is not an exaggeration to say that we have now, in the United States, lost our constitutional way. We have lost our generalized understanding of the relationship between the two normative objectives: political equality among citizens, summarized under the rubric democracy, and the liberty or independence of each citizen from the coercion of the state – an objective that was presumably to be achieved by constitutional constraints on governmental authority. The American structure as initially imagined, and to a surprising extent realized over long periods of our history, was accurately described as a *constitutional democracy*. And I emphasize that both words are important, with *constitutional* taking precedence over *democracy*, if, indeed, any such ordering is desired. Unfortunately, it is the constitutional understanding that has been largely lost from public consciousness, with consequences for all to see.

Citizens in the former socialist countries live now in the post-revolutionary moment during which there may exist opportunities to design and construct elements of political-economic orders that, once emplaced, will prove difficult to reform. The urge towards democratization is surely easy to understand, and the association between nondemocratic political structures and the suppression of individual liberties leads perhaps naturally to a neglect of the potential democratic danger to individual autonomy. The institutionalization of democratic procedures of governance may produce consequences desired by no one unless these procedures are limited by constitutional boundaries.

In the second section of this chapter, I shall discuss the relationships between political democracy and the market economy, both of which are nominally listed as objectives for post-revolutionary institutional reforms in the countries that were previously organized on socialist principles. In the third section, I shall summarize briefly the distinction between constitutional politics and ordinary politics, and I shall discuss the relevance of this distinction for the viability of a market economy and, indirectly, for a liberal society. In the fourth section, I shall sketch out the operation of a politics within rules, and, in the fifth section, I follow this sketch by outlining specific implications for areas of policy. The final section presents a general statement of position.

DEMOCRACY AND THE MARKET

Reformers in the countries that were classified as socialist prior to the revolutions of 1989–91 are as one in their stated twin objectives: (1) political reorganization towards introducing democracy and (2) economic reorganization towards introducing a market economy. (China, whose authoritarian leaders crushed its incipient revolution, is identified by its difference here. China seeks to shift towards economic organization based in part on market principles while putting down pressures towards democratization of its political structure.) As regards the reform leaders in the societies of Eastern and Central Europe and the republics of the former Soviet Union, it is, I think, appropriate to ask whether or not the relationships between political democracy and a market economy are well understood.

It is, of course, easy to understand why the historical experiences under the totalitarian rule of the Communist Party have generated urges towards democratic reform in politics and economic reform towards markets. Individuals seek to be able to exercise political voice, to sense that they, individually, can at least share in the decisions that shape their own lives. At the same time, and for different reasons, individuals simply observe the economic failure of attempted command-control institutions to produce economic value. The system did not deliver the goods, as measured by the size, quality and content of the bundle ultimately desired, and furthermore the bundle was not growing larger over time.

But do the political reformers, both those who have attained positions of authority and those who might aspire to authority under fledgling democratic procedures, understand that the necessary conditions for the effective functioning of a market economy require that the range and scope of democratic authority be limited? At one level of discourse, there seems to be near universal acknowledgement that private or several ownership of productive resources must be substituted for collective or state ownership-control. But the secure ownership that is required for viability of an economy implies protection of holdings against political takings, including takings that may be orchestrated through the auspices of democratic politics. Almost by definition, a market economy both requires and itself facilitates a restricted range for the operation of government, independently of whether or not the actions of government are subject to the indirect controls of democratic politics. Indeed, I would suggest that this political function of the market economy is, in some evaluative sense, more important than the economic function, as measured by the size of the bundle of valued goods generated.

Properly understood, therefore, the revolutions were, and are, directed toward the devolution or decentralization of political authority, or depoliticization, which only a market organization of the economy makes possible, and, further, only within which genuinely democratic processes of decision can attain some semblance of meaning. The organizational-institutional implications of such an understanding are clear: the range and scope for political authority must be restricted, preferably by constitutional constraints that may be strategically introduced during the post-revolutionary moment and before particularized interests emerge. Explicit constitutional limits on the intrusion of politics into the market have the further advantage of providing expectational stability for persons and groups, internal and external, who might make long-term investments.

CONSTITUTIONAL POLITICS AND ORDINARY POLITICS

On many occasions, I have emphasized the necessity for a constitutional understanding, by which I mean an appreciation for and an understanding of the two stages or levels of political decision making that must describe the functioning of any political order that can claim either legitimacy or tolerable efficiency. There is, first, the design, construction, implementation and maintenance of the basic rules, the fundamental law, the constitution, that defines the parameters within which what we may call ordinary politics is to take place. And there is, second, the operation of such ordinary politics within these rules, so defined.

In some ultimate descriptive sense, there must always exist such a two-stage, or even perhaps a multi-stage characterization of politics as it is actually observed. But the explicit recognition of the distinction, and, more importantly, of the operational implications, is often neglected, with the result that ordinary politics is allowed to proceed as if there are no limits. It is critically important that the logic of the distinction between the stages informs thinking about politics, both during moments of constitutional choice and in the post-constitutional periods described by the workings of ordinary politics.

There are, literally, hundreds of familiar nonpolitical analogues to the two-stage structure of politics emphasized here and elsewhere. Consider word processing. The user must first choose a software programme and, second, choose what to write within the constraints imposed by the programme. Or, consider the purchase of any durable good, say, an automobile. The capacities of the car limit to some extent the activities that may be performed in using it. Or, consider planting a fruit tree, where the initial choice is among an apple, peach, plum or pear tree. Once this choice is made, it necessarily constrains the activities involved in cultivation, and also the type of output to be expected. For economists, the Marshallian distinction between the long-run choice of a fixed facility or plant and the short-run choice concerning the level of operation of the plant, as given, is familiar, and this distinction is directly analogous to the constitutional choice-ordinary politics choice introduced here.

Constitutional politics involves setting the rules, selecting the parametric framework within which ordinary political decisions are to be made and carried out. Such politics defines the manner of selecting those who seek to govern others, the extent of the voting franchise, the timing and procedures for elections, the voting rules, the terms for eligibility for office, methods of representation and many other procedural details that are necessary for democratic processes to operate at all. These constitutional parameters for democracy will be almost universally acknowledged to be both necessary and to differ in kind from the objects upon which ordinary politics operates, even in those settings where there exists no explicit constitution, as such. But the extension of constitutional parameters to include more than these formal procedures for governance must also be recognized to be important for ensuring stability of expectations. The range over which governments are allowed to act, even governments that are procedurally legitimate in the democratic features listed above, must be known, at least in terms of well-defined boundaries beyond which political intrusion shall not extend. Such constitutional limits may lay out protected spheres for personal liberties, as in bills of rights, and also for economic liberties, without which any market order remains highly vulnerable to piecemeal interferences generated by interest-motivated coalitions.

A domain for the exercise of constitutional politics may be described, but the existence of limits does not, itself, imply that there is little or no room left for the play of ordinary politics, the spaces within which the activities of governments, as we know them, may be observed. Clearly, governments may do many things, whether these qualify as good or bad by any criterion, that are within the constraints defined in almost any constitutional structure. But it is folly to think that governmental activities are appropriately constrained only by the feedbacks on voter attitudes that the formal procedures of democracy make possible.

POLITICS WITHIN RULES

Politics, as we observe it and talk about it, is, therefore, strictly a politics within rules or, in the reductionist classification of the preceding section, strictly ordinary politics. A well-functioning polity will, indeed, be described by stability in its basic constitutional structure, which translates into an absence of activity aimed towards continual constitutional change and discussion of such change. But the politics within rules that describe the well-functioning polity operates effectively only if the rules are themselves both understood and respected. A politics that seems to proceed as if a constraining set of rules does not and should not exist must fail in several dimensions. An imperialistic ordinary politics ensures the removal of stability-predictability from the whole political-legal-economic order and thereby guarantees both economic stagnation and the loss of individual liberties.

To suggest that the constraints on the operation of ordinary politics that are embodied in a constitution, whether these constraints be formal or informal, whether they emerge through an evolutionary process or as a result of deliberative design, are not subject to continual change does not, of course, imply that genuine constitutional politics, the politics involved in changing the basic rules, is out of bounds for discussion or that genuine constitutional reform is taboo. The suggestion is only that constitutional rules should be treated as 'relatively absolute absolutes' by any comparison with the operation of within-rule politics and that these rules, if changed, be considered to be quasi-permanent, and that they be analysed as if they are and must become elements in genuine political capital (Buchanan, 1989). Politics loses meaning if every moment becomes constitutional in the sense that efforts are made to modify the basic structural parameters of the system. Genuinely constitutional moments are identified in part by their singularity, by their extraordinary presence, by their intrusion of sorts into the ongoing compromises of conflicting interests that describe and define ordinary political experience.

Democratization may be introduced with reference either to constitutional or to ordinary politics, but it is essential that the domains be understood to be separate and apart. Democracy, defined as ultimate equality of influence over collectively determined results, may characterize procedures through which, at some appropriate moment, the structural parameters are chosen. On the other hand, and by contrast, these parameters may be imposed nondemocratically, for example, the MacArthur constitution for modern Japan. But independently of how the rules are themselves selected, these rules themselves may or may not provide for ordinary politics to operate democratically in the standard meaning. The rules may dictate that, within the boundaries specified in the constitution, individual citizens are guaranteed the exercise of equal ultimate influence over particular outcomes, with modern Japan again offering an example.

It is important to note, however, and as the discussion should have made clear, that there are limits to any democratization of constitutional politics imposed by the necessary quasi-permanence of the rules. If the parameters of structure are to remain in place over a sequence of periods during which the processes of ordinary politics are expected to take place, it is necessary that citizens, acting politically in any arbitrarily chosen period, cannot expect to exercise an influence comparable to that exercised in the ordinary politics that is bound within the existing constitutional rules. In a very real sense, the electorate for an effectively democratic constitutional politics must include participants over the course of many periods. Political equality may be retained as a normative democratic ideal, but individuals must reckon that the influences exerted spill over through time periods as well as among participants within any time period. That is to say, the set of participants who may claim idealized equality of influence is larger, in a temporal dimension, in constitutional than in ordinary politics.

CONSTITUTIONAL MISUNDERSTANDING: EXAMPLES FROM MODERN UNITED STATES

In the introduction, I stated that the United States has lost its constitutional way, that constitutional understanding has been allowed to slip from public consciousness and that modern experiences drawn from the United States may usefully serve as precautionary warnings to those who are actively engaged in constitutional design for countries that remain in a formative moment. In order to support this claim, it is necessary for me to summarize very briefly elements of the constitutional history of the American republic.

In James Madison's grand design, the central or federal government of the United States exercised extremely limited authority, but within such authority its sovereignty was unchallengeable. The separate state governments were not to restrict the free flow of commerce over the inclusive territory; the extensive internal market was to remain open, allowing for full exploitation of the specialization of labour, producing advantages that became relatively more important as technology developed. Because of this guarantee of a large internal open market, there was relatively little need for explicit and extensive constitutional constraints on the domain for ordinary politics of the several state governments. The competition, both actual and potential, among these several units within the large open market acted to ensure that any excesses of ordinary politics, motivated by coalitions of conflicting interests, be kept within reasonable bounds. The competitive politics of a viable federalism can substitute for the explicit constitutional politics that would be necessary in a unitary polity. (This is a simple principle that the nations of the European Community should learn and act upon. Unfortunately, the constitutional moment during which a viable federal structure might have seemed possible may already have been missed [Buchanan, 1990b]).

Madison and his peers overlooked the requirement for constitutional guarantees for openness in the external market, that is as between domestic and foreign traders. The central government was empowered to regulate external commerce, and the absence of explicit constraints allowed the ordinary politics of interest to generate welfare-reducing and regionally discriminatory restrictions on trade. These observable excesses of ordinary politics were at least in part responsible for the intense interregional conflict that provided the origins for the bloody Civil War in the mid-nineteenth century. And the outcome of this war itself ensured that the effective federalized structure of American governance would, over time, disappear. Over the course of a century, the central government, without any threat of secession on the part of states, predictably assumed increasing authority, with the result that the modern United States is, basically, unitary in a descriptive sense. The central government is overwhelmingly dominant in any and all potential conflicts with the states.

This change in political structure was not accompanied by any recognition that the demise of the competitive politics as among the several states should have dictated the imposition of additional constitutional constraints on the powers of the central government, over and beyond those that Madison thought to be necessary at its formation. As the operation of the internal market of the United States came increasingly under the regulatory control of the ordinary politics of the single central government, there was no effective constitutional barrier to the intrusive interferences with the workings of the market, either internal or external. And the intrusion, once commenced, took on a dynamic of its own. Those interests that were successful in securing the artificially created profits or rents from politicized protection became attractors for other interests seeking, and getting, similar treatment. There were parallel extensions through the emergence of the transfer sector. The financing of genuinely collective functions from revenues raised from broad-based and general taxes was supplemented and expanded to include the financing of transfers, in money and in kind, to designated recipient groups, and taxes were deliberatively modified to ensure nongenerality in liability.

Many of these changes might have been tolerated without major damage to the constitutional fabric if they could have been considered as quasi-permanent. But, instead, the whole expenditure-tax structure in the modern United States has been allowed to become the primary object for the machinations of ordinary politics. The fiscal system is not treated as a part of the framework within which the decisions of participants in the market sector are made. The whole budgetary process reflects little more than the continuing compromises of the conflicting interests through ordinary politics. Everything seems up for grabs, and each legislative period is marked by proposed revisions in what should be structural parameters for the economy. Modern American political leaders, regardless of party, have no understanding at all of the need for, and the potential benefits from, stability in the rules, as applied to the whole of the regulatory-fiscal framework. The quasi-stagnation of the American economy in the 1990s is directly attributable to the failure of political and intellectual leaders to recognize that a more limited politics, as reflected in stability in rules, can be a more productive politics, if productivity is measured either in economic growth or in the liberties of citizens.

CONCLUSION

The US constitutional experience must be avoided if the emerging democracies and market economies are to have reasonable prospects for success, especially with the past and recent history of the failed socialist experiments. It is critically important that the private property rights, as, if and when established, be guaranteed against politicized takings, whether in the form of direct seizure, the imposition of particularized punitive legislation or indirect and onerous burdens of taxation. It is imperative that the constitutions for the formerly socialist countries contain the guarantees for procedural democracy (elections, franchise and so on) for personal liberties (speech, press, religion and so on) and for protections against politicized (even if democratic) invasions of private property rights. Because of the historical memories of the politicized economy, property owners can be assured on the last point only by a specific constitutional listing of the allowed scope and range for the workings of ordinary democratic politics. The public goods that are to be financed by taxes must be specified, along with the basic structure of taxes to be used. A fiscal constitution is an essential element in any constitutional democracy, but it is more important in a setting where the distrust of ordinary politics and politicians is deeply imbedded in the psyche of citizens.

I am not so naive as to predict that any of the countries facing the constitutional moment of the 1990s will meet the ideal standards that I might suggest. Without a heritage of experience that embodies some understanding of the central logic of effective constitutionalism, any implementation of constitutional democracy will be difficult to achieve. But the logic remains, as does the tremendous and unique opportunity. The logic is simple, however, and appropriate leadership can influence public attitudes and opinions. And, once again, the force of potential competition cannot be overlooked. If only one of the countries in question should achieve the reforms required for a leap into genuine constitutional democracy, the exemplar offered to other countries in this age of instantaneous communication would almost guarantee generalization to other settings.

19.   Property, politics and liberty[1]

The classical, and familiar, defence of a regime of private property as originally articulated by Aristotle, which concentrates attention on the role of incentives to use and care for holdings, may be supplemented (perhaps supplanted) by a quite different defence – one that concentrates attention on *liberty*. To the extent that a person genuinely owns property, in the legally protected sense, such a person is independent from the control of other persons, separately or collectively. And independence, or liberty, is valued, as such, and quite apart from any instrumental relationship with other objectives, including the generation of economic value.

I first introduce lengthy citations from what may seem a surprising source, but which do serve to offer support for the position to be developed. Following these citations, a bit of conjectural history presents the argument in its simplest form. This is followed, in section four, by an emphasis on the importance of private ownership of personal capacities. The inquiry is then extended in section five to nonhuman assets, and I examine the notion of self-production in relation to the demand for consumer goods. In section six, the analysis proceeds to temporal aspects of private ownership and then to financial assets and inflation in section seven. I conclude the chapter with a brief summary of the implications for social organization.

Much of the argument will be familiar, especially to persons who have actually experienced life in a political regime in which private property rights were severely restricted. In this sense, the whole argument may seem to be a trituration of the obvious. Nonetheless, it may be useful to draw out the foundational logic of the property-liberty relationship.

RERUM NOVARUM

An encyclical was issued under the auspices of Pope Leo XIII in 1893 – an encyclical that is widely known by its Latin title, *Rerum Novarum* (1893, [1939]). The author(s) of the passages cited below did not base the central criticism of socialism, and the explicit defence of private property, on an understanding of the classical efficiency-incentive argument of Aristotle and those who followed him. Nor is there any clear indication that they even understood elementary economic theory. But the reasoning does reflect a clear appreciation of the critical relationship between the rights of persons to acquire and to hold property separately and individually and their liberty to live as independent human beings.

The citations are from the early pages of the encyclical. The relevant page numbers are noted.

> the *Socialists*, working on the poor man's envy of the rich, endeavour to destroy private property, and maintain that individual possessions should become the common property of all, to be administered by the State or by municipal bodies. They hold that, by thus transferring property from private persons to the community, the present evil state of things will be set to rights, because each citizen will then have his equal share of whatever there is to enjoy. But their proposals are so clearly futile for all practical purposes, that if they were carried out the working man himself would be among the first to suffer. Moreover they are emphatically unjust, because they rob the lawful possessor, bring the State into a sphere that is not its own, and cause complete confusion in the community.

Private Ownership

> It is surely undeniable that, when a man engages in remunerative labour, the very reason and motive of his work is to obtain property, and to hold it as his own private possession. If one man hires out to another his strength or his energy, he does this for the purpose of receiving in return what is necessary for food and living; he thereby expressly proposes to acquire a full and real right, not only to the remuneration, but also to the disposal of that remuneration as he pleases. Thus, if he lives sparingly, saves money, and invests his savings, for greater security, in land, the land in such a case is only his wages in another form; and, consequently, a working man's little estate thus purchased should be as completely at his own disposal as the wages he receives for his labour. But it is precisely in this power of disposal that ownership consists, whether the property be land or movable goods. The *Socialists*, therefore in endeavouring to transfer the possessions of individuals to the community, strike at the interests of every wage earner, for they deprive him of the liberty of disposing of his wages, and thus of all hope and possibility of increasing his stock and of bettering his condition in life. . . .
>
> . . . it must be within his (man's) right to have things not merely for temporary and momentary use, as other living beings have them, but in stable and permanent possession; he must have not only things that perish in the using, but also those that, though used, remain for use in the future. . . .
>
> And to say that God has given the earth to the use and enjoyment of the universal human race is not to deny that there can be private property. For God has granted the earth to mankind in general; not in the sense that all without distinction can deal with it as they please, but rather that no part of it has been assigned to any one in particular, and that the limits of private possession have been left to be fixed by man's own industry and the laws of individual peoples. . . .
>
> We are told that it is right for private persons to have the use of the soil and the fruits of their land, but that it is unjust for anyone to possess as owner either the land on which he has built or the estate which he has cultivated. But those who assert this do

not perceive that they are robbing man of what his own labour has produced, for the soil which is tilled and cultivated with toil and skill utterly changes its condition; it was wild before, it is now fruitful; it was barren, now it brings forth in abundance. That which has thus altered and improved it becomes so truly a part of itself as to be in a great measure indistinguishable, inseparable from it. Is it just that the fruit of man's sweat and labour should be enjoyed by another? (pp. 2–4)

The empirical proposition in these passages is that persons desire ownership of property in order to secure and maintain liberty over the disposal of resources, without which liberty there could be no hope of bettering the conditions of life.

Note that the hope for betterment is individualized. The individual may, if secure in a regime that allows the acquisition of property, along with the maintenance and increase in value through time, *on his own account*, better his condition, and quite independently of any complementary collective action, beyond that minimally required for the functioning of a legal order. Note that these passages provide no consideration at all for the prospect that the betterment of the working man's condition may be achieved through collective or community ownership.

A STYLIZED EXAMPLE

Let me now introduce the argument through a simple imaginary example. Consider a community of peasant farmers who live and work on the land. There are two basic ownership arrangements. The land may be common property, or the land may be subdivided and separately assigned to farmers, each of whom controls the use of an assigned holding. Initially, let me assume away the incentive effect differences between these two arrangements. Assume that farmers work and maintain common property in the same way they work and maintain assigned private plots. Hence, in straightforward efficiency comparisons, there is no difference between the two regimes.

But let us look at the dependence relationships in the two settings. Under common ownership, each person remains maximally dependent on the actions of every other person in the community. By dramatic contrast, under private or separable ownership, each person is maximally independent of the behaviour of others. If the aggregate value of product is identical under the two regimes, any person, if allowed the choice at some constitutional stage, would surely prefer the setting that allows for greater independence.

Suppose, however, that there are advantages of specialization. Suppose that, even in the regime of private ownership, farmers in the community can secure more value by specializing in production followed by trade with others who are differently specialized. Does not any such shift from a stylized setting of self-sufficiency towards a network of specialization and market exchange reintroduce dependence akin to that which is present under full collective ownership?

Consider a specific example. Under full self-sufficiency each farmer produces his own requirements for two goods – potatoes and pigs. But each farmer in the community can get more of both goods by specialization and trade. So some farmers specialize in potatoes and others specialize in pigs. Each farmer becomes dependent on the 'blind forces of the market'.

What is the advantage of private property in a complex market order? Participants are dependent on the market, even if not on particularly defined persons. The simple example here is helpful in suggesting that the ownership of land, upon which each farmer may produce either potatoes or pigs, offers a protective benchmark of independence. If, having specialized in the production of potatoes for sale, a farmer then finds that the market has collapsed, he can, if necessary, resort to the production of his own pigs – a step that would be impossible in the absence of private ownership of the basic resource. Total dependence of the market is mitigated to the extent that there exists a self-production backup.

PROPERTY IN PERSON

A person is in private ownership of a productive asset if he or she controls the usage of that asset, and control here implies both the right to exclude others from access and usage and the right to dispose of the asset as desired. We can refer to private ownership in person, in the individual's own capacities to produce economic value. Such property-in-person exists when the individual is at liberty to choose when to submit to the direction of others concerning the use of his or her own labour services and when there exists also freedom to choose among locations, occupations and professions, both as offered by the market and as potentially created by the individual's own entrepreneurial initiative. A person is a 'wage slave' only if there is only one demander for services, and if entry into other relationships is somehow prevented. Freedom of entry is especially important here, not only because it offers the individual options for choice, but also because, with free entry extended to all persons in the nexus, any single person is insured against undue exploitation. If a person can make a contribution to economic value in excess of a wage being offered by an employer, there arises an opportunity for some other employer to enter the market and secure differential gains.

To the extent that the market order works effectively, the individual participant confronts multiple choice options in all markets, both for goods and for resource inputs, thereby reducing, and, in the limit, eliminating dependence on others. But the market order, in turn, only works effectively if all persons are, indeed, private owners of their own personal productive capacities, including the rights to enter and exit any relationship with potential trading partners.

PRIVATE OWNERSHIP OF NONHUMAN ASSETS

The simple example introduced earlier is misleading if it is interpreted to suggest that a regime in which all persons (families) might be assigned private-ownership rights in land is a possibility in the complex urbanized modern economy. If interpreted differently, however, the example need not be misleading at all. It may be taken to suggest that *any* productive asset, under private ownership, allows the owner to self-produce the services of that asset thereby securing independence from the market.

In a setting that would appeal only to economists, we could imagine an individual who owns absolutely nothing beyond his or her own person. Such an individual would enter the market and purchase all services directly: a house or flat with its furnishings would be leased or rented, an automobile would be leased or taxicabs and public transport used as needed. Simple observation suggests, however, that almost all persons prefer ownership of many assets that yield valued services, and that they become owners when circumstances permit. Houses and automobiles are owned outright rather than leased. How do we explain this preference, which seems almost universal?

Consider private ownership of a house. As the owner of this asset that yields services over time, the individual is producing these particular services for himself or herself. To the extent that such self-production is made possible, the owner is insulated from direct dependence on the market. In the equity ownership of a house, the requirement to enter the market for housing services is reduced, just as is the case of the farmer who, if necessary, can use his land to produce pigs.

Consumer durables (houses, furnishings, automobiles) provide means through which persons increase their liberties – increases that would not be possible under a regime that precludes private ownership. This important feature of private property is absent from the classical argument, but it may well be more important in public attitudes.

PRIVATE PROPERTY AND TIME

To this point, I have neglected the temporal aspects of private property ownership – aspects that are emphasized in the earlier citations from the papal encyclical. But it is clear that, if persons are to be able to adjust flows of income and outlay to some preferred temporal pattern, and to do so on their own account and without collective action, there must exist some institution that allows partitionable claims to value that extend beyond a current period. Ownership of human capital, in the sense discussed earlier, will go some distance towards satisfying this requirement, but private ownership of nonhuman assets is a necessary supplement.

My concern is not with the macroeconomic results that may stem from the relationship between private ownership and aggregate rates of capital accumulation in an economy. Again let me note that my interest is exclusively in the relationship between private property ownership and human liberty.

As suggested earlier, property ownership offers the individual the opportunity to withdraw, wholly or partially, from the market nexus. An owner of a productive asset may, if desired, increase current period expenditures over and beyond current income receipts; a share in capital value may be 'eaten up'. Or, conversely, an income earner may reduce current period expenditures below income and acquire ownership of productive assets; capital may be accumulated. Through asset accumulation, the owner's choice set is expanded; the owner remains 'free to choose' among a widened range of options. As Samuel Johnson suggested indirectly, a person is really most at liberty when he or she owns valued assets that are *not* dissipated or used up (Boswell, 1755 [1946]).

Even the person who may not be at all concerned about too much dependence on the blind forces of the market, and who may have no precautionary motive for acquiring and owning property, as such, will still desire partitionable claims to allow adjustment to the inexorable forces of life lived in real time.

There are implications to be drawn for the form of property preferred. For the person who places full trust in the competitive market process and wants to own assets solely for the purpose of adjusting incomes and outlays through time, the most preferred form of asset is that which is most readily transformable into other repositories of value. And, of course, money, or claims in money, best meet this criterion. The person who finds no advantage in the opportunity for self-production of services in kind from property and seeks a store of value exclusively for intertemporal adjustment, will opt for the purchase of financial claims rather than real assets.

PRIVATE PROPERTY, MONEY AND INFLATION

Money is, indeed, the asset that is most readily transformable into all forms of value. But in the economies that we observe, money is not a commodity, or bundle of commodities, that is produced and sold through markets. Money is, instead, a creation of the state, and its supply bears no relationship to its production cost. For the individual who holds property claims in money or in financial assets denominated in money, there will arise a demand for protection against, and independence from, the exploitation of the money-creating authority by the state, rather than against the workings of the market, as such.

Hence, we have here a quite different sort of precautionary motive for holding real assets that more than counterbalances that which was discussed earlier. The person who seeks protection against the blind forces of the market in affecting the real value of particular assets must be concerned, if the property is in the form of monetary claims, with protection against the actions of political agents who can effectively destroy capital values through inflating the money issue.

There is a balance to be struck. Real assets may be demanded neither for their self-production of services nor for measured rates of yield, but, rather, for their potential value accretion as the money-goods terms of trade shift against money. Clearly, individuals can be made more independent – can be secure in more liberties – in a regime that embodies predictability in the money–goods exchange rate.

The general implications are straightforward. A regime that includes legal protection for private property is severely limited in its efficacy if predictability in the value of its monetary unit is absent. And any regime that moves to expand private ownership in real assets must accompany such privatization by implementation of a monetary constitution that will offer guarantees against the exploitation of the money-creating powers. So long as the state retains effective authority to confiscate property values that are designated in monetary units, the whole legal structure of private property and contract is severely crippled. The potential efficacy of the institution of private property in protecting liberties remains only halfway realized.

FINAL SPECULATIONS

It is not easy to measure the amount of liberty in a political-economic order. However, an indirect measure is available in the observed share of product that is privately controlled. To the extent that individuals are subjected to coercive taxes, revenues from which are used to finance both public services and transfers, there can exist no separable claims. Individuals are locked more deeply into positions of dependence with each increase in the size of the collectivized sector of the economy.

In the United States, we refer to 'tax freedom day', which now occurs in early May of each year. Up until this date, we say that the average American works for, or earns income for, the state. Only beyond this date, or for the remaining months of the year, does the average American have the liberty of working for himself or herself to earn income to be disposed of as privately preferred. In Germany, the comparable tax freedom day would be moved up until early

July. The average German citizen works for the collective for more than one-half of each year. The argument made here is that even if the overall size of the collective or politicized sector should be optimal in terms of ordinary efficiency criteria, the value of personal independence or liberty would still dictate a reduction. And, of course, no one could seriously suggest that there is an efficiency argument for a public sector that commands one-half of gross product. A substantial reduction in the size of the politicized sector could both increase efficiency in the utilization of resources and, at the same time, expand the range of individual liberties.

Private property serves as a guarantor of liberty, quite independently of how political decisions are made. The direct implication is that effective constitutional limits must be present in order to prevent particular political intrusions into rights of property while, at the same time, imposing checks to the overall growth of politicization. If individual liberty is to be adequately protected, constitutional limits must be in place prior to and separately from any exercise of democratic governance.

An understanding of priorities in this respect should offer the basis for an extension of constitutional constraints on majoritarian legislative processes in modern democratic politics, and perhaps notably with reference to potential monetary and fiscal exploitation. The omnipresent confusion that has corrupted Western attitudes involves the failure to recognize that 'constitutional' must be placed in front of the word *democracy* if the political equality of citizens is to be translated into a meaningful measure of liberty and autonomy. The tyranny of political majority is no different from any other, and it may be more dangerous because it feeds on the lingering idealistic illusion that participation is all that matters.

NOTE

1. This chapter offers a concise version of an argument that is developed more extensively in a monograph, *Property as a Guarantor of Liberty* (Buchanan, 1993b).

198-207
(91)
P 16
P71
D72   D2/0

20.   The minimal politics of market order

> The economic progress of the twentieth century has fully confirmed that only a market economy is capable of ensuring high efficiency in national economy. (Leonid Abalkin, 1990).

The basic meaning of Abalkin's statement is clear. As I have put the same point elsewhere, there is now general agreement that the market economy works better than the socialist or centrally directed alternative. Further, we now agree on what is meant when we say that an economy 'works better'. Such an economy produces a larger bundle of goods and services, as measured by the evaluations of persons who consume them. The economy organized on market principles produces more value than an economy organized on nonmarket principles.

Abalkin refers to 'efficiency' in the production of value. A market economy is relatively more efficient for three reasons: it makes the incentives of participants compatible with the generation of economic value; it exploits fully the localized knowledge available only to participants in separated and decentralized circumstances, and it allows maximal scope for the creative and imaginative talents of all participants who choose to act as potential entrepreneurs.

I shall not discuss these familiar, and now acknowledged, characteristics of a market economy further. My purpose here is to suggest that over-attention to and over-concentration on the efficiency-generating features of the market economy may prompt neglect of the closely related corollary feature that is equally, if not more, important. The economy that is organized on market principles effectively *minimizes* the number of economic decisions that must be made *politically*, that is, through some agency that acts on behalf of the collective unit. In practical terms, we may say that an economy organized on market principles minimizes the size and importance of the political bureaucracy. If he had chosen to emphasize this feature rather than efficiency, Abalkin could have said: 'the logic of the structure fully confirms that only a market economy is capable of allowing for a minimal politicization of the national economy'. And should he have wanted to extend this statement, he might have added: 'and only through such minimization of politicization-bureaucratization (or at least through some reduction) could meaningful individually based social objectives be secured, whatever these objectives might be'.

In the second section of this chapter I shall describe the relationship between politicization and market organization as I develop the distinction between political pricing and market pricing. In the third section I shall discuss the implications of political pricing for the whole set of relationships among citizens and groups of citizens in an economy. The analysis, which utilizes modern contributions of public-choice theory, identifies sources of possible waste of economic value, as well as circumstances where persons are placed in dependency status in confrontation with others. The normative implications are evident. The fourth section discusses the necessary role of political or collective action in the design, construction, implementation and maintenance of the structural framework within which any market economy is allowed to function. Collective choice among alternative sets of rules is required, but any such choice is constrained by the feedbacks from value generation and from bureaucratic intervention. In the fifth section I shall return to the distinction between political price and market price to illustrate how possibly agreed-on 'social' objectives might be advanced without overt politicization of markets. I shall also introduce the notion of a politically influenced market price, and I shall demonstrate the limits of applicability. The final section presents conclusions.

POLITICAL PRICE AND MARKET PRICE

A characteristic feature of socialist regimes involves the use of politically determined prices for selected goods and services, presumably motivated by both distributional and paternalistic considerations. The goods and services so selected are made available to consumers at demand prices that reflect political judgements rather than the results that emerge directly from the interaction of demand and supply. The listing of such goods and services is empirically familiar: medical services, educational services, child care, urban transport, housing, milk, bread and so forth. Some or all of these selected goods or services are made available to consumers or users at prices below those that would be established by market forces.[1]

Consider a single and highly simplified example. Suppose a collective political decision is made to supply bread to consumers at a price of zero, which may be called a 'political price' since it is divorced from any relation between costs of production and demand. If political action is limited to an announcement of this political price, the response is readily predictable. Potential consumers will demand large quantities of bread at the zero price, and there will be no potential suppliers willing to put bread on the market at that price. Political decision makers who initially try to meet potential consumers' demands must direct large quantities of resources into bread production, either by direct requisition or by some scheme for subsidizing potential suppliers. That is, even if sufficient bread is available to meet all demands at the artificial political price, some additional political action must be taken, over and beyond the setting of price itself, in order to make the pricing operational. Resources must be drawn from other uses into bread production, and demanders are encouraged by the artificially low price to use bread wastefully. (The illustration from Soviet experience that is often adduced here is the story of peasants feeding bread to cattle.)

As noted earlier, however, I do not want to stress the wasteful or efficiency-reducing effects of political pricing. Let us heroically assume, therefore, that political decision makers, the planners who act on behalf of the collectivity, direct resources into bread production in some rough approximation of the quantity that would be forthcoming under market pricing. This combination of zero-demand price, along with roughly optimal supply, will ensure the presence of two results: there will be an excess demand for bread, and the costs of producing and supplying that quantity must be financed from sources other than people who consume the bread. Political decisions and political actions are required on two institutional dimensions over and beyond the setting of price.

We can compare such a regime of political pricing with a regime of market pricing by supposing that there is no politicized interference with the market for bread; thus the price is allowed to emerge from the interaction of demand and supply. In this setting, suppliers and producers may offer bread to prospective purchasers on terms of their own choosing, and potential consumers may choose to purchase or not, in whatever quantities they choose. We know that in this setting roughly the efficient supply of bread will be placed on the market ('efficient' as measured in terms of the value scales of demanders throughout the economy). In addition, under this regime of market pricing, the two results emphasized as characteristic of political pricing will be absent. There will be neither an excess nor a deficient demand for bread; there will be neither an excess nor a deficient supply of bread. And there will be no requirement that other persons in the economy, other than bread consumers, must finance the production of bread. The political decisions involved in (a) setting the political price, (b) allocating the available supply among potential demanders and (c) financing the production of the available supply are unnecessary under the market pricing regime.

There are, of course, distributional differences between the two regimes. Those consumers who succeed in getting bread at the zero price under the political pricing regime may be better off than they would be under the market pricing regime. (Although they may not be better off when the full price, including time in queues, is taken into account.) But these possible gains to consumers are fully offset by losses suffered by whomever in the economy must finance the supply that is made available. Political pricing must, in some sense, embody value transfers between users and nonusers of the goods that are politically priced. By contrast, no across-market transfers need take place under market pricing.

POLITICAL PRICING, BUREAUCRATIC DISCRETION AND SOCIAL WASTE

Market pricing incorporates two important coordinating functions that political pricing fails to perform. The available supply is rationed among potential demanders, and the quantity supplied is brought forth to meet the potential demand. If political price is set lower than market price, some means of rationing other than price must be brought into being, unless supply is adjusted to meet whatever demand emerges. In that case, massive wastage of economic value must ensue.

Under excess demand conditions, nonprice rationing may take any one of several forms, singly or in combination. Available supplies may be allocated by some explicit rationing mechanism, for example, by issuing ration coupons that are required for purchase. Or rationing may be accomplished by some variant of a first-come, first-served scheme that involves waiting periods and long queues in shops. Or, finally, the people who control access to supply may ration goods through private pricing. In each scheme emerges a necessary role for bureaucratic agency that market pricing would make redundant.

Similar implications for the necessity of a bureaucratic agency emerge when we examine supply-side coordination. If voluntary adjustment to market-related supply price is not allowed to take place, producers must, somehow, be encouraged to bring forth the politically chosen quantity of goods. Production may be directly organized through state enterprise, or private suppliers may be subsidized. In any case, some collection of revenues from other sources in the economy is required – collection that, again, depends on bureaucratic agency. Or production may be directly requisitioned, in which case suppliers must be subjected to coercive bureaucratic command.

Political pricing requires extended supplementary bureaucratic agency to achieve plausibly meaningful coordination of objectives. Individual citizens, both as demanders and users of the economy's end items but also as suppliers of the inputs that are combined to produce such items, are necessarily subject to the discretionary direction of bureaucratic agency to an extent not present under market organization. This dependency of the citizen on bureaucracy exists quite independent of personal behavioural characteristics of people in bureaucratic roles. Even if all those bureaucrats should behave ideally in terms of widely shared criteria of fairness, the dependency relationship continues to exist.

As modern public choice theory suggests, however, bureaucratic agents are not likely to be different from other persons in the community; at least, models of behaviour should not be constructed that presume totally different behaviour. The bureaucrat will, as will others, seek to maximize his or her utility subject to the constraints that are faced. And because the institutional structure under a regime of political pricing places other persons in a dependency relationship, the bureaucrat can scarcely be expected to refuse, deliberately, to exercise this power of discretion so as to maximize his or her own utility. Favouritism, discriminatory treatment, both positive and negative and arbitrary classifications – these features are almost necessary characteristics of any system that places people in dependency relationships with bureaucrats who are living, breathing human beings.

These characteristics will be present in regimes of political pricing even if there is no corruption in the ordinary meaning of the term. Bureaucrats who possess discretionary authority to allocate or distribute access to economic value will, of course, have opportunities for pecuniarily beneficial trades for the simple reason that the allocative-distributive authority itself has value. And there is surely some positive correlation between opportunities for, and the exploitation of, gain.

But the problems of bureaucratic discretion do not lie exclusively, or even primarily, with bribery. First, these problems exist because of bureaucratic discretion itself, which implies that choices must be made among claimants on some basis other than economic value. In this respect, the introduction of bureaucratic discretion made necessary by political pricing becomes a source of the relative inefficiency of the whole structure. Second, the dependency relationship introduced between those persons who hold discretionary authority and those who are subject to that authority creates arbitrary class distinction. Third, and perhaps most important, the artificially created scarcities under political pricing become objects of socially wasteful investments. People find it privately rational to invest resources in efforts to secure differentially favoured access to the economic power inherent in bureaucratic discretion. This rent seeking on the part of those who compete for the scarce access to valued goods (such as those who demand bread at the zero price) represents wasteful investment on the part of all people who are unsuccessful in the competitive effort.

There should be little or no dispute concerning the positive analysis of effects of political pricing on the size, range, discretionary limits and secondary behavioural repercussions of bureaucratic agency. There are no normative implications to be derived directly from the analysis, as such. Nonetheless, to the extent that analysts and observers can agree that these effects are, in themselves, undesirable characteristics of political pricing regimes, the relative advantages claimed for such regimes in comparison with market pricing regimes are reduced in significance. The minimization of politicization-bureaucratization of economic interaction, which market pricing makes possible, must be reckoned to be a relevant factor in the ultimate comparative judgement over and beyond the closely related and more familiar argument from efficiency.

THE POLITICAL CONSTITUTION OF ECONOMIC ORDER

Until now, I have referred to regimes of political pricing and market pricing without direct mention (other than the introduction to this chapter) of the constitutional structure that defines the framework within which any regime of economic interaction operates. It is important to emphasize that political or collective action is necessary in establishing and maintaining the regime's structure, under any and all circumstances. The minimization of the range and scope of bureaucratic discretion, discussed in the previous two sections, refers exclusively to the setting for economic interaction within the structure of rules, that is, within the constitution of the economic order. As the analysis suggested, market pricing tends to minimize bureaucratic discretion relative to that which is required under political pricing. But market pricing will function effectively only within a set of framework rules that must, themselves, be established or maintained collectively. At the level of constitutional choice, there is no escape from politicization.

I shall limit my discussion to an outline of those features of constitutional structure that will allow market pricing to emerge and to function. I shall not discuss how the basic constitutional choice among sets of rules is made. First, there must be a dispersed and decentralized distribution of the capacities to produce economic value, along with an explicit political and legal acknowledgement of this distribution. Property or property rights, both in human capacities and in nonhuman assets, must be widely dispersed in ownership, and the pattern of ownership itself must be afforded explicit legal protection. Second, private owners must be allowed to exchange owned rights to property among themselves, and there must be political-legal enforcement of voluntary contracts made for the exchange of these rights.

Under such a dispersed, decentralized pattern of private ownership, along with political and legal acknowledgement, protection and contract enforcement, the basic elements for the constitution of a market regime will be in place. Resource capacities will be allocated among separate possible uses; production will be organized through combinations of productive inputs and goods and services will be produced, supplied and priced to consumers who demand them. Nobody in either a private or a political role is directly required to attend to the particular features of the outcome, or pattern of outcomes, of the interdependent market process. This outcome, or pattern of outcomes, will emerge from the interactive, interdependent choice behaviour of many persons. The allocative and distributive results will be chosen by no one.

It is precisely at this point that an overemphasis on the efficiency criterion for evaluating the performance of a market economy may be misleading. The efficiency that is, indeed, achieved by market interaction is, itself, defined by such interaction. The value scale itself emerges from the market choices made by all participants; such a scale does not exist independently. There need be no relationship between the performance of a market economy and the efficiency relative to a value scale chosen by the planner or political decision maker. Only if decision makers are willing to allow the market itself to define efficiency can Abalkin's statement be valid.

A market order, of sorts, will emerge once the basic elements are in place. But the constitutional structure may be extended to include other rules or institutions that may be expected to facilitate the inclusive exchange process. The political agency, the state, may take on the responsibility of defining the monetary unit for the economic order, and may, ideally, seek to maintain stability in the value of such unit. There may also be specialized institutional arrangements aimed at promoting competitive forces, especially those that promote freedom of entry into production and prohibit cartel agreements. Other collectively consumed or public goods (for example, protection of environmental quality) may be brought within the state's authority, and constitutional rules may be introduced that specify the means through which state-supplied goods and services are to be financed.

MINIMAL BUREAUCRATIZATION AND THE SOCIAL MARKET ECONOMY

Attention to, and emphasis on, the relationship between the coordinating properties of market pricing and the range of bureaucratic discretion have implications for the efficiency of political intervention that may be undertaken in the furtherance of social objectives. Political decision makers, either those who act as agents for a ruling elite or those who claim to represent electoral constituencies in democracies, may reject the efficiency norm as defined by operation of the market economy, even if the collectivized sector is extended to include the financing of nonexcludable collectively consumed goods. These agents, for the same distributional and paternalistic reasons that motivated many of the socialist experiments in economic *dirigisme*, may seek to use political authority to modify, at least in part, the results of the market system.

At the same time, the advantages of market organization both in generating economic value and in minimizing the role of bureaucratic discretion may be accepted. How might the coordinating properties of markets be retained while using political authority to modify the distributive-allocative patterns towards those patterns more desirable to the decision makers (planners)?

Suppose that the basic structural rules of a market economy are established. Property rights are then decentralized, and voluntary contracts are enforced. Recall my earlier discussion in the second and third sections. If supplies are sufficiently provided to meet all demands at the politically determined demand price that faces potential consumers-users, there is no need for a supplementary rationing scheme. If all supplies offered at the politically determined supply price are taken, there is no need for rationing sales permits among potential suppliers. Price may be used, therefore, both to ration demand and to stimulate supply. But the additional market equilibrium characteristic may be absent. The demand price at which a good is offered to consumers may not be brought into equality with the supply price offered to suppliers. As noted, under any scheme of political pricing, some cross-market transfers of value must take place. If the political decision makers encourage market participants to purchase more of a good than their preferences will dictate in an undisturbed market pricing structure, a wedge must be driven between the demand price at which the good is offered to consumers and the supply price that is offered to producers. The demand price must fall below the supply price. Even if these separate prices fully accomplish their rationing function, means must be found to finance the difference.

The political decision makers must, in this case, be willing to introduce a wedge of the opposing direction in the market for some other good (or goods). That is, demand price must be made higher than the supply price in some other market (or markets) to generate the revenues sufficient to finance the subsidy for the favoured good or service. As in the first market, prices can be used to eliminate the need for bureaucratic discretion in supplementary rationing roles. But recognition of the across-market transfer of value here suggests that the budget must balance. That is, the revenues collected from the disfavoured good must be precisely equal to the subsidies paid to the producers and consumers of the favoured good. Production and consumption of one good can be encouraged; production and consumption of the other good can be discouraged. The alleged social objective can be accomplished within the set of constraints imposed by participants' preferences in the economy in their roles as demanders and suppliers of the two goods (or bundles of goods).

A Tale of Bread and Vodka

The discussion here may be clarified by a simple example. Suppose that the political decision makers, whoever they may be, modify the allocative and distributive results of the market economy in a specific way. The declared social objective may be to encourage the production and consumption of bread, to discourage the production and consumption of vodka and, at the same time, to minimize both efficiency loss and bureaucratic discretion.

Bread production may be differentially subsidized, and vodka production may be differentially taxed. Under such arrangements, both goods continue to be marketed at prices that are politically influenced although they remain, in one sense, market prices. For such a scheme to work effectively, the two sides of the account must balance. Further, the solution must be brought into adjustment with the demand and supply schedules of both goods, as revealed through the independent behaviour of demanders and suppliers.

The political decision makers cannot simply impose a per unit tax on vodka independent of the per unit subsidy on bread. Given the behaviour of vodka demanders and suppliers, any specified tax per unit on vodka will generate a defined revenue total that will then be available for subsidizing bread. But the size of the per unit subsidy will depend, in this case, on the behaviour of demanders and suppliers of bread. Political decision makers cannot simply select any per unit subsidy for bread, if they want to minimize the need for bureaucratic discretion in bread distribution. Conversely, any preselected per unit subsidy on bread will, given the behaviour of demanders and suppliers of bread, require a defined revenue outlay. So that this outlay may be financed from the tax on vodka, the per unit size of tax will be fixed, given the behaviour of demanders and suppliers of vodka.

Political decision makers might desire many solutions that may simply be inconsistent with the behaviour of participants in the economy. For example, revenues required to finance a full subsidy on bread, to allow it to be offered at a zero price as in our earlier illustration, may be beyond the limits that could be generated by a tax on vodka. The demand and supply behaviour of participants in all markets, which must be allowed to take place without bureaucratic coercion, will place constraints on the ability of political decision makers to modify market results. Within such limits, the structure of market prices may be very substantially modified in presumed furtherance of social objectives.

CONCLUSION

In any economy, resources must be allocated and combined to produce useful outputs that must, in turn, be distributed to consumers. An economy that is organized on market principles will accomplish this set of tasks more efficiently, and more economic value will be generated than in a centrally directed economy. My purpose has been to emphasize the importance of the corollary feature of the market economy, which relates the organization of the economy to the range of political and bureaucratic discretion. If resources are not allocated and products distributed through the workings of a market system, then the allocative and distributive functions must be performed directly by political-bureaucratic agency. In this direct and obvious sense, markets, to the extent that they are allowed to operate, constrain bureaucratic intervention into the lives of citizens.

This conclusion does not imply that markets or market organizations eliminate, as if by magic, the elemental constraints imposed by the scarce resources. By increasing efficiency in resource use, markets may reduce the severity of these ultimate constraints. Yet the basic limits on resources remain; markets replace the implementation and representation of constraints through coercive intrusion of personalized bureaucracy by the impersonal price structure. The discretionary power or authority of the bureaucrat is replaced by the impersonal authority of prices, with the accompanying differences in interpersonal relationships.

The market order minimizes the range of bureaucratic discretion, but this order operates only within a constitutional framework that must be politically established and sustained. The basic elements – dispersed private ownership of property and enforcement of contracts – are necessary to allow markets to emerge and to generate patterns of outcomes upon which preferences of participants place the highest value, as expressed through market behaviour.

Politics, as it operates and no matter how the decision structure may be organized and how decision makers are selected, may not willingly confine its activities to establishing and maintaining the constitutional framework. Politicians, both on their own account and as representatives of constituencies of citizens, may seek to modify some outcomes that would emerge from the uncontrolled workings of market process. Many citizens may share in categorizing certain goods as 'worthy of encouragement' (sometimes called 'merit goods') and other goods as 'worthy of discouragement' (sometimes called 'sumptuary goods'). In almost every polity, attempts will be made to modify the results of market interaction to encourage the first set of goods and to discourage the second set.

There are better and worse means of intervening in the workings of markets if minimizing bureaucratic discretion along with efficiency is accepted as a norm. The objectives for a social market economy may be furthered by schemes of appropriately selected taxes and subsidies that are adjusted to the demand and supply behaviour of participants.

NOTE

1. Administrative inefficiencies in distribution may, of course, be so large as to make the inclusive prices for such goods higher than free-market prices, despite the intent of the planners.

21. Politicized economies in limbo: America, Europe and the world, 1994[1]

This year, 1994, is useful for stocktaking. We are five years on from the revolutions of 1989; we are a decade past the celebration of George Orwell's *1984*. We knew, long before 1984, that Orwell's precautionary predictions would be falsified, just as we should have known well before 1989, that the Communist socialized regimes in Central and Eastern Europe and the Soviet Union were not sustainable over a long term. But we paid little or no attention to what the extensively politicized economies of the West or East would look like in the era following the long Cold War, when Germany was reunified and there was no longer the hovering threat of superpower nuclear conflict. If only Francis Fukuyama's grand predictions could have become reality. Or, more soberly, if only we could, in 1994, discern signs that the world is moving in the directions that Fukuyama dreamed.

Yes, indeed, there is a science of economics. Economists find their *raison d'être* in laying out, for public and politicians alike, the conditions that must be met if economies are to grow and to prosper. But there is a difference between the applicability of the economists' scientific teachings and that of the natural scientists. I shall discuss this difference in some detail in the second section. In the third section I shall shift perspective and offer some suggestions about the failures of 'economic science' to find emplacement in democratic political reality. In the fourth section I examine the prospects for an equilibrium of interests in the politicized economies of modern democracies. How much aggregate value will be sacrificed to the 'black holes' of distributional politics (Magee, Brock and Young, 1989)? And is there some natural limit? In section five I introduce the necessary competitiveness of nations as the phenomenon of modern history that may check the implosion of value that majoritarian democracy seems to promise. In the discussion I shall examine the role of a European confederation and the workings of competitive federalism more generally, both for Europe and beyond. Finally, in section six I shall return to familiar territory and discuss the constitutional interests that may reflect the teachings of economic science. Constitutional revolutions do occur, and the interdependence of the global economy can serve political as well as economic purpose.

THE SCIENCES OF NATURE AND THE SCIENCES OF MAN

Recall Fukuyama's prediction to the effect that, with the dramatic historical falsification of the hypothesis that command and control of economic activity can generate value at levels comparable to those generated under market institutions, nations everywhere would reorganize their economies to reflect a final, if sometimes begrudging, acceptance of the truths of classical political economy. Markets would become the normal or standard form through which persons and groups carry on their ordinary economic activities. Governments would, presumably, back off from an activist, interfering stance and would limit themselves to the establishment, maintenance and enforcement of the supportive constitutional-legal framework.

Fukuyama's prediction shows no sign of becoming reality. There is no indication that economic science, in the broad sense relevant here, carries more respect and authority in the post-revolutionary moment of 1994 than it did, say, in 1984 or earlier. Observed political and policy discourse, whether in America or Europe, proceeds as if the revolutions of 1989 did not occur. The rhetoric of the Clinton administration in the United States marks a return to that of the 1960s, to an era when policy activism was in flower, and well before incentives were allegedly rediscovered in the 1970s and 1980s.

Why? The question is why economic science is so different from its natural science counterparts. Technological advances based on developments and experiments in the natural sciences generate changes that allow us to get more valued output from inputs. There are, of course, distributional losses imposed on persons who may have invested human or nonhuman capital in displaced technologies. At best (or worst), however, these persons, when organized, can secure political action that delays changes toward increased efficiency. Because, however, it remains always to the direct interest of some persons to introduce the technological advances consequent on scientific progress, the ultimate direction of change is guaranteed.

Matters are quite different with reference to changes in economic structure that may promise increases in the overall production of value. Potential gainers from applications of the teachings of economic science are likely to be spread among the whole population and to be large in numbers. There is unlikely to be high differential profit to anyone in particular upon the introduction of economic reforms that open up markets. Efficiency-increasing structural changes may be introduced only through concerted, collective action by the political unit and organized private support for such changes may be difficult to marshal, despite the promised increase in aggregate value. Even when reforms are proposed, organized groups may use the same avenues of political action deliberately to reduce or to destroy value potential.

Each person's direct economic interest is in the size of total value under his or her command. But this objective may be gained by getting a larger share in an aggregate that remains unchanged or falls and by holding the same, or even a smaller, share in a larger aggregate. Consider the person who thinks of the prospect of getting, through politically organized action, an increase in income from two to three dollars, even with the full knowledge that the aggregate value in the whole economy will fall by two dollars in the process. The person gains a dollar; others in the economy lose two dollars; the game is negative sum. In the distributional politics of modern majoritarian democracies there is little scope for the application of economic science.

THE WEALTH OF NATIONS

Who has a direct interest in the aggregate wealth of a nation? Who should have such an interest? Here arises a normative contradiction that confronts the classical liberal. Margaret Thatcher was roundly chastised for her statement that there is no society, as such. Her intent was to suggest that only individuals offer the loci of value and evaluation. But, taken literally, there could then exist no aggregative interest, no 'national purpose', no 'vision', for Germany, the United States or any other nation, state or group thereof.

Yet almost all commentators proceed as if such an aggregative interest exists, regardless of their own positions on the stylized ideological spectrum. It is as if we are forced, willy nilly, to adopt an organicist conception while simultaneously mouthing individualist norms in our philosophy.

There is indeed a problem here, and it finds acute historical placement in the post-revolutionary moment of the middle 1990s. During the long Cold War, the normative claims of individualism could be shunted aside and adherence to the rhetoric of national goals could go unchallenged and unchallengeable. Germany, the United States, the West generally – these entities took on moral significance and the wealth of nations, defined as the aggregate value of production along with its rate of growth, became a criterion of comparative measurement. To survive in the international conflict with Communism, the West required a productive economy. And there was a truly common interest in economic prosperity and growth over and beyond that reflected in the privately separable shares of value. Purely distributional objectives, with the consequent domestic conflict, could, and were, at least to an extent, sublimated to furtherance of the more comprehensive purpose. The Cold War held the welfare-transfer state in check.

The Cold War is over; the West has won. But what does this portend for private interests in the wealth of nations? Why should the citizen be concerned with other than his or her privately separable share in economic prosperity unless probabilistic calculations so dictate? Can we not predict a veritable explosion in the basic distributional politics of democracy once the partially relevant encompassing interest dictated by the Cold War disappears from public and political consciousness?

There is simply no calculus of interests that can stand as a bulwark against the political entrepreneurs who seek always to exploit opportunities for differential distributional gains. The only criterion for acceptability becomes political success. The winning coalition of interests legitimizes itself as it succeeds, and independently from an effect on aggregative value.

The politicized economies of Western countries are in deficit along many dimensions, including, of course, the obvious fiscal transfer of value from future taxpayers to current beneficiaries. Claimant client groups, whether organized geographically, as in Germany, or by age, as in the United States and elsewhere, or by other shared features, are sufficiently strong to prevent any political curbs on rates of growth in entitlement subsidies. On the other hand, productive income earners resist further tax increases that promise no return in measurable private benefits. De Jasay's 'churning state' (1985) is with us, but the transfers are not limited to those who are current givers or takers. Massive deficit financing burdens future taxpayers, thereby guaranteeing that the conflict between welfare-state dependents and productive income earners must be exacerbated in future years. Someone must pay for the spending that now goes through public budgets. Are the income earners of the new century likely to quietly accept their personal obligations to pay off the accumulated debts incurred in the 1990s? And why should they do so?

AN EQUILIBRIUM OF INTERESTS?

Almost all observers agree that the politicized sectors of Western democracies are 'too large', in the sense that more economic value could be produced from the available resources if the sectors could be reduced, however measured. Surely a national economy does not produce its highest value when more than one half of GDP was public outlay. (In Germany in 1994, the share was 55 per cent.) If socialism in the large failed so dramatically, how can socialism in the not so small be expected to work?

The question of relevance does not concern the absolute size of the public sector so much as the prospective change in this size. So long as the politicized sector remains stable relative to total product, the overall economy may work reasonably well, despite the obvious opportunity cost measured in lost value potential. But what are the prospects for either more or less politicization in Western democracies over the remaining years of this century and the early years of the next? Have we attained an equilibrium of sorts? Have all of the groups who might successfully secure profits through political action, even at the expense of overall economic productivity, exhausted their opportunities? Will such groups acquiesce in their currently measured claims on others? Will the United States shift its priorities from defence to transfer spending while maintaining its relatively low public sector share? Will the increase in transfer spending level off? Or will political interests succeed in moving America towards European levels?

I do not find a simple analytical logic that allows me to identify an equilibrium level for the politicized sector share, even in the stylized sense that economists prefer to use. Tax reaction functions, along with Laffer curve speculations with public choice models, might yield interesting results, but little that is generally definitive could be produced. As noted earlier, in the Cold War game between West and East there were both economic and military targets. And there was a trade-off point beyond which distributional interests might have been held in check. But absent such a trade-off point, where is the ceiling?

COMPETITIVENESS AMONG NATIONS

Limits on the destruction of potential economic value owing to the distributional politics of majoritarian democracy may be indirectly imposed by the necessary competitiveness among separate political units, the nation-states, in an increasingly interdependent worldwide economic nexus. In a very real sense, the emerging international competitiveness has replaced, and will replace, the economic elements of the Cold War, even if the results are generated very differently in the two cases. A single nation-state that is totally isolated from the world nexus may allow its internal distributional politics to destroy a very large share of potential economic value that the resource base would make possible. But to the extent that the economy is integrated with those of other political units, efforts to extend fiscal transfers as well as regulatory intrusions may be thwarted. A single country cannot readily impose rates of tax on its resources or goods that are much above those levels in other countries with whom trade takes place without setting off undesirable shifts in terms of trade. The basic discipline of the market emerges to place severe limits on the nonproductive enterprise of political rent seeking.

Technological developments, especially those stemming from the information-communications revolution, may guarantee increasing economic interdependence among nations (McKenzie and Lee, 1991). To the extent that this historical trend takes place, the value-destroying activities of rent seeking coalitions are internally inhibited. The over-extended welfare-transfer state may find its days numbered, unless coalitions among several states can effectively cartelize the welfare-transfer sectors of several states, thereby preventing the pressures of international competitiveness.

It is useful at this point to discuss briefly the prospects for the countries of Western Europe in the movement toward European confederation. As I have stated elsewhere (Buchanan, 1994c), I think that Europe has probably missed out on a once-in-history opportunity to achieve economic greatness through integration into a genuinely competitive federalism, in which the advantages of a larger market might have been secured while at the same time the forces of interstate competition could have been relied on to forestall undue internal politicization. Prospects for Europe are not so bright in 1994 as they were in 1990, largely because of the offsetting forces of Brussels' bureaucratization and nationalistic intransigency. The urge towards regularization and harmonization of the several economies, and as dictated by Brussels, and as reflected in the Maastricht treaty, runs counter to any unleashing of the potential efficiency-enhancing forces of interstate competitiveness.

A strong, but severely limited, central authority for Europe is needed – an authority that can effectively enforce the free flow of resources and goods across national frontiers. But this authority should not extend to include the imposition of regularization requirements on the separate political units, nor should a single currency and a single central bank be a part of the whole competitive federalism scheme. Europe has faced an almost ideal time for the introduction of Hayek's proposal for competitive monies. Each nation's central bank could be allowed to issue its own currency, but each and every citizen of Europe should be constitutionally protected in the liberty to make contracts in any currency, including the payment of taxes.

I realize, of course, that the Europe of 1994 seems a long way from attaining the ideal of competitive federalism that seemed more possible in 1990. But there are forces of history still at work, and the failure of the *dirigistes* to secure docile acceptance of Maastricht offers lingering hope to all those who are true federalists.

CONSTITUTIONAL INTEREST, ECONOMIC SCIENCE AND INTERNATIONAL INTERDEPENDENCE

My aim in this chapter has been to offer a broad and inclusive summary assessment of the politicized economies of the world, particularly America and Western Europe, in 1994. I have deliberately added 'in limbo' to my title in order to suggest that so much remains in transition from where we were, pre-1989, to somewhere else. A post-Cold War equilibrium has not been attained.

I have organized my remarks around a theme stimulated by Fukuyama's optimistic and provocative prediction that economic science will emerge triumphant and that polities, everywhere, will reorganize their economies along market principles. But why have we not witnessed more support for markets and marketization in the highly politicized economies of Western Europe and America? Why has the public sector continued to grow as a share in GDP?

There is no respected challenge afoot to the basic principles of economic science. We know that markets which allow for free entry and exit and for prices to be set by supply and demand unrestricted by political intrusion generate more economic value, as measured by standards that emerge in the market process itself, than any other organizational structure. And economic value is valued by everyone. Each of us prefers to live in a community, a region, a nation and a world that is prosperous and provides an abundance of goods and services, with increasing abundance through time. Each of us, no matter who or where we are, has an abiding constitutional interest in economic prosperity.

But we have no direct action-motivating interest. Instead we have nongeneral, nonconstitutional interests which are measured in gains for our own small, less than totally inclusive, communities – geographically, occupationally, industrially, professionally, institutionally organized interests that come into conflict with the general, or constitutional, interest. And it is these particular group interests, as they come to be exploited in the politics of majoritarian democracy, that prevent the emplacement of the basic teachings of economic science into observed institutional reality. There always remains, of course, some residual ignorance of basic economics, even among sophisticated political leaders, and even as late as 1994, but the primary force that prevents the dominance of constitutional interest is the presence of particularized distributional interests, not ignorance (Olson, 1982).

How can the constitutional interests of all members of a polity be advanced? How can persons be persuaded to act politically in pursuit of their generalized interest even if in opposition to their particular distributional interest? I have, personally, spent a good part of a lengthy academic career trying to address such questions as these. I am no closer to answers in 1994 than I was in 1954, about the time I commenced to be concerned with such issues.

I do not, however, despair, because I sense the possibility in the offing that somewhere, sometime, there will emerge a set of political entrepreneurs in some polity that will put in place their own institutional variant of what are essentially the principles of classical liberalism. That is to say, one country's leaders may act to further their citizenry's constitutional interests and the internal politics may be such as to leave time for the experiment to work. In this way, there may arise one or more exemplars for other leaders to emulate. The countries on the Asian rim come to mind here, along with those of Latin America. The United States and the countries of Western Europe may be goaded out of the political arteriosclerosis of the extended welfare-transfer state by the observed growth of the smaller nations.

NOTE

1. This chapter was initially presented as a lecture at the University of Catania, Sicily, Italy, in December 1994 and published as a monograph in Italian and English. The perspective is explicitly dated, as the chapter's title suggests. I have made no attempt to update the argument.

22.   Society and democracy[1]

My thesis is simple: 'society' takes precedence over 'democracy'. By this statement I mean that while democratic processes of governance, in which all persons have some participatory role, may well be necessary in any well-functioning civic order, the converse relationship does not hold. The presence of democracy as such does not guarantee, or even promote, the construction and maintenance of those constitutional-institutional parameters which inclusively define the civic order (or 'society'). In the absence of such parameters that define the very framework within which government, as well as private agencies, operate, no civic order or society can exist that warrants positive evaluative designation.

I can summarize my argument by repeating here a statement made in Chapter 19. I stated that the political structure of any society that embodies respect for individual liberty must be one that is described by the term *constitutional democracy*, but of the two words in this couplet, *constitutional* is prior to *democracy*.

I propose to develop this thesis with reference to the demonstrated proclivities of modern democratic politics to extend beyond meaningful constitutional, or within parametric, limits and to take on attributes of a negative-sum contest that becomes akin to a game without rules. In a very real sense, the distributional politics of what Anthony de Jasay (1985) has appropriately termed 'the churning state' has become this age's version of the Hobbesian war of each against all. Particular interests seek to get, and succeed in getting, the assistance of the state at the expense of others all within the processes of democratic institutions. Until and unless we come to an understanding that the principle of generality must be operative in politics in some manner that is at least akin to that which is ideally present under the notion of equality before the law, the observed excesses of democracy will continue to undermine the public's confidence in our ability to govern ourselves.

POLITICS WITHOUT ROMANCE

My inaugural lecture at the Institute for Higher Studies in Vienna, Austria, in 1979, was entitled 'Politics without Romance'. I have since found this three-word title to be quite useful in summarizing the whole research programme in public choice – that programme within which my own work has been classified. This title is descriptively accurate because it contrasts the public choice conception or explanatory model of politics and political process with the traditional alternative – one that could be described as 'politics with romance'. Surprising as this may seem to realists, such a romantic model has been central in political theory since the ancient Greeks. In this traditional conception, the whole enterprise of politics is understood to be a continuing search for what is good, true and beautiful for the polity. To the extent that individual participation is explicitly considered at all in this conception, the emphasis is on participation in the ongoing dialogue and discussion. The teleological nature of the whole enterprise suggests that the good and the true, once discovered, are to be universally accepted and acclaimed by all 'right-thinking' and 'morally responsible' citizens. In this romanticized conception of politics, the specific features of a decision rule that may be used to close off discussion, temporarily or permanently, do not demand critical analytical attention. What matters is that the uniquely determinate results be attained and implemented – not that individual expressions of preference be embodied in such results. To the extent that separate individual preferences are counted or measured in some amalgamation process, such procedure qualifies only as one possible means of discovering that which exists. I have often referred to the multi-person jury as a means of determining guilt or innocence in criminal proceedings as an analogue to the place of democratic voting procedures under this conceptualization of politics. Individual preferences differ, only because persons may be differently informed or may have differing theories as to how the good and the true may be generated. In this model, they do not differ because individuals have differing interests or purposes for the whole political enterprise.[2]

The realist or nonromantic conceptual model of politics is dramatically different from that just sketched out. First, there is no room for the notion that there exists some ultimate truth in the political enterprise, just waiting to be discovered. Second, the basic legitimization of politics, and of government as a coercive force, lies in the expressed consent of individuals, who judge that collective action is necessary for them, individually, to accomplish purposes that they cannot readily achieve through private action. And, in the organization of collective action, that is, in the activity of politics, individuals express their own interests, which may differ, as well as their own theories. Politics is an enterprise in which persons and groups seek to further shared, but still private, purposes.

In this realist conception of politics, which informs the public-choice research programme, it is immediately evident that individual participation matters in quite a different way from its role in the romantic or idealist conception. Precisely because individuals do have separable interests, which may conflict, it becomes relevant and important that they be allowed access to the participatory enterprise.

And not only potential access, but also the specific features of the decision rule become significant. A vote is more than a voice. Further, the domain of society over which politics is allowed to enter and to dominate emerges as a critical variable. In sum, politics as a 'compromise of interests' is different in kind from politics as a 'discovery of the good or the true'.

THE ELECTORAL FALLACY

The intellectual leaders of the eighteenth-century Scots Enlightenment and the American founders, in particular, were political realists; they were highly sceptical of politics, government and politicians as promoters and guarantors of the public or general interest of the ordinary citizenry. They sought to constrain governmental intrusions into the lives of citizens, whether economic or personal. They interpreted constitutions to have such constraint as a primary purpose, and they did not distinguish between forms of government in terms of the applicability of constitutional limits. Whether or not governments qualified as democratic was not considered directly relevant to the need for constraint on the domain of society over which politics was allowed to operate.

Unfortunately, confusion emerged as previously despotic regimes came increasingly to be replaced by constitutionally guaranteed, democratic electoral systems. What I have called 'the electoral fallacy' emerged in the nineteenth century and was reflected in the notion that, so long as there existed constitutional protection that guaranteed universality in the franchise – open and periodic elections, freedom of entry into the formation of political parties and the generality of enforcement of laws enacted through majoritarian processes – politics would be kept within bounds. Democracy was considered to be the guarantor of the discipline that it imposed upon itself. There was little or no understanding that electoral democracy, in particular, requires its own constitutional constraints. This absence of understanding was exacerbated by the resurgence of the romantic image of politics in early nineteenth-century political philosophy. The constitutional wisdom of the eighteenth century was lost, and democracy, treated as almost synonymous with majoritarianism, was allowed to move almost at will into areas of civic society that remained unprotected by constitutional barriers.

THE NATURAL LIMITS OF MAJORITY RULE

In much modern discourse, democracy means majority rule. But this understanding is seldom followed up by its consequence. Majority rule means rule by the majority which, in its turn, means that those in the minority are ruled. They are coerced into an acceptance of political results that they do not prefer. This very elementary definitional starting point is too often overlooked because of an implicit assumption that the alternatives for collective or political selection are themselves exogenous to the process or rule through which selection is made. In such case, while individuals in the minority may prefer some alternative other than the one imposed by the majority, there is no overt exploitation of the minority, as such. In this conceptual framework, the collective selection process contains elements of a coordination game within which members of both the dominant majority and the minority are predicted to benefit from the result, quite independently from status.

But where do the alternatives for political action come from? Are these alternatives out there as potentialities, waiting for some process, any process, to make a selection and put one of them into being? Or are the alternatives for political action themselves created endogenously by political entrepreneurs, who seek to further the interests of those persons and groups whom they represent? Do political entrepreneurs emerge to invent and discover alternatives for political action that are aimed primarily, if not exclusively, to promote the interests of those represented in the relevant coalition? In this perspective on democratic politics, the alternatives among which some selection is to be made do not exist independently at all. And in this perspective it is perhaps clear that, while alternatives may well be 'public' along some relevant dimensions, the differential interest of members of the majority coalition is likely to be furthered by 'private' elements (Flowers and Danzon, 1984). It is equally clear that the set of political alternatives brought up for consideration will depend upon the decision rule in operation. A voting rule that requires only a simple majority of a legislative assembly will generate quite different options than would a voting rule that requires a five-sixths qualified majority.

Unless there exist explicit constitutional constraints on the type of alternatives to be considered, or, more generally, on the activities of society subject to politicization, the natural tendency of majoritarian decision processes is to move towards actions that benefit members of the majority at the expense of members of the minority. Aided and abetted by imaginative political entrepreneurs, majority coalitions will succeed in securing political approval for programmes that provide differential or special benefits to their own members, while imposing costs, either generally on all citizens or differentially on members of the dominated minority. Or, conversely, majority coalitions will secure approval for programmes offering general benefits to the whole citizenry while being primarily financed by taxes imposed differentially on members of the minority. Or, in further extension of this natural proclivity of political majoritarianism, programmes that quite explicitly involve overt transfers from minority to majority members may become commonplace.

In any realist model or understanding of political process, majority rule becomes more than either a means of closing off discussion or of discovering truth. Majority rule becomes a means through which the interests of those who make up the successful coalition may be advanced, if necessary, at the expense of those who are outside this coalition. And when it is recognized that the make-up of majority coalitions shifts through time, we should scarcely be surprised at the growth of the politicized sector of society in the age of majoritarian democracy.

GENERALITY IN POLITICS

What can be done to keep democracy within some appropriate limits? How can the natural extension of majority rule be held in check, while at the same time preserving those elements of political equality that are deemed necessary for the functioning of civic order? How can the game that is majoritarian politics be controlled to ensure against minority exploitation? How can steps be taken to guarantee that this game be positive sum – that political action generates net benefits to all members of the inclusive polity?

These are, of course, questions that have been discussed through the ages. But they are, nonetheless, as relevant at the end of the twentieth century as they were in Athens in the centuries before Christ lived. The fears of democratic excesses expressed by the early Greeks also describe modern attitudes. The central problem of democracy has by no means been resolved.

James Madison, the most important of the American founders, sought to forestall the emergence of coalitional or factional politics by incorporating several procedural checks and balances into the constitutional structure. Governmental authority was to be deliberately divided between executive, legislative and judicial branches – each responsive to a different constituency and with differing institutional traditions. The legislative branch was to be further limited by bicameralism, with separated, if overlapping, constituencies for the two bodies. Further, power was to be divided between the central and regional, or provincial, governments with central domination restricted by the potential for secession. These several structural parameters for governance were to be implanted in an explicit constitution which also stipulated the limits on the extension of political power, no matter how exercised.

We now know that the Madisonian enterprise failed. The great American Civil War in the 1860s removed forever the threat of secession by the states. This basic constitutional change more or less ensured that, eventually, the United States would be transformed into a centralized majoritarian democracy with few, if any, checks on ultimate political authority. In this modern setting, democracy dominates society.

The parliamentary democracies of Western Europe were even less successful in holding back the forces for Leviathan. Confused by the electoral fallacy discussed above, these societies were allowed to drift into the politicized domination reflected in the modern social democracies of the expanded and intrusive welfare state, with little or no discussion of the appropriateness of limits to majoritarian control.

Observation suggests that democracy, in modern practice, is out of control. The great revolution of 1989–91, which displaced centralized collectivism as a viable form of economic order, seems to have exerted little or no influence on the continued overreaching of majoritarian democracies and on the ideas that sustain this movement. Is it possible even to imagine some means through which democracy can be limited, without, at the same time, replacing majority voting itself, which, unfortunately, has come to represent the meaning of democracy, at least in public attitudes? We do, indeed, find ourselves caught up in contradiction here. We want to define democracy as 'majority rule,' while, at the same time, we recognize that, under any realistic modelling of politics, majorities will act to exploit minorities.[3]

I suggest that the application and enforcement of the *principle of generality* can remove the contradiction here. We can reform our politics so as to reduce substantially, if not totally eliminate, majoritarian exploitation without in any way removing majority voting from its central place as the basic decision rule and also without placing specific areas of social activity beyond the boundaries for politicization. The principle of generality is almost self-explanatory. If political or collective action is to be taken at all, it must be general in application over all persons and groups in the political community. Politics cannot be allowed to take differential or discriminatory action. This principle would, indeed, close off many options for majoritarian choice. But within the whole set of alternatives that satisfies the generality criterion, majority voting may be allowed to make final determination.

The importance of the principle of generality was emphasized by Professor F.A. Hayek in his comprehensive treatise, *The Constitution of Liberty* (1960), although he did not discuss its applicability in the context of majoritarian politics. Hayek recognized, however, the relevance of generality as traditionally embodied in the rule of law, which he identified as a central norm in any society that would lay claim to classification as a liberal order. 'Equality under the law' as a norm implies that specific exemption or special treatment is out of bounds. In enforcing legal rules, the judiciary is simply not allowed to differentiate among individuals and groups. Of course, this principle of generality, even in law, has existed, and exists, only as a widely acknowledged norm for judicial action rather than a strictly followed directive for behaviour. Violations have, and do, occur. Nonetheless, the rule of law continues to retain its viability as an ongoing principle for legal order in all Western societies.

Why have social scientists and social philosophers, other than Hayek, failed to recognize that differential or discriminatory treatment in politics is, at base, equivalent to differential or discriminatory treatment in law? Why can a legislative or parliamentary majority pick out particular constituency groups for special treatment, either favourable or unfavourable, when a judge, in enforcing law, is prevented from comparable discrimination? The answer lies in the combination of the idealist model of politics and the electoral fallacy, both of which were discussed earlier in this chapter. Majority coalitions, both because their authority is presumed subject to electoral feedback, and they are presumed to be engaged in a search for truth rather than advantage, have been essentially immunized from critical behavioural scrutiny. And, indeed, the modern role for members of legislative assemblies has been transformed into one that involves the promotion of differential constituency interest as its defining characteristic.

Only if, as and when effective constitutional constraints are imposed on the discriminatory actions of majority coalitions can modern democratic politics be forced back into some appropriate relationship to the more inclusive society. It may be helpful at this stage to note several examples that would illustrate how a principle of generality would work if applied to politics.

Consider trade policy. The differential interest of each producer group (or industry) is to secure protection of its own market from potential competition by foreign suppliers. There are profits to be gained by investing in political activity that will impose such protection. And if a sufficiently influential coalition of producer groups can be organized, majoritarian politics will install the desired protectionist regime (Buchanan and Lee, 1991). The groups that succeed in this effort will, however, increase profits only if the restrictive policy remains nongeneral. If a principle of generality is in place, protection for any industry or producer group would require that like protection be extended for all industries. But, in this case, the differential or particular interest of any single group in protection no longer exists. Given an effective generalization requirement, the interest of each group is in a nonrestrictive regime of free trade. Support for protectionist majority coalitions would largely disappear.

As a second example, consider the familiar patterns of special interest spending. A single legislator is deemed praiseworthy by constituents if a governmental project is located in his or her district, quite independently of the overall net benefits of the project. Under a principle of generality, the approval of any locationally-specific project would require the comparable location of other projects in all districts, rather than only in those areas represented by the members of the majority coalition. In such case, the interest of the electoral constituency shifts and support for cost-ineffective projects disappears, but without in any way subverting the ultimate authority of a majority to take decision for the whole electorate.

As a third, and final, example, consider taxation. Somewhat interestingly, some elements of the generalization principle do describe tax structures in modern democratic regimes. Overtly discriminatory tax treatment of persons and groups as classified by political status would be deemed constitutionally out of bounds and attempts to impose such treatment would be prevented by judicial mandates in most jurisdictions. But important features of constitutionally acceptable tax structures clearly violate any generality norm. Democratic majorities can impose discriminatory taxes on particular sources and uses of income, on particular professions, occupations, industries or products and services and, perhaps, most importantly, rates of tax can be different for persons in differing income categories. The progressive income tax clearly represents a departure from the generality principle, and only a uniform proportional or flat rate tax, without exemption, deduction or shelter would fully qualify.

CHANGING THE PUBLIC MIND-SET: FROM THE PARTICULAR TO THE GENERAL

One way of interpreting the central argument advanced here is as a reconciliation between the teleological feature of the romantic notion of politics and the reality of interest-seeking political behaviour. Politics, as an activity, should be aimed at furtherance of 'good' for society. But political activity, as it is observed to take place in majoritarian democracy, does not match this philosophically legitimating purpose. The infusion of the generality principle or norm as a restriction on the domain of politics, as a limit on any ability of politics to further the defined interest of one group over another, would go far towards closing the gap between the ideal and the reality of democracy. Individuals will, of course, continue to seek to further their own interests, and these interests will differ among separately classified groups of persons. But potential disagreement over policy alternatives that are known to be generally applied are likely to be dramatically less intense than disagreement over nongeneralizable polity options.

A shift in the public mind-set towards politics is required if the generality principle is to gain adherence as a prospective avenue for structural reform. The remaining residues of the romantic image of a disembodied political authority seeking the 'good' and the 'true' must be swept away. In such an image, the good might, of course, involve the furtherance of the particular. The genuinely benevolent government might discriminate among groups in terms of criteria for overall goodness. But in the absence of any plausible presumption of benevolence, the general welfare cannot be promoted by other than general measures. Particular interests can be arrayed in support of generally applied alternatives only if and when the differentially superior profits from nongeneral alternatives are eliminated. A majority coalition will, of course, select a somewhat different mix of the feasible generalizable options than that mix preferred by members of the minority. But the difference would be reduced to a dimension along which all relevant alternatives tend to generate mutual advantage to all participants. The game of democracy would tend to be a positive sum.

SOCIETY AND DEMOCRACY

Only through the accomplishment of structural reform along the lines broadly suggested by the argument here can 'society' and 'democracy' be brought into the ultimately necessary symbiosis that is preferred by everyone. Democracy, as a basic organizational form, becomes the means through which persons in a civic order (a society) can secure the mutual benefits of peace and prosperity. Democracy cannot be allowed to trump society in the sense that the basic structure of civil order is determined by the relative success or failure of particular coalitions of persons and groups.

As such reform is implemented, politics, politicization and the outreach of the state must recede from the extended current margins as elements in the inclusive civic order. Within its own limits, as defined by its constitutional structure and as guided by the generalization norm, the state can, and should, remain strong. A weak state ensures only that factionalism, whether private or public, will emerge to subvert the genuinely productive collective action that a properly functioning constitutional democracy can facilitate.

Is it naive to hope that individuals can begin to think more seriously about the relationship between society and democracy so as to allow constitutional entrepreneurs to organize public support for specific reform? Until and unless there comes to be a general public understanding of the philosophical grounding of democracy *in* society, rather than the other way around, the march of history offers little basis for optimism. Such an understanding, translated into practice through structural reform, can help to create a twenty-first century that is dramatically different from the twentieth and better by all standards of comparison. Are living and future members of the post-socialist world up to the challenge?

NOTES

1. This chapter was initially presented as a lecture in Madrid, Spain, in December 1993.
2. For further discussion, see Vanberg and Buchanan (1989).
3. Norman Barry (1993) identifies a comparable contradiction in Hayek's position on parliamentary sovereignty.

23. Notes on the liberal constitution

No existing or proposed political constitution contains sufficient constraints or limits on the authority of the agencies of government over the activities of individuals and groups, and most notably over their economic activities. There is no *liberal* constitution in existence or in prospect. In this sense, all existing constitutions are failures, and almost all serious proposals for reform fall short of any promise of full success. I advance this blanket criticism of existing and proposed constitutional structures without knowledge of particular details but in full and conscious awareness of the historical fact that, for well over a century, all political discourse has been informed by, and the institutional results thereby influenced by, the 'fatal conceit' (Hayek, 1988) that political direction can facilitate rather than retard economic progress. All constitutions that have been put in place since the eighteenth century, and all that have been reformed (either explicitly or by usage and interpretation since that time) must reflect, to some degree, the romantic image of the benevolent state, whether actual or potential, the image that was introduced by the political idealists on the one hand and by the visionary socialists on the other.

The constitution that embodies 'politics without romance' (Buchanan, 1979) exists nowhere today, and no reform proposals that reflect such a realist model of politics enter directly into any ongoing dialogue. Residues of such a vision may be found only in some of the Madisonian elements that remain in the US documents and records and in the arguments of the relatively small number of classical liberals now extant. Despite this negative assessment, which may seem to be nearly total in its condemnatory sweep, there may be bases for some optimism as we look far enough forward into the post-revolutionary epoch, and especially into the next century. Ideas do have consequences, and we have lived with the consequences of false ideas for almost two centuries – far too long to have expected shifts to occur by the mid-1990s. But consequences, or rather events, also feed back on ideas, and, after the unpredicted revolutions of 1989–91, the romantic image of the benevolent and capable state must prove increasingly difficult to sustain. The theories of political failure, advanced sparingly by classical liberals throughout the period of socialist hegemony only to have been treated with scorn and derision, have been corroborated by history in what was perhaps the grandest of all experiments in social science. And unless we totally despair of human capacity for rational action, we must

225

anticipate that, sometime in the post-socialist century, men and women will exhibit constructive constitutional capabilities that can now be scarcely imagined.

In this sense, Francis Fukuyama (1992) is surely right. Call it what one will, something of historical note did effectively end with the great revolutions of 1989–91. And Fukuyama is also correct in suggesting that economic science, which explains how the market economy operates independently of politicized direction and control so as to produce the largest bundle of goods and services available within given resource constraints, has finally been vindicated. But is Fukuyama also right when he predicts that this scientific result will be incorporated into institutional-constitutional reform? To agree with him here, we, perhaps, must think beyond the horizon of a few decades.

As a start, it may be useful to extend our hindsight into the pre-romantic, pre-socialist epoch, back to the eighteenth century, to try to recapture the constitutional understanding that so excited the philosophers as well as the politicians. Until and unless such a shift in the modern mind-set is somehow achieved, all efforts at constitutional dialogue aimed at basic reform will essentially be wasted. Governments, no matter how organized, will remain basically unchanged, and the politicians-bureaucrats will continue to facilitate the mutual exploitation of each by all, as in Anthony de Jasay's 'churning state' (1985). Economies will founder, and, increasingly, potentially valued product will disappear into the 'black hole' of that which might have been (Magee, Brock and Young, 1989).

THE CONSTITUTIONAL ORDER OF CLASSICAL LIBERALISM

The classical liberals of the eighteenth century, whether represented by the members of the Scots Enlightenment or by the American founding fathers, were highly sceptical about the capability and willingness of politics and politicians to further the interests of the ordinary citizen. Governments were considered to be a necessary evil, institutions to be protected from, but made necessary by the elementary fact that all persons are not angels (Madison, 1787, [1966]). Governments, along with those persons who were empowered as their agents of authority, were not to be trusted. Constitutions were necessary, primarily as a means to constrain collective authority in all of its potential extensions. State power was something that the classical liberals feared, and the problem of constitutional design was thought to be that of ensuring that such power would be effectively limited.

The devices aimed to accomplish this purpose are the familiar ones: sovereignty was split among several levels of collective authority; federalism was designed to allow for a deconcentration or decentralization of coercive state power; the separate functional branches of government were deliberately placed in continued tension, one with another, at each level of authority. In some polities, the dominant legislative branch was further restricted by the constitutional establishment of two bodies, each of which was organized on a separate principle of representation.

It is important to recognize that these basic organizational-procedural elements of political constitutions were designed, discussed and put in place by the classical liberals within the context of a shared aim or purpose, which was that of checking or constraining the coercive power of the state over individuals. The motivating force was never one of making government work better in the accomplishment of some arbitrarily selected public good, or even one of ensuring that all interests were somehow more fully represented.

The organizational-procedural elements of the classical liberal constitution (those listed above and others) were deemed to be less important than those provisions that laid out the range and scope of activities that were appropriately to be undertaken by collective authority. That is to say, the constitutional instructions as to what governments might and might not do were always considered to be much more important than how governments do whatever it is that they, in fact, do. This critical distinction, which was central to the whole classical liberal conception of social order, was essentially lost to the public consciousness during the ascendency of electoral democracy, especially during the nineteenth and twentieth centuries. There was generalized acceptance of the fallacy that equated the emergence of electoral democracy with a reduced need for explicit constitutional constraints on the range and scope of governmental activity.

In the classical liberal constitutional order, the activities of government, no matter how the agents are selected, are functionally restricted to the parameters for social interaction. Governments, ideally, were to be constitutionally prohibited from direct action aimed at carrying out any of the several basic economic functions: (1) setting the scale of values, (2) organizing production and (3) distributing the product. These functions were to be carried out beyond the conscious intent of any person or agency; they were performed through the operation of the decentralized actions of the many participants in the economic nexus, as coordinated by markets, and within a framework of laws and institutions that were appropriately maintained and enforced by government.

This framework-maintenance role, properly assigned to government in the classical liberal order, included the protection of property and the enforcement of voluntary contracts; the effective guarantee of entry and exit into industries, trades and professions; the ensured openness of markets, internal and external, and the prevention of fraud in exchange. This framework role for government also was considered to include the establishment of a monetary standard and in such fashion as to ensure predictability in the value of the designated monetary unit. (It is in this monetary responsibility that almost all constitutions have failed, even those that were allegedly motivated originally by classical liberal precepts. Governments, throughout history, have almost always moved beyond constitutionally authorized limits of their monetary authority.)

A central principle inherent in the classical liberal constitution dictated that, regardless of what governments do, and whether or not collective activities are contained within the indicated limits, all persons and groups are to be equally treated. The generality principle, applicable to the law, was to be extended also to politics. There was no role for governmental action that explicitly differentiated among separate factions or classes of persons. In the classical liberal conception, successful majority coalitions could not impose differential taxation on members of political minorities, even for purposes of 'doing good' (Buchanan, 1992b).

THE CONSTITUTIONAL ORDER OF SOCIALISM

The classical liberal vision of a constitutional order did not command widespread public and philosophical acceptance for more than the several decades that straddled the turn between the eighteenth and nineteenth centuries. In small part, the reaction against this vision was due to the zealotry of those advocates who extended the central *laissez-faire* precept too enthusiastically, even to the rejection of a collective-governmental role in setting the parameters for economic interaction. But, primarily, the reaction against classical liberalism stemmed from the generalized unwillingness of participants in the body politic to accept the spontaneous allocative and distributive results generated in the operation of a market economy. These results were not taken to be natural; they were not understood to be the working out of the whole complex of separated choices made by persons in their many capacities. The results of market process were taken to be artifactual – produced rather than emergent and, hence, subject to direct manipulation, change and redirection by politicized collective action.

The reaction against classical liberalism was specifically stimulated and fuelled by two separate sources. First, the genius of Karl Marx lay in his ability to isolate, identify and publicize those elements in the operation of market capitalism that seemed most open to criticism, especially in the intellectual context of an incompleted classical economic theory, along with prevailing confusion as to the distinction between constitutional and within-constitutional operations of governments. Marx concentrated on the vulnerability of capitalism to financial crises, on the tendency towards concentration in industry and on the alleged distributive exploitation of the proletariat. Second, political idealists for many centuries had implicitly used models of the state that involved presumptive benevolence and omniscience. Any failures of markets could, under this presumption of the idealized collectivity, be fully corrected by directed political action. The generalized Marxist critique, along with the presumption of idealized political governance, essentially destroyed the intellectual-scientific basis that had been constructed in justification of the classical liberal constitutional order.

From the middle of the nineteenth century, some vision of a socialist order emerged to capture, in varying degrees of enthusiasm, the minds of persons in all developed societies, even in those societies where Marxism, as such, was able to secure relatively little direct support. At base, the socialist vision categorically rejected the classical liberal conception of a self-regulating economy that operates within a set of constitutional limits enforced by government which, in turn, is itself limited largely, if not totally, to the enforcement role. And, if the self-regulating, or nonpoliticized, economy is rejected as the basic organizing principle, the controlled or regulated economy becomes a necessary component of any alternative model for social organization. This shift from the self-regulating model of an economy to that of a controlled or regulated economy may be, but need not be, directly related to issues that involve organizational-procedural changes involving ways and means that agents and agencies of governance are selected, along with constitutional dictates concerning how the control and regulatory functions are to be performed.

The socialist constitutional order, whether this be defined in application to a single party, a self-appointed authoritarian regime or a social democratic parliamentary majority, necessarily extends the range and scope for politicization well beyond the narrowly defined limits of collective authority under the classical liberal order. If the whole economy is opened up for control and regulation in the general interest, there can be, by definition, little or no prior constitutional constraint on the definition of what such interest is by those agents and agencies charged with the responsibility for allocative and distributive results. Whereas governments in a classical liberal constitutional order have only a limited responsibility for the results that emerge from the interaction of persons in many capacities, governments in the socialist constitutional order have full or total responsibility for all results, including the size, composition and distribution of the bundle of value generated in the whole system. This ultimate responsibility remains with government even if the market, as a means of organization, is allowed to operate without detailed direction over wide areas of interaction. In the socialist model of government, there is, and can be, no constitutional guarantee offered to economic actors, whether persons or firms, against politically generated intrusions into liberty of commerce, whether this be marginal or total. In a genuine sense, with reference to the structure of the economy, the very term *socialist constitution* is oxymoronic. At best, the constitutional order of socialism embodies constraints only on the procedures of politics and the behaviour of political agents in carrying out those procedures; it cannot extend to include constraints on politicization of the economy, as such.

As we now know, as we have been informed by the great revolutions in Central and Eastern Europe in 1989–91, as well as by the cumulative historical experience from other parts of the world, as supplemented by analytical argument, the central principle for socialist order is fatally flawed and has been from the outset of its promulgation. The presumption that politicized control-regulation of economic relationships can, and will, generate a satisfactorily large bundle of goods and services, as valued by participants themselves, has been shown to be grounded in fallacy, both by argument and experience. In sum, the grand socialist experiments of the century did not work, and improved variants on these experiments cannot work, given the motivational, epistemological and imaginative limits of the human animal. There is now generalized acceptance of the proposition that only market organization of the economy, which exploits the human potential, can produce an acceptably adequate aggregate of economic value.

THE POST-SOCIALIST CONSTITUTIONAL CONTRADICTION

The set of public, professional, political and philosophical attitudes that seems most descriptive of the immediate post-socialist years of the 1990s is internally contradictory. The socialist vision of politicized control-regulation of economic interaction has by no means been exorcised from the modern mind-set despite the evidence from reason or from history. The belief that persons, acting jointly through their membership in collectivities, can effectively improve on the spontaneously generated outcomes of market processes remains embedded in the modern psyche. Despite the overwhelming strength of the evidence, and despite supporting argument, persons cannot readily acquiesce in the stance suggested by post-socialist reality. The romance of socialism, which is dependent both on an idealized politics and a set of impossible behavioural presuppositions, has not yet disappeared.

Whether or not the romance will, in fact, fade away as we move further beyond the post-revolutionary turbulence of the 1990s and into the next century, cannot be settled outside futuristic speculation. Several questions may be posed: will truth finally triumph over romance? Will the constitutional order of classical liberalism return, in some form, and come to command acceptance as the only order that combines personal liberty and economic prosperity? Will the public's interest in aggregative economic growth, in economic progress itself, finally carry the day and be reflected in genuine constitutional reforms? Or, may we expect the emergence of some new ideology that will offer renewed sustenance to a romantic image of collectivized utopia? Without the emergence of such an ideology, can we expect public acquiescence in authoritarian grabs for power? Without some equivalent of the Marxist class struggle as an ideological crutch for sloganeering, can the politicians escape sceptical censure by the public, even if there is little understanding of the functioning of the market? Is some tacit knowledge of constitutionalism likely to surface as the twenty-first century approaches?

The politics of my own country, the United States, does not offer much basis for short-term optimism in putative response to these questions. The rhetoric of class warfare is used to generate support for an enlargement of the already swollen governmental sector of the economy, and the provisional scepticism of the 1980s about the efficacy of regulatory efforts seems to have been replaced by reversion to nostrums of a half-century past. 'Socialism in the small' is on the ascendency, as if the demise of 'socialism in the large' is totally irrelevant. Politics aimed at improving on the outcomes of market processes is presumed capable of succeeding, despite the working of the selfsame incentive incompatibilities, knowledge limitations and entrepreneurial disregard that produced the background for the great revolutions of 1989–91.

As noted earlier, if we are to find grounds for constitutional hope, it may be necessary to extend our sights, both temporally and locationally. We must recall Keynes' insistence on the long-range influence of ideas. Perhaps the post-socialist period is simply too short for us to have expected shifts in public and political attitudes, especially in those societies that did not themselves go through the revolutionary upheavals. Perhaps any rebirth of classical liberalism must be expected to occur in those societies that did indeed suffer the revolutions; perhaps only in those countries has there been a sufficient loss of belief in politics and politicians to allow some reconstruction of the eighteenth-century ideal of constitutional order.

Only one prediction seems safe here. The constitutional prospect for the next century will be one of surprises.

CONCLUSIONS

I have discussed only briefly the whole set of constitutional issues that involves organizational and procedural alternatives of governance. I have not addressed such issues as republican versus parliamentary forms of government; proportional representation versus two-party structures; effective federalism versus political centralization. But my neglect of these issues has been quite deliberate. All such organizational-procedural matters fade into insignificance by comparison with the constitutional challenge of placing constraints on the authority of government over the operation of the economy. Until and unless the government is severely constrained in its economic overreaching, along more or less classical liberal principles (including the principle of generality), the particular choices made among the organizational and procedural alternatives become relatively insignificant.

A democratically elected parliamentary majority imbued with socialist ideas and vision can destroy the potential value that might be forthcoming from an unfettered market economy as much or more than the activities of an authoritarian regime. To the extent that constitutional constraints do effectively limit governments in their regulatory, financial and taxing powers, the particular constitutional form for governance itself assumes secondary rank. To the extent that the powers of government remain open-ended and nonconstrained, the forms of government may seem to matter. But in some final sense, the overextended politics must surely fail, regardless of structural particulars.

In almost all countries, the continuing dialogue and discussion is centred on the establishment, maintenance and preservation of 'constitutional democracy.' My central argument may be summarized in the statement that *constitutional* is the critically important one of the two words here. Economic prosperity and progress, as measured in value produced and consumed, can only occur in settings where the activities of government are constitutionally constrained, quite independently of how governmental agents are selected.

24. Reform without romance: first principles in political economy[1]

At an Austrian meeting in August 1994, a distinguished philosopher surprised his audience by an emphatic insistence that he was no guru – that his role did not include the proffering of advice on this or that major issue of the day. I want to do the same thing. I want to preface any remarks by emphasizing that I am not sufficiently familiar with the historical, institutional or environmental particulars of any country to speak in a detailed way either on current economic policy or on ordinary politics. But I am a *political economist* – a scientist who does try to understand how political and economic structures actually work. And from this understanding certain first or basic principles emerge – principles that may be used to design reforms, provided that an agreed-upon set of objectives exists. But these principles are general, and they must in every case be applied in the knowledge of the particular time and place. My role is, therefore, to present and defend the general principles that can, indeed, tell us how economic prosperity, personal freedoms and domestic tranquillity can be achieved.

HUMAN NATURE

Let me first explain my title 'Reform without Romance'. My primary emphasis is on 'without romance'. In many countries, decades (even centuries) have passed with far too much intellectual effort exerted in elaborating idealized or stylized constructions of how a political economy might work. Unfortunately, analysis and examination of how political and economic interaction takes place in nonromantic or realistic institutional settings, as populated by real persons, were largely ignored. The public choice research programme is basically aimed at correcting this error.

Once this basic shift in perspective is taken, we are well on the way towards understanding. Ordinary persons, no matter what roles they may occupy in political, administrative, bureaucratic or business structures, respond to private, personal incentives in roughly similar ways. That is to say, there are uniformities in behaviour patterns that can be used to help us in deriving some of the general or first principles about which I spoke. In this fundamental sense, persons do not behave differently over time and space. Persons in the nineteenth century responded to incentives in much the same way that persons respond in 1994. And persons in Romania respond similarly to persons in Austria, America or Africa. I am not denying the importance of culture here. I suggest only that the differences that we observe are to be attributed largely, even if not entirely, to the differences in the separate incentives structures, which range as widely among historical epochs as among polities.

CLASSICAL POLITICAL ECONOMY

The great eighteenth-century classical economists who called themselves moral philosophers, notably Adam Smith and David Hume, were successful in generating genuine and independent intellectual excitement with their discovery of how the basic uniformities in human behaviour, in human nature, could be institutionally channelled so as to serve the generally desired objectives of economic prosperity (as measured in terms of growth and stability) along with personal liberties and domestic tranquillity. Their discovery now seems simple enough, even if its implications are denied in practice in any and all political regimes in existence today, whether East or West. But a review might be useful.

Thomas Hobbes, who wrote a full century earlier than Smith and Hume and whose great book *Leviathan* was published in 1651, did, indeed, see through the romantic blinders when he looked at politics. Hobbes recognized that persons and groups have conflicting interests; that war, not peace, was the natural setting and that man's life would be nasty, brutish and short unless a political sovereign was established to maintain security and order. What he failed to recognize, however, was the prospect for controlling the interpersonal conflicts of interest by means that did not require the surrender of extensive personal liberties to the political sovereign. Hobbes failed to see that, provided only that the political authority establishes and maintains a regime that defines, protects and enforces a regime of private ownership of property (including property in person), the incentives for persons to promote their separate interests through voluntary exchange would result in benefits for all of a nation's citizens. And it is precisely this discovery that marks the contribution of the moral philosophers of the eighteenth century, as articulated best in Adam Smith's great book *The Wealth of Nations*, published in 1776.

Let me concentrate on the most familiar statement in *The Wealth of Nations*, the argument that the butcher offers meat for purchase not from some motivation of benevolence but, instead, out of regard to his own self-interest. The butcher has an incentive to sell us meat for supper because he secures money in exchange – money that he may then use in other exchanges to secure those goods which he most desires. That is to say, the whole interlinked chain or network of voluntary reciprocal exchanges allows all persons, as producers and consumers, to secure the bundle of goods they separately desire while, at the same time, retaining the liberties to do as each pleases, subject to no direct control by political authority.

NATURAL LIBERTY

The simple system of natural liberty, to use Adam Smith's own designation, or as we would say, the market organization of economic activity, serves two functions simultaneously. Resources are directed by private owners into the most productive activities, as determined by the demands of final consumers, who get, in turn, the largest possible bundle of goods, again as measured by individuals' own evaluations. At the same time, however, over and beyond this economic or efficiency-enhancing function, the market reduces or eliminates the need for collective or political choices to be made concerning what, how and how much is to be produced and consumed, and by whom. That is to say, the market serves a *political* as well as an *economic* function – one that may well be the more important of the two. Efficiency and economic liberty are two consequences of the same structural order of social interaction.

This summary sketch of the first principles of classical political economy is perhaps sufficient to suggest the excitement that was generated by the discovery of these principles in the eighteenth century. And a genuine understanding of these principles remains the basis for the arguments that place market organization at the centre of any institutional reform today, regardless of the current historical setting and independently of existing relationships.

LAWS AND INSTITUTIONS

These first principles do not, however, specify the nature of the political-legal-ethical framework within which individuals might be expected to carry on the many activities that make up an efficient and ongoing market economy. These first principles have been, and are, used by *laissez-faire* ideologues to suggest that free markets work well, anywhere and everywhere, and quite independently of the political-legal-ethical setting. Adam Smith did not make this mistake. He was careful to say that the market order, the system of natural liberty, works well only within the appropriate set of 'laws and institutions'. But Smith, perhaps, paid too little attention to precise definitions of these institutional requirements.

We, as political economists, have learned something in the two-and-one-quarter centuries since Adam Smith. We can now extend the first principles to include a specification of the political-legal-ethical framework that must be in existence for market order to work well – a framework that must be the central focus of any and all efforts at reform.

A preliminary principle emerges even prior to any such specification, however. A categorical distinction must be made between collective or political action directed at changes or reforms in the structural or constitutional framework for the market order and collective or political action directed at changes in resource usage within this order. An understanding of the first principles sketched out above should suggest that political reforms are or may be appropriate if aimed at the constitutional structure but are not often appropriate if aimed at modifying patterns of resource use within the operation of markets themselves.

But what are the political-legal-ethical parameters that must exist in order for a market economy to function effectively?

PRIVATE PROPERTY

First of all, persons must be in possession of full ownership rights to the means of producing economic value, whether these means are in the form of human or nonhuman capacities. Only with private ownership can the appropriate incentives be exploited. The basic argument for private ownership has been known since Aristotle. Persons will care for, maintain and direct the use of productive resources properly only if there is a reciprocal relationship between effort expended and reward anticipated. A central Marxian socialist fallacy was the neglect of this ancient Aristotelian principle. How could persons be expected to produce economic value if the linkage between productive effort (work as well an entrepreneurship) and the distribution of rewards is severed. In a paper I wrote several years ago, I referred to the impossible socialist idyll of 'consumption without production' (see Chapter 13; Buchanan 1993c).

Viewed from the Aristotelian perspective, any and all attempts to operate an economy on collective-command-central principles were foredoomed to failure. In modern terms, the structure of any such economy is incentive incompatible, quite apart from other central problems of management, such as the utilization and acquisition of knowledge concerning both consumer wants and producer capacities.

FREEDOM OF ENTRY

The assignment of private ownership rights is a first principle for viable economic order, and a basic political task is the enforcement of such rights. But privatization and enforcement are not, of themselves, sufficient to secure a well-functioning market economy. The ideologists of *laissez-faire* often neglect to note the limits that must be placed on the behaviour of those who participate in market dealings, even as fully protected owners of private property. Persons and groups must be prevented from erecting barriers to entry into and exit from productive activity. Adam Smith's butcher offers meat for purchase out of his own self-interest, but this action is kept within nonexploitive limits only by the presumption that other prospective butchers, who may offer to sell at competitively determined prices, are present. The rights of private property cannot be extended to include rights to establish and enforce monopoly positions in markets.

The assignment and enforcement of rights to private ownership of property, along with the guarantee of rights to free entry into and exit from economic activity, are appropriate framework parameters, responsibility for which must be placed directly with the political-legal authorities. The market, standing alone and independent from political authority as defined by these basic functions, cannot be expected to accomplish the genuine miracle that remains possible if the parametric framework is in place.

MONETARY STABILITY

Beyond private ownership and free entry, what else is required that is appropriately guaranteed by legal-political authority? Recognition that viable activity – production, exchange and consumption – can take place only in a monetary economy draws direct attention to the function of money and to a possible political-legal role in establishing stability in monetary value. If exchanges are to be made in units of monetary value, if relative prices of goods and resource units are defined in nominal monetary terms, the vulnerability of the whole economy to unpredictable shifts and swings in the value of money becomes clear. Stability in monetary value becomes a much desired characteristic of the framework for market order.

There are certain advocates of markets who argue that *laissez-faire* will generate the emergence of a market-based monetary unit and that the forces of entry and exit will ensure adequate stability in its value, thereby leaving little or no monetary role for the political-legal authorities. I do not, personally, accept this argument, although I recognize its persuasive features. For my own view, I look upon monetary stability as a necessary element in the parameters of a viable market economy, and I think that such stability should be, and can be, guaranteed by political action. In saying this, I can be (and have been) accused of political naiveté, of myself maintaining a romantic vision of how politics actually works. Governments and politicians, anywhere and everywhere, have used their money-creating powers to extract value from citizens. Why, then, should I suggest that politics can, indeed, guarantee monetary stability?

Recall, however, that my self-assigned task in this chapter is to introduce some first principles for reform in the organization of a market economy. I am not, at this time, offering a realistic or hard-headed positive analysis of just how politics, or markets, work. The elementary fact is that throughout time governments may be observed to allow property rights to be confiscated or eroded to serve the interests of politicians; they may be observed to erect barriers to entry and exit in exchange, again to the interests of politicians, and they may be observed to use money-issue powers to extract value. This record does not, in any way, imply that such behaviour remains impervious to any institutional-organizational-constitutional reform. The whole normative purpose of the enterprise of 'constitutional political economy' is to lay out first principles for institutional change that may constrain the natural proclivities of politicians to subvert the genuine interests of citizens as participants in the network of market exchange.

ETHICS

Private property, freedom of entry and exit, monetary stability – is the attainment of these objectives sufficient to allow the prediction that prosperity, peace and order will emerge? To this point I have said nothing specific about the place of ethical or moral norms in the workings of a market economy. The discussion has been grounded on the presumption that there exist behavioural uniformities in all cultures that allow the derivation of principles for institutional-organizational reforms independently of time and place. Nonetheless, the cultural norms of behaviour, which may differ substantially among nations and over time, can affect the efficacy of any efforts to apply the general principles for reform which have been outlined above. An economy in which participants behave, generally, in accordance with what we may call 'the morality of the marketplace' will produce more economic value than an economy in which participants seek maximally to exploit each and every opportunity to realize personal gain, even at the direct expense of trading partners. There will exist productivity differences even if the formal institutional parameters are identical in the two settings. The ethical norm that dictates fairness in trading, rather than fraud, can be highly beneficial in generating mutually desirable results.

The importance of ethical standards in the successful workings of a market economy should, I think, be stressed in any discussion of first principles for reform in post-communist countries. A half-century's experience of life under command-control economic regimes has surely led to some erosion of the behavioural traits conducive to a regime of market exchange. The command-control economy, with its ubiquitous shortages, offered perverse incentives towards behaviour aimed opportunistically in order to secure differential advantage. Changes in behavioural attitudes should not be expected to occur suddenly, regardless of the institutional reforms that may be put in place.

I think that the years since 1989 have already done much to remove the early romantic dreams about the ability of the quick fix that seemed to be promised by dramatic reforms. But I fear that in some countries and among some observers the pendulum has already swung too far in the negative direction. There is no basis for any abandonment of the first principles of reform – principles that retain their validity and that continue to offer the best, and indeed the only, means through which citizens of a country can serve the joint blessings of liberty, prosperity and peace.

NOTE

1. Material in this chapter was presented in a lecture in Romania in September 1994.

PART IV

Federalism

25. National politics and competitive federalism: Italy and the constitution of Europe[1]

In this chapter, I propose to examine, in a general and abstract sense, the constraints that are placed on the autonomy of a single political unit by its membership in an effective federal union or federalism that is described basically or primarily by an integrated and open economic nexus. Italy's membership in the emerging federalism of Europe becomes the obvious exemplar for my analysis here, even if detailed interpretations of the pre-Maastricht, Maastricht and post-Maastricht institutional prospects are not within my ken.

Italy's 'constitutional interest' in the European federalism seems to me, as an external observer, to be unique. To summarize my conclusion at the outset, let me say that Europe and Europeanization offers to the Italian citizenry the necessary opportunity for the implementation of internal reforms without which Italian politics and politicians might continue the regime of fiscal profligacy well into the next century. Italian citizens-voters face a rare opportunity to put their fiscal house in order, as their political leaders are forced into fiscal responsibility, perhaps 'kicking and screaming' on behalf of their special-interest constituencies, but moving nonetheless in the directions dictated by considerations of the general interest. In my view, far too much attention has been given, in the post-Maastricht discussions, to the need to constrain the powers of the potential federal authority of Brussels relative to the constraining influence on national politics and politicians that such federal authority might itself exert.

SUPRANATIONAL ECONOMIC INTEGRATION AND LIMITS ON NATIONAL SOVEREIGNTY

Let me first define some terms, and, as economists always do, let me set up a model that will facilitate analysis and discussion. I want to examine the relationship between the range and extent of 'the economy' or 'the market' on the one hand and the range and extent of 'the polity' on the other. My particular focus is on the problems that arise when the economic nexus is more extensive than the political nexus and not vice versa.

In one sense, of course, the economic nexus is world-wide; at least some markets are world markets in the true sense and would remain so almost regardless of political boundaries. And, in yet another sense, some economic relationships remain very localized; some markets are necessarily local. I want to cut through possible ambiguity here and stipulate that for my purposes, I shall presume that the size of the economic nexus is well-defined by the limits within which economic or trading relationships *may* take place without politicized interferences. And the specific object for attention is the setting in which this economic nexus includes within its territorial dimensions several separately organized political communities, separate 'nations', each of which has a history of national autonomy or independence.

The economy is characterized by freedom of trade in goods and services, by freedom of movement for persons and resources, including labour and capital, throughout the territorial limits. The necessary institutional structure is described as competitive, although, within limits, 'public' as well as 'private' ownership may be present. But there must be freedom of entry and exit into and out of all relevant productive and distributive processes. I shall leave aside analyses of possible economic interactions between persons or organizations inside this economy and persons and organizations beyond the defined limits. In other words, the trade that is external to the federalism is not under discussion here.

It is necessary to specify precisely how political authority (or 'sovereignty') is divided as between the separate national political units within the federal union or federalism and the central political authority of the federalism itself (the 'federal government'). I shall analyse that setting in which the central authority is severely restricted; it is constitutionally empowered only to enforce the guarantees for openness across the whole economy, to ensure that trade and resource flows across national boundaries are not restricted or protected by actions of national political units. This central government authority is minimal, and the authority mirrors in effect the results that would emerge if the separated national units should join in a genuine free-trade zone, with some full enforceable guarantee against the violation of terms by the autonomous units. Also, and importantly, this model becomes descriptive of an integrated economy as driven by forces of technology coupled with a psychological shift in public attitudes away from nationalism *per se* and toward supranational loyalties. It does not seem unrealistic to suggest that the Europe of the late 1990s and early 2000s will be described by some combination of these institutional forms.

In the setting stipulated, the separate national polities – the nation-states – retain authority over all elements of potential policy except those that allow overt interference with the free flow of goods, services and resources across national borders, as within the federalism. I want to analyse the internal and indirect constraints that membership in the integrated and open economy, within the territory of the federalism, will impose on the political choices of the member nation-states. For example, how will membership in an open and integrated economy constrain national choices with respect to monetary and fiscal policies? How will such membership affect national choices to provide genuinely public goods financed by general taxes? How will membership in the federal union with a supranational economy affect the ability of national political units to implement transfer schemes through which some citizens are taxed to finance payments to others?

THE PROTECTIVE STATE AND THE PRODUCTIVE STATE

These questions may be addressed by classifying political activities, the actions taken on behalf of the national unit, 'the state', into several sets, as these have been discussed in basic political philosophy. There is, first, that set of activities that are necessary to define the rules of social interaction – activities that provide the framework for any economic and social relationships between and among individuals and groups. This set includes the familiar requirements for a legal order, those institutions that allow for the definition and enforcement of claims to valued endowments, both personal and nonpersonal. Private or separate property and the enforcement of contracts of exchange in rights to property – these are the recognized bases for social order, commonly recognized to be necessary elements in what I have called 'the protective state', and which others have variously called 'the night-watchman state' or 'the minimal state' (Buchanan, 1975).

These most basic of all political functions are important with reference to the central questions examined here. In an integrated supranational economy, what would happen if the separate national units should differ widely among themselves in the performance of the protective state role? Suppose, for example, that the legal-political authority in one national state does not protect persons and properties to the standards that are descriptive of the other nations in the federalism. Suppose that fraud, theft, brigandage, assault, plunder and other intrusions on persons, endowments, claims and contracts are more widespread in one polity than in others.

The economic results are easy to predict. Owners of productive resources will invest less in the national unit that fails, relatively, in its role of the protective state, at least less than they would otherwise invest. Rates of return would necessarily include a margin for losses that need not be included at all in more 'orderly' units. Because of the relative shortfall in capital investment, competitively-determined wage rates for comparable labour capacities will tend to be lower in the less orderly units. The differential in wage levels will, in turn, offer incentives for an outmigration of workers to other units in the free-trade zone. In the economic equilibrium across the whole territory of the integrated market, the less orderly unit pays for its political-legal failure by generating a lower-valued product than its basic resource potential would make possible.

But how will membership in the integrated economy of a supranational federalism affect this result, which would seem to emerge whether or not the national state in question enters in the inclusive economic nexus? Membership in the more inclusive market – one that extends across national political boundaries – will generate a more dramatic differential as among levels of national product and, for this reason, will impose relatively higher costs on persons who remain in nonproductive roles in the less orderly unit. Owners of productive resources – labour and capital alike – can act to ensure against the exploitation inherent in the failure of the state to fulfill its protective function; they can do so by migrating to more orderly polities within the federalism. These owners need not remain among the continuing net losers under the failures of the protective state. Those citizens who do not, or cannot, take advantage of the possibilities offered by the widened economic nexus must lose out in the equilibrating process. They do so because they cannot secure benefits from the exploitation of those resource owners who can, and do, act on the opportunities offered by exit.

As this prospect comes to be recognized, the natural proclivity of governments might seem to point towards politically orchestrated interferences with the flow of resources beyond national boundaries, efforts that would, of course, violate the basic terms of federalized integration. And it is precisely to prevent such efforts that a strong, if limited, central federal authority is presumably established. Further, the prospect that such efforts may come to dominate the internal politics of nations undermines the argument to the effect that a supranational free-trade zone, without a central authority, may be a superior institutional form.

The analysis of the effects of possible differential performance in the role of the protective state by the separate national units in a supranational economy, as organized politically in a federal union or federalism, can be repeated, more or less without change, for the relative performance of nations in their roles as productive states. The classical Italian writers on the *scienze delle finanze*, and especially Antonio De Viti De Marco, stressed that the state can be productive as well as protective. Political units can provide services that are equivalent to inputs into the production of goods and services, and these inputs enhance the value productivity of complementary privately-supplied inputs. In modern terminology, the governmental or political supply and financing of elements of economic infrastructure can, possibly, make the privately-organized sector of the economy more rather than less efficient in producing final goods and services.

The ultimate test lies, of course, in the comparative results. And the primary, indeed, the central effect of economic integration into a supranational nexus is the direct demonstration of the comparative political efficiencies of the separate political units – the separate member states. If a single nation-state, through the complex operation of its internal political institutions, succeeds in offering a mix of tax-financed public goods (infrastructure) that is economically more productive than its national counterparts (competitors), private investment will become marginally more productive in that unit, thereby providing an attractor for the inflow of capital and, ultimately, labour. By contrast, if a single nation-state essentially defaults in its productive-state role, through the tax-financing of resource-wasting, 'public' projects that affect private productivity negatively, its citizens must lose out, relatively, in the competitive federalism, with the losses observable in net resource outflows to other units in the federalism.

The competition among the separate national units within the supranational federal arrangement that defines the inclusive territory for the economic nexus will, over time, tend to produce an observable 'regularization' and 'harmonization' of the economic activities geographically classified as located in the separate states. The relative productivities of publicly-supplied infrastructure will tend towards some degree of equality. The national politics that fail to meet the competitive standards determined by the operation of competitive national politics in other units will be effectively forced to modify the mix of public-goods supply. But note in particular here that such regularization and harmonization *emerge* as a result of a potential and ongoing competitive process; these results do not, and cannot, emerge from dictates laid down in advance by the central authority, since this authority itself has no means of knowing what quality and quantity of infrastructure investment by the political units will prove, in the end, to be economically most efficient.

THE MONETARY-FISCAL ROLES FOR THE NATION-STATES IN A SUPRANATIONAL FEDERALISM

I shall not indulge in the taxonomic argument concerning whether or not the monetary-fiscal arrangements of a national state should be classified within the activities of the protective or the productive state. In any case, these monetary-fiscal arrangements warrant special consideration since it is the monetary-fiscal autonomy of the national units that may seem to be most directly affected by membership in a supranational federalism with an integrated economy. Recall that, in my discussion here, I do not stipulate any institutional centralization of monetary-fiscal authority. The separate nation-states, as separate polities, are at liberty to pursue internally chosen monetary-fiscal policies. I concentrate attention only on the indirect constraints imposed on such policy choices by the guarantee of openness of the market across the whole territory of the inclusive federalism.

We may presume that each of the separated nation-states would organize its monetary operation through the institution of a central bank that issues a national currency. The monetary unit of a national political unit is presumed to be freely exchangeable, at floating rates of exchange, against all other national monies in the federalism. (I shall not model the workings of fixed-rate schemes akin to the European EMS.) Internally politicized interferences with the movement of financial assets among the separate parts of the federalism are effectively prohibited by the central federal authority.

In this setting, if a single national central bank allows its own currency, and related instruments, to expand at rates that are higher, relative to internal demands, than comparable rates in competing units of the federalism, internal rates of inflation will exceed those observed elsewhere. Relatively higher inflation in a single nation-state will produce two predicted effects. There is empirical evidence to the effect that higher rates of inflation are accompanied by decreased predictability in the value of the monetary unit. This will increase the riskiness of investment and thereby reduce the flow of resources towards the inflating nation. Second, the indirect tax levied on all holders and users of assets defined in nominal money units will tend to reduce the net productivity of all resource investment, human and nonhuman, unless the tax proceeds are channelled into genuinely productive infrastructure spending. And although there is no necessary linkage here, it seems unlikely that government outlays financed by monetary expansion will be productive in economic value terms.

Monetary expansion by a national central bank is related directly to the budgetary stance of the government of the political unit. If internal political choices are made that generate rates of outlay in excess of projected revenues produced by explicitly legislated taxes, the budgetary deficit emerges more or less as a residual that must be financed, either by explicit issue of public debt or by money creation. As debt-financed deficits continue over a sequence of periods, and as the size (and consequent interest charges) of the national debt mounts, pressures increase for money creation by the central bank. Regardless of the organizational-institutional structure, the pronounced objective of maintaining some proximate stability in the value of the monetary unit becomes enormously more difficult as budget deficits increase and as these deficits come to describe permanent political reality.

These relationships between monetary and fiscal actions hold independently of the possible congruence or incongruence between the size of the polity and the size of the market nexus. But they clearly become more acute, and more readily apparent, in the setting that we are examining, where the separate national political units are smaller in territorial reach than the inclusive free-trade and resource-flow zone that is coincident in size with the supranational federal union. All government spending must be financed, one way or another, and any national government that spends nonproductively, relative to other units in the federalism, will reduce the rate of return on resource investment, with the resultant retardation in the relative rate of growth.[2] If the spending is financed, either by explicit public borrowing or by money creation, the differential between the rates of return between the 'offending' nation-state and its political competitors in the federalism is further increased. The competitive pressures among the separate member units in an integrated economy tend to act strongly towards inducing both central bankers and governments to limit severely the relative disparities between their own and others' behaviour patterns in monetary-fiscal matters. (Waves of competitive inflation-financed deficit regimes cannot totally be ruled out, but the presence of even one national unit that adheres to 'responsible patterns' of policy would make such situations unlikely to occur.)

Once again, however, the point to be emphasized is that these pressures towards regularization, towards relative conformity in policies as among the separated polities in the federalism, emerge from the competitive process itself. An empowered central federal authority is neither required nor desirable to secure the results. (In this context, some of the Maastricht Agreement's requirements about national debt and deficit limits reflect simple misunderstanding of the workings of the competitive process.)

THE TRANSFER STATE

To say that a government spends nonproductively is not equivalent to the charge that the spending is either frivolous or that the decision to spend was not motivated by worthy purpose. 'Nonproductive' in the context used here refers only to inefficacy in generating final product as evaluated in the marketplace and as measured in the national accounts. Nonproductive spending includes, therefore, all spending on transfers, whether these be directed towards the welfare support of those deemed deserving: the young, the old or the poor. And it also includes those transfers to members of constituencies that succeed in manipulating the political game to their advantages in securing transfer rents, for little or no legitimate purpose.

All political units engage in transfer spending of all varieties, and they finance this spending variously through some combination of taxation, debt and money creation. The issue of relevance to our discussion involves the relative importance of the transfer sector in the separate member units of the supranational federalism. If a single nation-state, among the competitive set of states, attempts to use the governmental budget to implement transfer levels that are significantly larger (as shares in national product) than other units, the net productivity of resource investment will be reduced, with the same consequences traced out earlier with reference to other politically-generated differentials in resource returns. Regardless of the purpose of the transfer activity, whether in furtherance of genuine welfare or of self-seeking group interests, the combined revenue raising-spending package must reduce the share of product value received by the owners of productive inputs, human and nonhuman. And if one of a set of economically interlinked polities gets out of line with its competition along this dimension, it will observe its relative productivity diminishing.

There is, however, a major distinction to be drawn between the effect of interunit competition with respect to transfer spending and the other activities that have been previously examined. Interunit competition within the integrated market nexus tends to force the separate political entities to fulfill their protective state roles effectively, to provide economically productive infrastructure investment, to maintain monetary stability and to attain fiscal balance, all in a relative sense. Each of these results, as forced upon the competitive nation-states, is intrinsically desirable, provided only that the enhanced value of national product is deemed to be 'good'. What critic can suggest that the achievement of these objectives is not desired?

Transfer activities are not different in one respect. Competition will put pressure on the separate governments to generate an *economically efficient* set of fiscal transfers. By contrast with the other activities discussed, however, the economically efficient set of transfers may be *socially nonpreferred*. It seems quite possible that citizens in a particular nation-state may (and by some substantial consensus) prefer a level of transfer spending directed towards welfare recipients that is in excess of that level which might be forced on them in an operative supranational federalism. And this result may be more likely if differences in the income levels of the separate nation-states are large. The relatively 'rich' nation-states may well choose levels of domestic transfer spending that are beyond the capabilities (and hence the preferences) of citizens in the relatively 'poor' units. At the same time, citizens (especially those in the relatively rich units) may be reluctant to cede their autonomous authority over redistributive actions of government to the competitive pressures that membership in an economically integrated federalism implies. To this extent, there may be an argument for explicit harmonization of policies, perhaps to be coordinated through the auspices of the central federal authority – an argument that could scarcely be advanced with reference to the other activities of the separate states.

Even here, however, caution is in order. Transfer activities that describe what Anthony de Jasay (1985) has called the 'churning state' can scarcely be justified as reflecting the preferences of citizens. These transfers back and forth among and between the politically successful and unsuccessful organized interests cannot be socially preferred in any meaningful and well-understood sense to the economically efficient level of transfers that would be forced upon national politics in an effective competitive federalism. And how are genuine welfare transfers to be distinguished, politically, from the 'churning' transfers? Once the grubby realities of national democratic politics are fully embodied in the sometimes idealized models of political redistribution, perhaps the sacrifice of political autonomy in this dimension does not appear large.

ITALY AND THE CONSTITUTION OF EUROPE

I have sketched out the elementary principles of the relationships between the political independence of the separate national governments and membership in an integrated economy that includes the territory of several such polities and which is politically organized as a competitive federalism with a limited central authority. I have not tried to use modern Europe as a descriptive or a normative example, but the parallels are clear. I now want to move to the second part of my title and to relate the argument specifically to Italy and to the Italian citizenry, while again emphasizing my illiteracy on matters of institutional history or current policy discourse.

There are many reasons why the citizens of a defined sovereign polity – a nation-state – might consider membership in a supranational federalism with a central authority that would enforce freedom of commerce over the whole territory. Since Adam Smith, we have known that the division of labour depends on the extent of the market and that resource productivity depends, in turn, on the division of labour. Citizens of all of the countries of Europe, whether these countries are large, medium or small in size, must expect to reap benefits from genuine economic integration, with the citizens of the relatively smaller units promised relatively greater differential gains. The geopolitical objective of securing protection by means of an included Germany may dominate the choices of many citizens who do not elevate economic interest to a dominant place.

My indirect emphasis has been on a basis for Italian membership in a federal Europe that is quite different from either the straightforward economic logic of a widened and more inclusive market or the geopolitical logic of an included rather than an excluded Germany. In my interpretation, a primary reason for securing membership in and promoting continued movement towards a genuinely integrated economy organized under a competitive federalism is that this institutional development offers a means of partial escape from the internal or domestic political exploitation suffered by ordinary citizens in the fully autonomous nation-states of nineteenth- and twentieth-century history. The ordinary citizen, of any member country, will, of course, secure benefits from the enlarged market area and may also sense greater security in an inclusive

Europe. But this ordinary citizen may be affected much more by the constraints, or limits, that the Europeanization of the economy will place on the powers and authority of the politicians *within* his or her own country, to interfere with his or her life, both economic and otherwise. A competitive federalism can prove to be efficacious in limiting domestic political intrusiveness in ways that no formal constitution can approach. The exit option offered by the widened market is overwhelmingly more significant than the voice option offered by participation in democratic politics. And we should note here that the exit option need be exercised only by a few marginal resource owners in order to yield spillover benefits to all citizens.

I suggest that these relationships may apply with special force to the citizenry of Italy – a citizenry that has possibly been subjected to as much or more exploitation by its own political institutions and politicians than other member units of the emerging European federalism. Italians 'need' the European federalism as an indirect constitutional means to force their own politicians to take the actions that are necessary for economic viability. And was it not, indeed, the prospect for Europeanization that, in October 1992, forced the Italian government into taking measures that were deemed to be beyond the reach of prior governments?

In general terms, Maastricht was wrongly directed; the provisional agreement reflected far too much of the Delors-Brussels mind-set that concentrates on top-down harmonization and far too little understanding of the efficacy of genuine competition among separate units in a federalism. But, as Maastricht is reevaluated and possibly revised, there remains ample opportunity to move towards a Europe that will be in the interests of all citizens in all of the member states. The latent fear of Brussels' bureaucratic dominance tends to be overemphasized in many of the arguments that have been advanced against Maastricht, and especially by those in the United Kingdom who associate themselves with Mrs. Thatcher's position.

Personally, my own reading of the tea leaves tells me that the Italians, French, Germans and others have passed the psychological threshold. These peoples are Europeans in so many senses that I do not foresee a twenty-first century Europe made up of autarkic nation-states as of old. Such a future is simply not in the cards. One way or the other, an integrated Europe economy is well on its way to becoming that which is. My advice and counsel to all Italians, as well as to all citizens in the other potential member countries, is to support, and enthusiastically, the Europeanization of their economies, while, at the same time, keeping a weather eye out for exploitation by all politics and all politicians, whether these be confined within national or supranational institutions. Competition remains, after all is said and done, the most effective element of any constitution that protects liberties.

NOTES

1. Material in this chapter was first presented in Catania, Sicily, in December 1994.
2. I am, of course, assuming that the monetary framework operates to ensure macroeconomic sufficient stability. Hence, there are no Keynesian-like arguments for fiscal stimulus.

254-62
(95)

H11
H77 K10
```

# 26. Federalism as (1) and ideal political order and (2) an objective for constitutional reform[1]

My aim in this chapter is to discuss *federalism*, as a central element in an inclusive political order, in two quite different but ultimately related conceptual perspectives. In Part I, I examine federalism as an ideal type – as a stylized component of a constitutional structure of governance that might be put in place *ab initio*, as emergent from agreement among citizens of a particular community before that community, as such, has experienced its own history. In Part II, the discussion shifts dramatically towards reality, and the critical importance of defining the historically determined *status quo* is recognized as a necessary first step towards reform that may be guided by some appreciation of the federalist ideal.

## 1. IDEAL THEORY

### Federalism as an Analogue to the Market

An elementary understanding and appreciation of political federalism is facilitated by a comparable understanding and appreciation of the political function of an economy organized on market principles. Quite apart from its ability to produce and distribute a highly valued bundle of goods (relative to alternative regimes), a market economy serves a critically important political role. To the extent that allocative and distributive choices can be relegated to the workings of markets, the necessity for any politicization of such choices is eliminated.

But why should the politicization of choices be of normative concern? Under the standard assumptions that dominated analysis before the public-choice revolution, politics is modelled as the activity of a benevolently despotic and monolithic authority, that seeks always and everywhere to promote the public interest, which is presumed to exist independently of revealed evaluations and which is amenable to discovery or revelation. If this romantic image of politics (see Buchanan, 1979a) is discarded and replaced by the empirical reality of
```

politics as observed, any increase in the relative size of the politicized sector of an economy must carry with it an increase in the potential for exploitation. The well-being of citizens becomes vulnerable to the activities of politics, as described in the behaviour of other citizens as members of majoritarian coalitions, as elected politicians and as appointed bureaucrats.

This argument must be supplemented by an understanding of why and how the market, as the alternative to political process, does not also expose the citizen-participant to comparable exploitation. The categorical difference between market and political interaction lies in the continuing presence of an effective exit option in market relationships and in its absence in politics. To the extent that the individual participant in market exchange has available effective alternatives that may be chosen at relatively low cost, any exchange is necessarily voluntary. In its stylized form, the market involves no coercion, no extraction of value from any participant without consent. In dramatic contrast, politics is inherently coercive, independently of the effective decision rules that may be operative.

The potential for the exercise of individual liberty is directly related to the relative size of the market sector in an economy. A market organization does not, however, emerge spontaneously from some imagined state of nature. A market economy must, in one sense, be 'laid on' through the design, construction and implementation of a political-legal framework – an inclusive constitution that protects property and enforces voluntary contracts. As Adam Smith emphasized, the market works well only if these parameters, these 'laws and institutions', are in place.

Enforceable constitutional restrictions may constrain the domain of politics to some extent, but these restrictions may not offer sufficient protection against the exploitation of citizens through the agencies of governance. That is to say, even if the market economy is allowed to carry out its allocational-distributional role over a significant relative share of the political economy, the remaining domain of actions open to politicization may leave the citizen, both in person and property, vulnerable to the expropriation of value that necessarily accompanies political coercion.

How might the potential for exploitation be reduced or minimized? How might the political sector, in itself, be constitutionally designed so as to offer the citizen more protection?

The principle of federalism emerges directly from the market analogy. The politicized sphere of activity, in itself, may be arranged or organized so as to allow for the workings of competition (which is the flip side of the availability of exit) to become operative. The domain of authority for the central government, which we assume here is coincident in territory and membership with the economic exchange nexus, may be severely limited, while remaining political authority is residually assigned to the several 'state' units, each of which is smaller in territory and membership than the economy. Under such a federalized political structure, persons, singly and/or in groups, would be guaranteed the liberties of trade, investment and migration across the inclusive area of the economy. Analogously to the market, persons retain an exit option; at relatively low cost, at least some persons can shift among the separate political jurisdictions. And, again analogously to the market, the separate producing units – in this case, the separate state governments – would be forced to compete, one with another, in their offers of publicly provided services. The federalized structure, through the forces of interstate competition, effectively limits the power of the separate political units to extract surplus value from the citizenry.

The Principles of Competitive Federalism

The operating principles of a genuinely competitive federalism can be summarized readily (see Brennan and Buchanan, 1980, Chapter 9, for more comprehensive treatment). As noted, the central or federal government would be constitutionally restricted in its domain of action, severely so. But, within its assigned sphere, the central government would be strong, sufficiently so to allow it to enforce economic freedom or openness over the whole of the territory. The separate states would be prevented, by federal authority, from placing barriers on the free flow of resources and goods across their borders.

The constitutional limits on the domain of the central or federal government would not be self-enforcing, and competition could not be made operative in a manner precisely comparable to that which might restrict economic exploitation by the separate states. If, for any reason, the federal (central) government should move beyond its constitutionally dictated mandate of authority, what protection might be granted, either to citizens individually or to the separate states, against the extension of federal power?

The exit option is again suggested, although this option necessarily takes on a different form. The separate states, individually or in groups, must be constitutionally empowered to secede from the federalized political structure, that is, to form new units of political authority outside of and beyond the reach of the existing federal government. Secession, or the threat thereof, represents the only means through which the ultimate powers of the central government might be held in check. Absent the secession prospect, the federal government may, by overstepping its constitutionally assigned limits, extract surplus value from the citizenry almost at will, since there would exist no effective means of escape open.[2]

With an operative secession threat, on the part of the separate states, the federal or central government could be held roughly to its assigned constitutional limits, while the separate states could be left to compete among themselves in their capacities to meet the demands of citizens for collectively provided services. Locational rents, differential preferences for publicly provided goods and services, scale efficiencies, the absence of residual claimancy – these and other factors would prevent even the idealized federal structure from attaining overall results that would be comparably efficient to those attained in the market economy, even when the shortfall of the latter from its idealized variant is acknowledged. Nonetheless, an effectively competitive federalism can be imaginatively constructed, and one that is consistent with the observed behavioural regularities of human nature. Such a construction surely belongs in the realm of the 'might be' rather than the realm of science fiction. In such an idealized political order, the individual citizen would be insured against undue fiscal or economic exploitation by either the federal or the state governments. The exploitation that might occur would be kept within threshold limits determined by the costs of personal and institutional work.

Some observers might be prompted to inquire: what political activities will the separate states perform in an effectively competitive federalism? The asking of such a question suggests a basic misunderstanding of the principles sketched out in this section.

Within each separate state of the federalism, both the dividing line between privately and publicly organized production-distribution activity and the allocational-distributional mix among the items within the publicly organized sector remain to be determined by the interworkings of the preferences of the citizenry and the internal political process. There is no external constraint that takes explicit shape here, whether emanating from the constitution, the central government or anywhere else. The separate states are free to do as they please, constrained only by the participation of their own citizens in the decision processes.

We should predict, of course, that the separate states of a federalism would be compelled by the forces of competition to offer tolerably efficient mixes of publicly provided goods and services, and, to the extent that citizens in the different states exhibit roughly similar preferences, the actual budgetary mixes would not be predicted to diverge significantly, one from the other. But the point to be emphasized here (and which seems to have been missed in so much of the discussion about the potential European federalism) is that any such standardization or regularization as might occur would itself be an *emergent* property of the competitive federalism rather than a property that might be imposed either by constitutional mandate or by central government authority.

2.   THE PATH DEPENDENCY OF CONSTITUTIONAL REFORM

From Here to There: a Schemata

The essential principle for meaningful discourse about constitutional-institutional reform (or, indeed, about any change) is the recognition that reform involves movement from some 'here' towards some 'there'. The evaluative comparison of alternative sets of rules, alternative regimes of political order, as previously discussed, aims exclusively at defining the 'there' – the idealized objective towards which any change must be turned. But the *direction* for effective reform also requires a definition of the 'here'. Any reform, constitutional or otherwise, commences from some here and now, some *status quo*, that is the existential reality. History matters, and the historical experience of a political community is beyond any prospect of change; the constitutional-institutional record can neither be ignored nor rewritten. The question for reform is then: 'how to get there from here?'

These prefatory remarks are necessary before any consideration of federalism in discussion of practical reform. The abstracted ideal – a strong but severely limited central authority with the capacity and the will to enforce free trade over the inclusive territory, along with several separate 'states', each one of which stands in a competitive relationship with all other such units – may be well-defined and agreed-upon as an objective for change. But until and unless the 'here' (the starting point) is identified, not even the direction of change can be known.

A simple illustration may be helpful. Suppose that you and I agree that we want to be in Washington, DC. But suppose that you are in New York, and I am in Atlanta. We must proceed in different directions if we expect to get to the shared or common objective.

Constitutional reform aimed towards an effective competitive federalism may reduce or expand the authority of the central government relative to that of the separate state governments in the inclusive territory of potential political interaction. If the *status quo* is described as a centralized and unitary political authority, reform must embody *devolution* – a shift of genuine political power from the centre to the separate states. On the other hand, if the *status quo* is described by a set of autonomous political units that may perhaps be geographically contiguous but which acts potentially in independence one from another, reform must involve a centralization of authority, a shift of genuine power to the central government from the separated states.

Figure 26.1 offers an illustrative schemata. Consider a well-defined territory that may be organized politically at any point along the abstracted unidimensional spectrum that measures the extent to which political authority is centralized. At the extreme left of this spectrum, the territory is divided among several fully autonomous political units, each one of which possesses total sovereignty, and among which any interaction, either by individuals or by political units, must be subjected to specific contractual negotiation and agreement. At the extreme right of this spectrum, the whole of the territory is organized as an inclusive political community, with this authority centralized in a single governmental unit. Individuals and groups may interact, but any such interaction must take place within the uniform limits laid down by the monolithic authority.

Figure 26.1   A constitutional reform schemata

An effective federal structure may be located somewhere near the middle of the spectrum, between the regime of fully autonomous localized units on the one hand and the regime of fully centralized authority on the other. This simple illustration makes it easy to see that constitutional reform that is aimed towards the competitive federal structure must be characterized by some increase in centralization if the starting point is on the left and by some decrease in centralization if the starting point is on the right.

The illustration prompts efforts to locate differing regimes at differing places in their own separate histories on the unidimensional scalar. In 1787, James Madison, who had observed the several former British colonies that had won their independence and organized themselves as a confederation, located the *status quo* somewhere to the left of the middle of the spectrum, and he sought to secure an effective federalism by establishing a stronger central authority to which some additional powers should be granted. Reform involved a reduction in the political autonomy of the separate units. In the early post-World War II decades, the leaders of Europe, who had observed the terrible nationalistic wars, located their *status quo* analogously to Madison. They sought reform in the direction of a federalized structure – reform that necessarily involved some establishment of central authority, with some granting of power independently of that historically claimed by the separated nation-states.

By comparison and contrast, consider the US in the late 1990s, the history of which is surely described as an overshooting of Madison's dreams for the ideal political order. Over the course of two centuries, and especially after the demise of any secession option, as resultant from the great Civil War of the 1860s, the US political order came to be increasingly centralized. The *status quo* in the 1990s lies clearly to the right of the spectrum, and any reform towards a federalist ideal must involve some devolution of central government authority, some increase in the effective independent power of the several states.

Constitutional Strategy and the Federalist Ideal

The simple construction of Figure 26.1 is also helpful in suggesting that the ideal constitutional structure described as competitive federalism may be difficult to achieve. Whether motivated by direct economic interest, by some failure to understand basic economic and political theory or by fundamental conservative instincts, specific political coalitions will emerge to oppose any shift from the *status quo* towards a federal structure, no matter what the starting point. If, for example, the *status quo* is described by a regime of fully autonomous units (the nation-states of Europe after World War II), political groups within each of these units will object to any sacrifice of national sovereignty that a shift towards federalism might require. And the strategic success of such groups is enhanced to the extent that the effective alternative is presented, not as a federal structure located somewhere in the middle of the spectrum, but as the highly centralized authority at the other extreme. If the antifederalists raise the spectre of central government domination, popular support for the federalist reform necessarily becomes weaker.

Similar comments may be made about the debates mounted from the opposing direction. If a unitary centralized authority describes the *status quo ante*, its supporters may attempt to and may succeed in conveying the potential for damage through constitutional collapse into a regime of autonomous units, vulnerable to economic and political warfare. The middle way offered by devolution to a competitive federalism may, in this case, find few adherents.[3]

The discussion of steps towards the constitution of the European Union, especially during the early 1990s, seems to reinforce the points made directly above. The discussion appears to have proceeded largely as if the genuine federalist structure is not considered as a constitutional alternative. The position represented as that of Jacques Delors, and much of the Brussels bureaucracy, envisages a Europe in which political authority is highly centralized, with the whole economy subjected to uniform regulation. By contrast, the position represented by the Bruges group, and promoted by Margaret Thatcher, more or less accepts the Delors thrust as the only effective alternative to the retention of full national sovereignty. From this base of interpretation, any talk of federalism becomes anathema. (For earlier analyses of the discussion, see Buchanan, 1979a, 1990b.)

As the construction in Figure 26.1 also suggests, however, the fact that the federalist structure is, indeed, 'in the middle', at least in the highly stylized sense discussed here, may carry prospects for evolutionary emergence in the conflicts between centralizing and decentralizing pressures. Contrary to the poetic pessimism of William Butler Yeats, the 'centre' may hold, if once attained, not because of any intensity of conviction, but rather due to the location of the balance of forces (Yeats, 1989).

Federalism and Increasing Economic Interdependence

In the preceding discussion, I have presumed that the economic benefits of a large economic nexus, defined both in territory and membership, extend at least to and beyond the limits of the political community that may be constitutionally organized anywhere along the spectrum in Figure 26.1, from the regime of fully autonomous political units to that of the centralized political authority. Recall that Adam Smith (1776) emphasized that economic prosperity and growth find their origins in the division (specialization) of labour, and that this division in turn depends on the extent of the market. Smith placed no limits on the scope for applying this principle. But we know that the economic world of the late 1990s is dramatically different from that of 1775. Technological development has facilitated a continuing transformation of local to regional to national to international interactions among economic units. And, consistently with Smith's insights, economic growth has been more rapid where and when political intrusions have not emerged to prevent entrepreneurs from seizing the advantages offered by the developing technology.

Before the technological revolution in information processing and communication in this half-century, however, politically motivated efforts to 'improve' on the workings of market processes have seemed almost a part of institutional reality. In this setting, it has seemed to remain of critical economic importance to restrict the intrusiveness of politics, quite apart from the complementary effects on individual liberties. And political federalism, to the extent that its central features were at all descriptive of constitutional history, did serve to facilitate economic growth.

The modern technological revolution in information processing and communications may have transformed, at least to some degree, the setting within which politically motivated obstructions may impact on market forces. This technology may, in itself, have made it more difficult for politicians, and governments at any and all levels, to check or to limit the ubiquitous pressures of economic interdependence (McKenzie and Lee, 1991). When values can be transferred worldwide at the speed of light and when events everywhere are instantly visible on CNN, there are elements of competitive federalism in play, almost regardless of the particular constitutional regimes in existence.

Finally, the relationship between federalism as an organizing principle for political structure, and the freedom of trade across political boundaries must be noted. An inclusive political territory, say, the United States or Western Europe, necessarily places limits on its own ability to interfere politically with its own internal market structure to the extent that this structure is, itself, opened up to the free workings of international trade, including the movement of capital. On the other hand, to the extent that the internal market is protected against the forces of international competition, other means, including federalism, become more essential to preserve liberty and to guarantee economic growth.

The United States offers an illustrative example. The United States prospered mightily in the nineteenth century, despite the wall of protectionism that sheltered its internal markets. It did so because political authority, generally, was held in check by a constitutional structure that did contain basic elements of competitive federalism. By comparison, in this last decade of the twentieth century, the United States is more open to international market forces, but its own constitutional structure has come to be transformed into one approaching a centralized unitary authority.

Devolution towards a competitive federal structure becomes less necessary to the extent that markets are open to external opportunities. However, until and unless effective constitutional guarantees against political measures to choke off external trading relationships are put in place, the more permanent constitutional reform aimed at restoring political authority to the separate states offers a firmer basis for future economic growth along with individual liberty.

The Europe of the 1990s offers a second example. If trade beyond the limits of the European Union's members remains open, the concerns about excessive centralization of political authority may be misplaced. However, to the extent that 'fortress Europe' becomes descriptive of political reality, the movement towards a genuinely competitive federalism takes on much more importance.

NOTES

1. This chapter was first presented in Mexico in January 1995, at a conference sponsored by the Fraser Institute and the Instituto Cultural Ludwig von Mises.
2. For a formal analysis of secession, see Buchanan and Faith (1987), and for a more general discussion, see Allen Buchanan (1991).
3. The theory of agenda setting in public choice offers analogies. If the agenda can be manipulated in such fashion that the alternatives for choice effectively bracket the ideally preferred position, voters are confronted with the selection of one or the other of the extreme alternatives, both of which may be dominated by the preferred option. See Romer and Rosenthal (1978).

H11
H77 D70

27. Economic freedom and federalism: prospects for the new century[1]

I commence this chapter with two separate presuppositions upon which there
should be no dispute. First, the performance of a market economy is superior
to that of an economy subject to command and control, with superiority being
directly measured by the size of the bundle of goods and services produced –
goods and services that are valued as end-items of consumption and use by
participants in the economies themselves. This proposition is surely confirmed
by recent historical experience, but it is also confirmed by scientific analysis
which now incorporates recognition of the epistemological as well as the
incentive advantages of market or market-like organizational structures. Second,
there is in the 1990s an ongoing worldwide process of institutional change that
involves depoliticization of economic activity – a process that appears variously
and in separate countries under several descriptive labels including:
denationalization, privatization, federalism, devolution, deregulation.

The two presuppositions are, of course, directly related; the institutional
process of change, which can be observed to be taking place, occurs as a direct
consequence of the near-universal recognition of the validity of the first
presupposition stated. The process of institutional change represents a decoupling
of the spheres of political and economic interaction. And this decoupling, or
divorce, emerges as a necessary consequence of collapse of the central-command
principle that was the basis of the socialist ideal.

Centralized command and control over the economic activity of a whole
national territory requires that the mapping of political authority correspond with
the extent of economic interaction. In the United States, it would make no sense
at all for a single state, among the fifty, to try to control the economic activity
of its citizens in detail when the state's borders remain open to the free flow of
goods and resources across state boundaries throughout the whole national
territory. Described in terms of the normative ideals envisaged by the central
planners of the early twentieth century, a socialized economy in the American
setting would have demanded the centralization of political power and authority
into the unit of control that is, territorially, correspondent with the limits of
economic activity. When we recognize this point, and when we also recognize
that the socialist ideology was omnipresent and significant in driving American
institutional change during much of this century, we should not really be at all

surprised that the central (federal) government in the United States increased its powers dramatically at the expense of those of the states. A viable federalism, in which political power, or sovereignty, is genuinely shared between the central government and the separate states or provinces, is simply incompatible with the command-control model of socialist economic organization. The philosophical logic of the socialist century dictated centralized political power.

We can understand why political power came to be centralized, everywhere, both in those nations that were defined to be in either the socialist or nonsocialist camps. With the intellectual-scientific as well as the practicable bankruptcy of the command-control model of economic organization, we should indeed sense the institutional mismatch that now exists. Institutional conservatives, from all across the ideological spectrum, are reluctant to acknowledge that the historical nation-state has lost its *raison d'être*, at least to the extent that political activity is considered to include directed control and regulation of economic life.

What is the political structure that is appropriate for the national units of the world, when, increasingly, internal economies are described by freedom of entry and exit to all markets, both for citizens and for foreigners?

To begin to get at an answer to this critically important question we must, I think, go back to the basic understanding of why the central-command models of economic organization failed, and why market models are so superior, at least in some comparative sense. As noted, the centrally-planned economy failed because it did not, and cannot, utilize either the knowledge of opportunities or the incentive structures that emerge more or less naturally in markets. But why and how do markets use knowledge? And why and how do markets exploit incentives? Is there some central principle that allows markets to be more effective along these dimensions?

The central principle is summarized in the word *competition*. Markets work well – they produce large bundles of goods and services wanted by participants – because they exploit the forces of competition. If markets are open to entry and exit, the existence of any potential profit opportunity will attract investment; and note that only one entrepreneur need recognize any opportunity. There is no need that the potential profitability be sensed by a committee, a board or by the whole membership of the political authority. The entrepreneur who first senses knowledge of the profit opportunity can anticipate gains, but his gains will themselves be quite limited by the freedom of entry for imitators and followers. Profits will be dissipated as more and more persons and firms enter the newly opened line of market activity. The initial entrepreneur who discovered the opportunity is restricted by the entry of others in the degree to which he can withdraw profits.

The consumer-user of economic goods and services is thereby protected against undue exploitation by prospective monopolists; he is protected by the competitive process, which ensures that profits, if and when they appear, will quickly be dissipated and, further, which ensures that any available profit opportunity will be discovered. The participant in an effectively functioning market economy can rest assured that there is no major source of current economic value that is mysteriously hidden from sight and waiting to be discovered. The competitive process of the market economy allocates resources to those uses that participants value most highly.

Why is it necessary to go through this lesson in elementary or introductory economic theory in order to get at the question posed earlier relating to the appropriate political organization for the nation-state in the post-revolutionary world economy? My answer is succinct: only a *federalized* political structure can effectively exploit the forces of competition in any manner at all analogous to the market process. The appropriate political structure is one of *competitive federalism*, whether the United States, for Europe, for Latin America or for China.

What competitive federalism does is to introduce into political order the disciplinary pressure of competition (analogous to that present in markets) even if necessarily attenuated by the nature of political authority. Note that I am not suggesting here that there is no role for political authority; I am not making a case for limiting political authority to the role sometimes described as the night-watchman, the minimal or the protective state. The point here is quite different. There may well exist goods and services that are desired by participants that cannot be efficiently supplied by markets. 'Public goods and services' in the definitional Samuelsonian sense of shared collective consumption may exist, and persons may organize political action to secure these goods through collective agency, through political units or governing bodies. But how can governments, charged with the responsibility of collecting taxes from citizens and using the revenues to supply commonly shared public goods and services, themselves be controlled so as to limit the exploitation of the principals, that is, the people themselves? Again, the answer is *competition*. If the public goods functions of collective or governmental organization can be federalized so that several units coexist side by side in an inclusive but economically open political nexus, no single unit can unduly exploit its monopoly position with respect to its treatment of either taxpayers or consumers-users of public goods. In an integrated economy, persons and capital investment can shift among units, and, further, the observations of differential treatment by different units will exert disciplinary pressure on deviant governmental units in a federalism.

Consider, as a first example, law enforcement of the ordinary sort. Assume that law enforcement is within the responsibility of the local unit of government, which includes a territory and a membership that is only a small part of an inclusive open economic nexus. If the local unit operates its law enforcement effort inefficiently, either from localized corruption or from laxness or severity in operation, the community becomes less attractive relative to its neighbours. It will lose members by outmigration as well as capital investment. The threat of this result will put pressure on the local agency to remain roughly efficient, in some comparative sense, in its operation.

Or, as a second example, consider government subsidy (or regulative favours) to a particular industry, that reduces economic productivity. If the political unit that practises such discrimination is integrated in an open trading network with other competing jurisdictions, the effects will be quickly noticed and will be measured by resource migration. Internal political discrimination will be severely constrained.

How far should devolution be carried? Even if the principle of competitive federalism be acknowledged, how much deconcentration or decentralization of political authority is implied? In one limit, of course, the principle might suggest that all political-collective activity should be privatized, thereby securing the maximal efficiency of competition. But we have suggested that there do exist genuinely public goods, for which there are perhaps major efficiency gains to be secured through collective provision. The principle of competitive federalism suggests only that the prospective efficacy of competition be put into the balance when other efficiency considerations are introduced. For example, just because the standard efficiency logic might dictate the financing and supply of a good or service by the central government does not suggest that only the central government should serve this function. To some extent, the advantages from decentralized provision stemming from the competitive process might offset the standard efficiency logic.

Consider the European Union and the prospects for a unified currency in 1999 or soon. An argument can, of course, be made that a single European currency unit would increase overall efficiency throughout the territory of the Union. The range of 'publicness' is Europe-wide. But this fact alone does not imply that the optimal monetary arrangements for modern Europe involve a common monetary unit or a single European central bank. My own view is that such arrangements would not be the most preferred at this juncture in history. A regime of separated national currencies, with competing national central banks, each of which remains in competition with others to secure the allegiance and loyalty of Europeans continentwide, seems to me to ensure greater net efficiency because the danger of centralized monopoly control is mitigated.

As this example perhaps suggests, the particular political arrangements for carrying out the separate public-goods functions may depend on the history that has settled the *status quo* in being. For any particular function, there is, of course, what may be called a 'natural' range of publicness – a natural size for the membership of the community of persons who might share in nonexcludable benefits. The argument from the principle of competitive federalism suggests that the potential, and dynamic, efficiency to be anticipated from competition always offsets, to a degree, the precise mapping of governmental units and ranges of provision.

Again, an example may be helpful, this time drawn from American experience in this century. On strictly efficiency grounds, an argument can be made that governmentally financed (and possibly provided) educational services might best be organized in large jurisdictional units, perhaps at the level of the separate American states. There is, however, ample empirical evidence now in place to support the finding that, as the centralization and consolidation of educational services have proceeded throughout the last half of the century, the delivery of services preferred by the final consumer-user has suffered. Attitudes of experts now suggest that education is best provided at and by local governmental units, which must operate in settings where competitive pressures are intensified.

We must, of course, remain wary of making evaluative comparisons across separated public functions and especially across national boundaries. Institutional structures of governance differ, and each historical developmental pattern differs from others. Nonetheless, the principle of competitive federalism, as such, can be helpful in any setting, as offering a normatively meaningful guide toward structural reform.

I have left one issue of central importance yet to be discussed. To what extent should the federalized structure of politics in a single large nation embody uniform or standard devolution of political authority and autonomy as among the separate subunits? Is it desirable to allow some states, provinces or regional units to assume more public-goods autonomy than others within an overall national jurisdiction? Or must a devolution of authority to any one unit necessarily imply devolution of like or similar authority to all other units in the national jurisdiction? Must the constitutional separation of powers be uniform, or can this separation be discriminatory or differentiated?

Modern Spain offers an example where the federalized structure is highly discriminatory; modern United States offers the converse case, where the granting of authority to one state must (with some rare exceptions) imply the granting of comparable autonomy to all states.

Consider, first, modern Spain. Confronted with separatist insurgence in the Basque Country, the national government in Spain granted extraordinary powers of autonomy to this region, while keeping the region within the national territory of and under the suzerainty of the nation-state. In separate action, Catalonia was also granted substantial autonomy, but not nearly so extensive as the Basque Country. Further, Valencia and other provincial governments were given particular status, with less autonomy than either the Basque Country or Catalonia, but yet more than some other regions in the Spanish national territory. Modern Spain is now best described as a discriminatory competitive federalism, which seems to work so long as the loyalties of citizens are sufficiently localized to forestall demands of equal treatment across all units. Internally, within Spain itself, goods and services and resources flow freely across provincial boundaries; the economic nexus is clearly national in scope. And as Europe opens up its markets generally, extending the market nexus across countries, we may expect that the within-Spain political differentiation among the separate provinces or regions will assume less significance.

In the United States, pressure for devolution from the central government to the separate states is strong, especially for the provision of welfare-state type services (essentially income transfers to the poor). The historical tradition and the institutional *status quo* suggest that differentiated treatment of the separate states in terms of autonomous authority is unlikely to take place. However, the Spanish example suggests that such differential autonomy is not out of bounds, while adhering to the principle of competitive federalism.

I am not, of course, sufficiently familiar with the situation in Hong Kong or in China to comment either positively or normatively on the policy and constitutional alternatives that will be faced in 1997 and beyond. But I should suggest the feasibility of looking to the Spanish model of devolution of political authority as a source of possible instruction and guidance.

To this point, I have discussed the possible efficacy of competitive federalism as a means of dividing political authority between central and smaller units of governance in a large territory with an integrated economic nexus. I have not examined the situation confronted by a relatively small state with limited membership and restricted territory. In this setting, the limits to devolution of authority and autonomy to units of government smaller than the central authority are obvious. How, then, can the equivalent of competitive federalism be achieved in such settings?

The smaller the national political unit, the more necessary it becomes to maintain open entry and exit for goods, capital and labour across its borders with other jurisdictions. In an open economic and trading network, the degree to which persons in any country can be politically exploited is severely limited, even in the absence of competition among separate political jurisdictions. In one sense, freedom of international trade does substitute for the competitive discipline imposed by federalized political structures. But history has surely taught us that we cannot depend on the internal politics of any nation, regardless of its ideology, to enforce freedom of trade between its citizens and those of other countries. A small nation must keep its borders open if it expects to maintain its place or to move up in the comparative league tables that measure economic value. A large nation may also ensure its own prosperity by free trade; but the large nation can, in addition, use the devolution of political authority within its borders to introduce competitive pressures over and beyond those emerging from international markets.

What does it mean to say that a person has economic freedom? To me, this means that the person has available exit options – that he or she has choices – concerning what to purchase and from whom, concerning what profession or occupation to enter, concerning what new enterprise to start up, concerning what to invest in. So long as, and to the extent that, persons possess these economic freedoms, they are independent of the power of any single person or group. These freedoms are understood to be characteristic features of a functioning market economy. What federalism accomplishes for the political sphere of action is some measure of economic freedom over and beyond those offered by the market in fully partitionable or private goods and services. In so far as persons combine through political agency to finance and share the benefits of commonly supplied goods and services, the potential exit option offered in competitive federalism places discipline on exploitation akin to that placed on the private-goods monopolist who must always know that any profit position is strictly temporary.

The thrust towards privatization, denationalization and devolution is by no means yet exhausted. It is difficult to predict just what the political equilibrium, in any country, or in the world, will look like in, say, two decades. I am firmly convinced that rapidly developing modern technology ensures that markets must be opened up further, not closed, and that political authority must, necessarily, lose out if it engages in belated efforts to reestablish controls over economic life.

It is to be hoped that political leaders, everywhere, will recognize that the constitutional framework can be reformed with an aim of exploiting the competitive forces that only federalized political structures expose and energize. The findings of modern economic science suggest that the wealth of any large nation can be increased by constitutional guarantees that, to the extent possible, political authority will be devolved from central to several, and competing, quasi-autonomous units integrated economically in a federal structure.

NOTE

1.   Material in this chapter was first presented in Hong Kong, June 1996.

References

Abalkin, Leonid (1990), 'What Hinders Reform?', *The Literary Gazette International* **1** (6), 6 (Moscow).

Akerlof, George (1970), 'The Market for "Lemons": Quality Uncertainty and the Market Mechanism', *The Quarterly Journal of Economics*, **84**, 488–500.

Alchian, Armen (1950), 'Uncertainty, Evolution and Economic Theory', *Journal of Political Economy*, **58** (3), 211–21.

Alchian, Armen (1977), *Economic Forces at Work*, Indianapolis: Liberty Press.

Alchian, Armen and Susan Woodward (1987), 'Reflections on the Theory of the Firm', *Journal of Institutional Theoretical Economics (Z. Ges. Staatswiss.)*, **143** (1), 110–37.

Ash, Timothy Garton (1990), 'Eastern Europe: The Year of Truth', *New York Review of Books*, **37** (2), 21.

Barry, Norman (1993), 'F.A. Hayek's Theory of Spontaneous Order', Liberty Fund Conference paper, Chicago.

Binmore, Ken (1994), *Game Theory and Social Contract*, vol. 1, *Playing Fair*, Cambridge, MA: MIT Press.

Boswell, James ([1755], 1946), *The Journal of a Tour to the Hebrides with Samuel Johnson*, London: Everyman.

Brennan, Geoffrey and James M. Buchanan (1980), *The Power to Tax: Analytical Foundations of a Fiscal Constitution*, New York: Cambridge University Press.

Brennan, Geoffrey and James M. Buchanan (1984), 'Voter Choice: Evaluating Political Alternatives', *American Behavioral Scientist*, **29**, 185–201.

Brennan, Geoffrey and James M. Buchanan (1988), 'Is Public Choice Immoral? The Case for the "Nobel" Lie', *Virginia Law Review*, **74**, 179–89.

Buchanan, Allen (1991), *Secession: The Morality of Political Divorce from Fort Sumter to Lithuania and Quebec*, Boulder, CO: Westview Press.

Buchanan, James M. (1954), 'Individual Choice in Voting and the Market', *Journal of Political Economy*, **62**, 334–43.

Buchanan, James M. (1959), 'Positive Economics, Welfare Economics, and Political Economy', *Journal of Law and Economics*, **2**, 124–38.

Buchanan, James M. (1962), 'The Relevance of Pareto Optimality', *Journal of Conflict Resolution*, **6**, 341–54.

Buchanan, James M. (1968), *The Demand and Supply of Public Goods*, Chicago: Rand-McNally.

Buchanan, James M. (1969), *Cost and Choice*, Chicago: Markham. Midway Reprint, University of Chicago Press, 1974.

Buchanan, James M. (1973), 'The Coase Theorem and the Theory of the State', *Natural Resources Journal*, 13, 579–94.

Buchanan, James M. (1975), *The Limits of Liberty: Between Anarchy and Leviathan*, Chicago: University of Chicago Press.

Buchanan, James M. (1978), 'Markets, States, and the Extent of Morals', *American Economic Review*, 64, 364–8.

Buchanan, James M. (1979a), 'Politics without Romance: A Sketch of Positive Public Choice Theory and Its Normative Implications', *Journal of the Institute for Advanced Studies*, 3, 1–11.

Buchanan, James M. (1979b), *What Should Economists Do?*, Indianapolis, IN: Liberty Press.

Buchanan, James M. (1982), 'Order Defined in the Process of Its Emergence', *Literature of Liberty*, 5 , 5.

Buchanan, James M. (1983), 'The Public Choice Perspective', *Economia delle scelte publiche*, 1, 7–15.

Buchanan, James M. (1989), 'Relatively Absolute Absolutes', in *Essays on the Political Economy*, Honolulu: University of Hawaii Press, pp. 32–46.

Buchanan, James M. (1990a), *Socialism Is Dead But Leviathan Lives On*, The John Bonython Lecture, Sydney, Australia: Centre for Independent Studies, pp. 1–9.

Buchanan, James M. (1990b), 'Europe's Constitutional Opportunity', in *Europe's Constitutional Future*, London: Institute of Economic Affairs, pp. 1–20.

Buchanan, James M. (1991a), 'The Domain of Constitutional Political Economy', *The Economics and the Ethics of Constitutional Order*, Ann Arbor: University of Michigan Press, pp. 3–18.

Buchanan, James M. (1991b), *Analysis, Ideology and the Events of 1989*, Zurich: Bank Hofmann.

Buchanan, James M. (1991c), 'The Gauthier Enterprise', in *The Economics and the Ethics of Constitutional Order*, Ann Arbor: University of Michigan Press, pp. 195–213.

Buchanan, James M. (1992a), 'Political Ethics as a Criterion for Constitutional Design', Fairfax, VA: Center for Study of Public Choice, working paper.

Buchanan, James M. (1992b), 'Markets, Politics, and the Rule of Law', Fairfax, VA: Center for Study of Public Choice, working paper.

Buchanan, James M. (1993a), 'Rights, Social Choice and Behavioral Feasibility', Fairfax, VA: Center for Study of Public Choice, working paper.

Buchanan, James M. (1993b), *Property as a Guarantor of Liberty*, Aldershot, England: Edward Elgar.

Buchanan, James M. (1993c), *Consumption without Production: The Impossible Idyll of Socialism*, Freiburg, Germany: Haufe, pp. 49–75; *Konsum ohne Produktion: Die unmögliche Idylle des Sozialismus*, pp. 17–47. (Chapter 13 in this volume.)

Buchanan, James M. (1994a), 'Choosing What to Choose', *Journal of Institutional and Theoretical Economics*, **150** (2), 123–44.

Buchanan, James M. (1994b) in 'In Celebration of Armen Alchian's 80th Birthday: Living and Breathing Economics', John Lott (ed.), *Economic Inquiry*, **34**, 412–26.

Buchanan, James M. (1994c), 'Catalonia and the Constitution of Europe', Fairfax, VA: Center for Study of Public Choice, working paper.

Buchanan, James M. (1995), 'Individual Rights, Emergent Social States, and Behavioural Feasibility', *Rationality and Society*, **7** (2), 141–50.

Buchanan, James M. and Roger Faith (1987), 'Secession and the Limits of Taxation: Towards a Theory of Internal Exit', *American Economic Review*, **77** (5), 1023–31.

Buchanan, James M. and Dwight R. Lee (1989), 'Cartels, Coalitions and Constitutional Politics', *Public Choice Studies* **13**, 5–20 (Japanese translation); (1991), *Constitutional Political Economy*, **2** (2), 139–69.

Buchanan, James M., Robert D. Tollison and Gordon Tullock (eds) (1980), *Toward a Theory of the Rent-Seeking Society*, College Station: Texas A&M University Press.

Buchanan, James M. and Gordon Tullock (1962), *The Calculus of Consent: Logical Foundations of Constitutional Democracy*, Ann Arbor: University of Michigan Press.

Buchanan, James M. and Yong J. Yoon (eds) (1995), *The Return to Increasing Returns*, Ann Arbor: University of Michigan Press.

Buchanan, James M. and Viktor J. Vanberg (1989), 'A Theory of Leadership and Deference in Constitutional Construction', *Public Choice*, **61**, 15–27.

Buchanan, James M. and Viktor J. Vanberg (1991), 'The Market as a Creative Process', *Economics and Philosophy*, **7** (2), 167–86.

Carens, Joseph H. (1981), *Equality, Moral Incentives and the Market*, Chicago: University of Chicago Press.

Coleman, James S. (1968), 'The Marginal Utility of a Vote Commitment', *Public Choice*, **5**, 39–58.

Congleton, Roger and Viktor Vanberg (1992), 'Rationality, Morality, and Exit', *American Political Science Review*, **86** (2), 418–31.

de Jasay, Anthony (1985), *The State*, Oxford: Basil Blackwell.

di Pierro, Alberto (1990), 'Istituzioni e modelli produttivi', *Politeia*, **6** (18), 4–6.

Downs, Anthony (1957), *An Economic Theory of Democracy*, New York: Harper.

Flowers, Marilyn R. and Patricia M. Danzon (1984), 'Separation of the Redistributive and Allocative Functions of Government: A Public Choice Perspective', *Journal of Public Economics*, **24** (3), 373–80.

Frisch, Ragnar (1959), 'On Welfare Theory and Pareto Regimes', *International Economic Papers*, **9**, London: Macmillan, pp. 39–92.

Fukuyama, Francis (1989), 'The End of History', *National Interest*, **16**, 3–18.

Fukuyama, Francis (1992), *The End of History and the Last Man*, New York: The Free Press.

Gauthier, David (1985), *Morals by Agreement*, Oxford: Oxford University Press.

Goetz, Charles J. and James M. Buchanan (1971), 'External Diseconomies in Competitive Supply', *American Economic Review*, **61**, 883–90.

Harsanyi, John (1953), 'Cardinal Utility in Welfare Economics and in the Theory of Risk-Taking', *Journal of Political Economy*, **61** (5), 434–5.

Hayek, F.A. (ed.) (1935), *Collectivist Economic Planning: Critical Studies on the Possibilities of Socialism*, London: George Routledge & Sons.

Hayek, F.A. (1944), *The Road to Serfdom*, Chicago: University of Chicago Press.

Hayek, F.A. (1960), *The Constitution of Liberty*, Chicago: Henry Regnery.

Hayek, F.A. (1976), *Law, Legislation and Liberty*, vol. 2, *The Miracle of Social Justice*, London and Henley: Routledge & Kegan Paul.

Hayek, F.A. (1979), *Law, Legislation and Liberty*, vol. 3, *The Political Order of a Free People*, Chicago: University of Chicago Press.

Hayek, F.A. (1988), *The Fatal Conceit: The Errors of Socialism*, Chicago: University of Chicago Press.

Hirschman, Albert O. (1970), *Exit, Voice, and Loyalty: Responses to Decline in Firms, Organizations, and States*, Cambridge, MA: Harvard University Press.

Hobbes, Thomas ([1651] 1943), *Leviathan*, London: Everymans Library.

Hume, David (1888), *A Treatise on Human Nature*, Oxford: Clarendon Press, p. xix.

Hutt, William H. (1936), *Economists and the Public: A Study of Competition and Opinion*, London: Jonathan Cape.

Kelman, Steven (1987), '"Public Choice" and Public Spirit', *Public Interest*, **87** (80), 93–4.

Kirzner, Israel (1973), *Competition and Entrepreneurship*, Chicago: University of Chicago Press.

Knight, Frank H. (1924), 'Fallacies in the Interpretation of Social Cost', *Quarterly Journal of Economics*, **38**, 582–606.

Leo XIII ([1893] 1939), *Rerum Novarum* , in G.C. Treacy (ed.), *The Condition of Labor in Five Great Encyclicals*, New York: The Paulist Press, pp. 1–36.

Levy, David (1990), ' The Bias in Centrally Planned Prices', *Public Choice*, **67** (2), 213–26.

Madison, James ([1787] 1966), *The Federalist No. 51*, in Roy P. Fairfield (ed.), *The Federalist Papers*, New York: Doubleday & Co, p. 160.

Magee, Stephen P., William A. Brock and Leslie Young (1989), *Black Hole Tariffs and Endogenous Policy Theory*, Cambridge: Cambridge University Press.

McKenzie, Richard and Dwight Lee (1991), *Quicksilver Capital: How the Rapid Movement of Wealth Has Changed the World*, New York: Free Press.

Mueller, Dennis C. (1979), *Public Choice*, Cambridge: Cambridge University Press.

Mueller, Dennis C. (1989), *Public Choice II*, Cambridge: Cambridge University Press.

Nove, Alec (1987), 'Socialism', in John Eatwell, Murray Milgate and Peter Newman (eds), *The New Palgrave: A Dictionary of Economics*, vol. 4, London: Macmillan, p. 398.

Nozick, Robert (1974), *Anarchy, State, and Utopia*, New York: Basic Books.

Olson, Mancur (1965), *The Logic of Collective Action*, Cambridge, MA: Harvard University Press.

Olson, Mancur (1982), *The Rise and Decline of Nations*, New Haven: Yale University Press.

Olson, Mancur (1991), 'Autocracy, Democracy, and History', College Park, MD: University of Maryland, working paper.

Polanyi, Michael (1962), *History and Hope*, London: Routledge.

Posner, Richard A. (1993), 'Richard Rorty's Politics', *Critical Review*, **7** (1), 33–49.

Prescott, Edward C. and Rajnish Mehra (1980), 'Recursive Competitive Equilibrium: The Case of Homogeneous Households', *Econometrica*, **48**, 1365–7.

Rawls, John (1971), *A Theory of Justice*, Cambridge, MA: Harvard University Press.

Robbins, Lionel (1932), *The Nature and Significance of Economic Science*, London: Macmillan.

Romer, T. and H. Rosenthal (1978), 'Political Resource Allocation, Controlled Agendas, and the Status Quo', *Public Choice* **33** (4), 27–43.

Rosenberg, Alexander (1992), *Economics – Mathematical Politics or Science of Diminishing Returns?*, Chicago: University of Chicago Press.

Samuelson, Paul A. (1954), 'The Pure Theory of Public Expenditures', *Review of Economics and Statistics*, **36**, 387–9.

Samuelson, Paul A. (1955), 'Diagrammatic Exposition of a Theory of Public Expenditure', *The Review of Economics and Statistics*, **36**, 350–6.

Schumpeter, Joseph A. ([1912] 1934), *Theory of Economic Development*, Cambridge, MA: Harvard University Press, English translation, *Theorie der wirtschaftlichen Entwicklung*.

Shackle, G.L.S. (1972), *Epistemics and Economics*, Cambridge: Cambridge University Press.

Sichel, Werner (ed.) (1989), *The State of Economic Science: Views of Six Nobel Laureates*, Kalamazoo: Upjohn Institute.

Smith, Adam ([1776] 1937), *The Wealth of Nations*, New York: Random House, Modern Library Edition.

Stigler, George J. (1987), 'Knight, Frank Hyneman' in John Eatwell, Murray Milgate and Peter Newman (eds), *The New Palgrave: A Dictionary of Economics*, vol. 3, London: Macmillan, p. 58.

Tullock, Gordon (1965), *The Politics of Bureaucracy*, Washington, DC: Public Affairs Press.

Tullock, Gordon (1967a), 'The Welfare Costs of Tariffs, Monopolies, and Theft', *Western Economic Journal* (now *Economic Inquiry*), 5, 224–32.

Tullock, Gordon (1967b), *Towards a Mathematics of Politics*, Ann Arbor: University of Michigan Press.

Vanberg, Viktor and James M. Buchanan (1989), 'Interests and Theories in Constitutional Choice', *Journal of Theoretical Politics*, 1, 49–62.

von Mises, Ludwig ([1932] 1981), *Socialism*, Indianapolis: Liberty Classics.

von Neumann, John and Oskar Morgenstern (1944), *Theory of Games and Economic Behavior*, Princeton: Princeton University Press.

Weber, Max (1930), *The Protestant Ethic and the Spirit of Capitalism*, London: Allen & Unwin.

White, Michael D. (1994), 'Bridging the Natural and the Social: Science and Character in Jevon's Political Economy', *Economic Inquiry*, 32 (3), 429–44.

Wicksell, Knut (1896), *Finanztheoretische Untersuchungen*, Jena: Gustav Fischer.

Yeats, William Butler (1989), 'The Second Coming', in Richard J. Fineran (ed.), *The Collected Works of W.B. Yeats*, vol. 1, *The Poems*, New York: Macmillan, p. 187.

Index